D1563922

THE COURAGE OF COMPOSERS AND THE TYRANNY OF TASTE

Also by Bálint András Varga and published
by the University of Rochester Press

György Kurtág:
Three Interviews and Ligeti Homages

Three Questions for Sixty-Five Composers

From Boulanger to Stockhausen:
Interviews and a Memoir

BÁLINT ANDRÁS VARGA

THE COURAGE OF COMPOSERS AND THE TYRANNY OF TASTE

REFLECTIONS ON NEW MUSIC

UNIVERSITY OF ROCHESTER PRESS

First published 2017

University of Rochester Press
668 Mt. Hope Avenue, Rochester, NY 14620, USA
www.urpress.com
and Boydell & Brewer Limited
PO Box 9, Woodbridge, Suffolk IP12 3DF, UK
www.boydellandbrewer.com

ISBN-13: 978-1-58046-593-9
ISSN: 1071-9989

Library of Congress Cataloging-in-Publication Data

Names: Varga, Bálint András, editor.
Title: The courage of composers and the tyranny of taste : reflections on new
    music / Bálint András Varga.
Description: Rochester : University of Rochester Press, 2017. | Series:
    Eastman studies in music, ISSN 1071-9989 ; v. 141 | Includes bibliographical
    references and index.
Identifiers: LCCN 2017002276 | ISBN 9781580465939 (hardcover : alk. paper)
Subjects: LCSH: Composers—Interviews. | Music—20th century—History and
    criticism. | Music—21st century—History and criticism. | Courage.
Classification: LCC ML390 .C826 2017 | DDC 780.92/2—dc23 LC record
    available at https://lccn.loc.gov/2017002276

This publication is printed on acid-free paper.
Printed in the United States of America.

Dedicated to my daughters Flora and Fanni
with many thanks for their encouragement

CONTENTS

INTRODUCTION

C reation springs at least in part from the will to communicate—in word, sound, color, and shape. The desire to give birth to a vision stands at the beginning of a process that will be influenced by tradition and contemporaries alike.

Creators are placed at the end and at the start of the history of their field of activity. They look back, they look around in the present, and cast a look ahead. How they will react to what they have perceived depends on the nature of their gifts. Are they going to be pioneers or will they take over the torch from their predecessors?

In any case, they will come upon ideas that may well surprise them: they emerge unannounced and produce unexpected situations in which the creator must make a decision. That decision will logically lead to others, opening up a road, pointing in a direction, with the goal possibly still vague.

What psychological barriers, if any, did James Joyce have to overcome to progress from *Dubliners* of 1914 via *Ulysses* of 1918–20 to *Finnegans Wake* of 1923–39? Did courage play any role? He was certainly aware of the risk he had taken in *Ulysses*: "That book was a terrible risk. A transparent leaf separates it from madness."[1]

The motif of risk-taking and courage also appears with Vincent van Gogh: "What would life be like without the courage to take risks?"[2]

What psychological barriers, if any, did Kazimir Malevich have to overcome to progress within a span of eleven years from his colorful *Spring Garden in Bloom* of 1904 to conceiving and releasing his abstract *Black*

1   Robert H. Deming, ed., *James Joyce: The Critical Heritage*, vol. 1, *1902–1927* (New York: Barnes and Noble, 1970), 22.

2   *Dear Theo: The Autobiography of Vincent van Gogh*, ed. Irving Stone and Jean Stone (New York: Plume, 1995), 83.

Square in a White Field? Did courage play a role there? Despair is probably a more fitting definition of his state of mind, for he described the creation of the black square as a "desperate attempt to free art from the ballast of objectivity."[3]

When I interviewed the German composer Jörg Widmann, he spoke of the "courage of despair," and also "fear of his own courage." No doubt about it: the new is born in labor, with despair and courage and risk-taking being synonyms of pain.

Fear was also shared by Anton Webern. In a lecture delivered in the early 1930s, he described the crisis he had faced in relinquishing tonality: "That was of course a fierce battle, inhibitions of the most frightful kind had to be overcome, the fear: 'Is that really possible'?"[4]

The fact that courage very well played a role in John Cage's decision to release to the public his silent piece *4'33"* of 1952 is testified to by his reply to the first of the three questions I put to a great many composers between 1978 and 2014.[5] The quote stands at the start of the list of similar examples in "Prompts."

Courage, then, is one of the psychological components in the decision-making process of creative people, even if some of them may vehemently deny it. It also has a sociological aspect: can creative people, in their effort to reach their potential public, ignore the latter's capacity or willingness to grasp their message? Can they ignore the opinions of their most immediate public: their colleagues as well as those whose job it is to mediate between them and society—conductors, festival directors, critics?

What role does taste play in the emergence and distribution of art? I wonder sometimes to what extent, say, Webern's oeuvre would have been influenced by the enthusiastic reception his music was to be accorded after 1945, had he experienced it during his lifetime. He would surely have composed far more, though probably not differently, if he had heard exemplary performances of his music and if he had been assured of its welcome by a group of admirers. I must think of the obeisant tone of his letters to Zemlinsky in which he thanked the older composer for his plan to conduct the *Passacaglia*, Op. 1 in Prague. Webern mentioned, almost in passing,

3 Kazimir Malevich, *The Non-Objective World: The Manifesto of Suprematism*, trans. Howard Dearstyne (Mineola, NY: Dover, 1926), 68.

4 A. Webern, Vorträge 1932/33, 48, quoted in Elmar Budde, *Anton Weberns Lieder Op. 3: Untersuchungen zur frühen Atonalität bei Webern* (Wiesbaden: Franz Steiner Verlag, 1971), 94. Translations to English are the author's unless otherwise indicated.

5 Bálint András Varga, *Three Questions for Sixty-Five Composers* (Rochester, NY: University of Rochester Press, 2015), 41.

that performances of the work he had heard had been wholly inadequate. He was, if anything, not spoiled by success.

To what extent are "I like it," "I do not like it" influenced by prejudice and ideology? Can you regard ideology as institutionalized taste? How strong is the herd instinct among artists, inducing them to belong to a group of like-minded colleagues and thereby gaining the reassurance of being abreast of the times? I am reminded of the scores of some Hungarian composers in the 1970s, in which wavy lines took the place of notes over lengthy stretches of music. They will have seen and heard pieces by their colleagues in the West, probably at the Warsaw Autumn Festival, and said to themselves: that is modern, that is how one is to compose today.

Ideology determined György Kurtág's relationship to Darmstadt. Here is an extract from our interview of 2007:

> Kurtág: The composers in Darmstadt did not appreciate it at all.[6] They never invited me back for thirty years.
>
> Varga: Would you have liked to belong among them?
>
> Kurtág: I thought I did. Now I no longer would.[7]

The role of taste or ideology and its fundamental significance for the career of a composer is demonstrated by what one might term the "Bornemisza Case": the work may not have appealed to most of those present, but it did impress a radio producer from Cologne by the name of Wilfried Brennecke (1926–2012). He recognized Kurtág's stature and went on to promote his music in his capacity as artistic director of the Witten Festival of New Chamber Music. The String Quartets opp. 13 and 28, as well as the *Kafka Fragments* op. 24 for soprano and violin owe their existence to commissions for the festival.

The story goes that the score of *Bornemisza* reached Pierre Boulez purely by chance. He had not heard of the composer, but the music made a tremendous impression, inducing him to commission Kurtág to write *Messages of the Late R. V. Troussova*, op. 17 (1976–80), a work for soprano and ensemble that was to secure Kurtág's international breakthrough. I believe the "Bornemisza Case" provides a cogent justification of the question

---

6 The reference is to György Kurtág, *The Sayings of Péter Bornemisza: Concerto for Soprano and Piano, Op. 7* (1963–68). It was performed at the Darmstadt Summer Courses in 1968.
7 Bálint András Varga, *György Kurtág: Three Interviews and Ligeti Homages* (Rochester, NY: University of Rochester Press, 2009), 58.

about the tyranny—the omnipotence—of subjectivity, ideology, in other words, taste.

Courage, fear, despair, tyranny: this book is an attempt to penetrate into the studios—the minds—of composers at work; their struggle with the material and their own limitations, with the rules they have inherited—rules inculcated in the course of their studies, so that even for a ninety-year-old composer like György Kurtág it takes a conscious effort to break them (see chapter 17). I hope, then, that this book will give an idea of the struggle underlying the notes that one gets to hear in concert halls; notes that one "likes" or "dislikes," each according to one's taste, intelligence, curiosity, and experience.

This book also attempts to throw light on the thinking of the "customers"—critics and festival directors. Are they aware of the subjective nature of their own judgment and decisions, and if so, how do they deal with it? As a former promotion manager for music publishers, I know from my own experience what an important role my taste played in my work. This awareness served as a permanent reminder not to take my subjectivity as a yardstick. It was a difficult tightrope act, for I could not bring myself to cynically promote works I did not believe in. I had to find a solution, and eventually I did find one.

Artur Rubinstein, the first major musician I interviewed (on October 19, 1966), warned me not to trust composers' statements about their music. They had no idea, he said, how their works were to be performed and they were apt to change their views more quickly than artists did.

I certainly attribute considerable significance to composers' statements and regard it as my duty to act as a bottle, preserving their message and communicating it to future generations.

PROMPTS

H ere is the list of relevant examples I sent to composers, inviting them to contribute to the book. In doing interviews with some of them, I would start by citing some of the examples below.

The Courage of Composers

John Cage related how he had been encouraged to realize his idea for the silent piece *4'33"* by the empty paintings of Robert Rauschenberg:[1]

> I think I had already had such ideas as far as the fusing of life and art went and they came to me from my study of Zen Buddhism with Suzuki. I had also thought of the silent piece two years before I wrote it. And the reason I did not write it when I thought of it was because I was aware that many people would take it as a joke and not seriously.
>
> That was why, when I saw the empty paintings of Rauschenberg, I was prepared to have, as it were, a partner in this serious departure from conventions. The French would call it démarche. In other words, I don't think I was influenced by him—I was encouraged in something that I was already convinced about individually.

In his autobiography *Hallelujah Junction*, John Adams relates: "John Cage was also instrumental in making me feel comfortable and in tune with new technology. His playful yet disciplined approach to objects of twentieth-century life like radios, loudspeakers, microphones, tape recorders, and even computers had for me the effect of empowerment. He gave me the courage to see technology as a fertile terrain for creativity."[2]

---

1 Varga, *Three Questions for Sixty-Five Composers*, 88.
2 John Adams, *Hallelujah Junction: Composing an American Life* (New York: Farrar, Straus and Giroux, 2008), 203–4.

Goffredo Petrassi drew courage from the works of Bruno Maderna and Alberto Burri:[3]

> I first heard Maderna's music around 1957—I think, his style had matured by then and his personality had grown independent from Darmstadt. The encounter with Maderna's art helped me a great deal—it gave me courage to make a big leap forward. I was ready for it intuitively but lacked self-confidence.
>
> A few years before, a painter had influenced me in a similar manner. I was insecure; I did not know how to master the serial technique. One day, I came face to face with pictures by Alberto Burri—I bought two on the spot. Burri is a great artist of international standing. He had broken with the traditional means of expression and experimented with new techniques and new materials: instead of brush and paint, he worked with tar, sackcloth and a wide range of other, very simple materials. For all that, his pictures made a strong impact on me. I thought I ought to have the courage, too, to turn my back on my earlier concept of music, make a leap and confront my own personality, my scale with serial techniques.
>
> I met Burri around 1951 and Maderna in 1957 or so. The works I composed after that have nothing to do with Maderna's style but they do demonstrate that I had bidden farewell to my clichés and was able to compose more freely, with broader inner horizons. The first such piece was the *Serenata* (1958) for five instruments.

In an interview published on his seventy-fifth birthday in 1998, I asked György Ligeti if it had taken courage for him to compose his Horn Trio—a work he himself described as a detour (together with the opera *Le grand macabre*).[4] He replied: "Composition is not a question of courage or cowardice: you do your thing and spare no thought about the impression it may make. He who cares about it is lost. He should go to Hollywood and write film music." However, in his "Report on My Own Work" (written for the world premiere of his *Lontano* on October 22, 1967, in Donaueschingen), Ligeti writes:

> It was around the year 1950 that I came to the realisation that it was no longer possible for me to continue in the post-Bartókian style in which I had composed until then. . . . It was at that time that I conceived of the first ideas about static music reposing in itself that no longer had anything to do with development or traditional rhythmic patterns. To begin

---

3   Ibid., 197.
4   Bálint András Varga, *From Boulanger to Stockhausen: Interviews and a Memoir* (Rochester, NY: University of Rochester Press, 2013), 54.

with, those ideas were vague, and at that time I had neither the courage nor the compositional and technical means to translate them into pieces of music.

In our first interview (1982/85), György Kurtág discussed the significance of the Budapest New Music Studio for his compositional thinking in the early 1970s: "The idiom of the New Music Studio that was emerging at the time played a major role at the start of *Játékok*: it gave me courage to work with even fewer notes."[5] When I reminded him of that comment in a telephone conversation in late December 2015, he said: "When I was not really fit to compose, the notes would immediately multiply."

In his book of interviews with Fiona Maddocks, *Wild Tracks*, Harrison Birtwistle remembers how he was taken by Alexander Goehr to see a painting by Picasso where Picasso revisits and reinterprets Velazquez's *Las Meninas*.[6] That painting gave Birtwistle courage to arrange works of the *Ars subtilior*, Dunstable, or Bach. Sometime in 2015 I rang and asked him where courage had come in. He explained that he had been reluctant to do any arrangements, perhaps because he was aware what his reaction would be were a colleague of his to tamper with his own pieces. He added, "Arranging a piece of music is a way of owning it."

The Tyranny of Taste, Ideology, and Prejudice

The title of this volume could also have been: *Courage in the Face of the Tyranny of Tastes and Ideologies*. Most of the following examples demonstrate how closely the two are bound up with each other as well as with (music) history in the second half of the twentieth century.

The idea to add the tyranny of taste to the original subject of the book, the courage of composers, arose on reading the following paragraph in the contribution by the Danish composer Karl Aage Rasmussen:

> As an artist, however, you are unlikely to totally avoid a sense of pressure from whatever artistic lingua franca is surrounding you, and the fear of becoming a pariah is deeply rooted in most people. As a student of composition in the late sixties, among not particularly academic modernists, I was nonetheless acutely aware that openly admiring—just as an

---

5   Varga, *Three Questions for Sixty-Five Composers*, 143. *Játékok* is the title of nine books of music for piano solo, piano duet, and two pianos.

6   Harrison Birtwistle, *Wild Tracks: A Conversation Diary with Fiona Maddocks* (London: Faber and Faber, 2014), 136.

example—the late Strauss of the *Metamorphosen* required an assurance that I did not possess at the time. And speaking fondly of, say, Prokofiev's music was inconceivable, so you kept your fascination secret. Some of Adorno's one-liners ("you can hardly hear a note without having to hide a smile") was an ongoing slap on the wrist, creating an anxiety about always attempting "the right thing"—or nothing at all. A mind model that enveloped my every artistic viewpoint during my early years.

I would cite that paragraph again and again in the course of my contact with composers.

In 1998, György Ligeti may have rejected the idea of courage in the creative process, elsewhere, however, in remembering his early years as a composer, he did not hesitate to admit to the absence of it at a time when he was badly in need of it (see above the quote from his "Report on My Own Work").

In the following extract, "courage" is not named expressly but it must nevertheless have played a role: Ligeti was surely aware that some of the means he employed in composing his wind quintet *Six Bagatelles* would fall foul of the Composers' Association:

At the end of September 1956, the Budapest Franz Liszt Academy organized the first Days of New Hungarian Music. On the initiative of the Jeney Quintet, my Bagatelles for wind quintet were finally performed. However, they were called Five Bagatelles, for No. 6 contained too many minor seconds even for the political thaw of the time: dissonances and chromaticism were "cosmopolitan," "music of the public enemy," only less so in the autumn of 1956 than in previous years. The audience made up of musicians and intellectuals were at their wits' end, not knowing whether they were supposed to like and applaud it. One of my former teachers made an attempt to cautiously congratulate me on my "success": he shook my hand and in his embarrassment kept shifting from foot to foot.[7]

Another example of courage in the face of the tyranny of ideology is reported by Péter Eötvös in his book of conversations with Pedro Amaral.[8] It concerns the courage of János Viski, his professor of composition at the Budapest Academy of Music, who eventually succumbed to the ideological

7   György Ligeti, "Zu meinen Bläserquintetten." In *György Ligeti: Gesammelte Schriften*, vol. 2 (Mainz: Schott, 2007), 156.
8   Péter Eötvös and Pedro Amaral, *Parlando-Rubato: Beszélgetések, monológok, és egyéb kitérők* (Budapest: Rózsavölgyi, 2015), 216.

and existential pressure to which he was subjected and died.[9] The following excerpt also shows the extent to which composers behind the Iron Curtain were cut off from music that was supposed to be ideologically damaging (such as the Second Viennese School) and the enormous effect made by an encounter with the oeuvre of someone like Anton Webern on a young composer such as Péter Eötvös at the end of the 1950s.

> He was an amazing man, something of a martinet but warm and humane, a true master, a real guardian angel for the young man that I was. After a year and a half of working with me, he invited me to his house. He made me sit next to an awe-inspiring, huge Grundig tape recorder and said: "Now I am going to show you music you have never heard before. I am going to leave you to listen to it by yourself." And then he added: "They are the works of Mr. Anton von Webern."
>
> I was astounded, or shall I say enchanted? I had had no idea that music could be like that. Incredulously, I experienced an undreamed-of sound world opening up in all its richness before me. It bowled me over straight away. It was one of the most beautiful moments of my whole life. Absolutely unique.
>
> To use a rather childish metaphor, I crawled into that music like a wasp into a pot of honey and could not crawl out of it for many years to come. Do not misunderstand me: I was never tempted to compose in a Webernesque style, but the pureness of his musical idiom, its transparency, its natural geometry infinitely fascinated me. So much so that this music also exerted a negative influence, in that for a good many years, it did not let me discover my own idiom, my own style, my own personal world. I felt his form of perfection was beyond reach, I could never build my structures with such clarity, I failed to achieve his technical, artistic, and spiritual mastery. Webern's clarity was too blinding; his oeuvre proved an insurmountable hurdle I could not overcome for a long time. . . .
>
> After discovering Webern, I began to compose music that no longer had much to do with Kodály; I had moved toward a more modern style that bore traces of Western music. That is, the kind of idiom that was beyond the pale for the Soviet system. Khrushchev was of course not Stalin but spiritual oppression was still in place and the slightest sign of sympathy for Western culture was construed as an indication of dangerous political contagion to be rooted out forthwith.

---

9 János Viski (1906–61) was a successful composer before World War II, with some of his orchestral works performed all over Europe, under conductors such as Willem Mengelberg. He was appointed a professor of composition at the Budapest Academy in 1942, a position he kept until the end of his life. Eötvös was his pupil between 1958 and 1961.

The director of the Budapest Music Academy was Ferenc Szabó. He was not only a composer but had also been an officer in the Red Army and he was tasked by the Russians to report any suspicious phenomenon in Hungarian cultural life. Szabó was an adherent of Stalin and dedicated several of his works to him. In the second half of the 1930s, at the time of the devastating purges in the Soviet Union, Szabó is supposed to have been involved in the notorious Moscow trials when several of his close comrades were summarily sentenced to death or deportation. He was a dangerous man, with the power to have anyone imprisoned if he deemed that the person represented the artistic principles of Western culture.

In the course of one of my examinations at the Budapest Academy of Music, I presented my compositions to Ferenc Szabó. On detecting in them rather suspect aesthetic principles, this man summoned my professor and questioned him about how and why he had permitted me to compose music of that kind. I never learned what had actually happened at that conference—all I know is that on reaching home, Professor Viski's heart stopped beating. Nobody could prove a direct link between the conference and Professor Viski's death, it might have been pure coincidence, but in my mind, I have always suspected a connection between the two.[10]

I remember meeting the Czech composer Miloslav Kabeláč (1908–79) in a Prague café. He was officially under a cloud at the time, so that in presenting me with a number of his scores, he suggested I carry them with the title pages turned inward, so that nobody in the street could see his name. I was shocked.

My encounter in Budapest with Tikhon Khrennikov (1913–2007), the all-powerful general secretary of the Soviet Composers' Union, and his reaction to the names of some advanced Russian composers I mentioned, made all too clear to me the conditions under which such composers had to work and live.

I also remember the Hungarian composer Sándor Balassa (b. 1935) and his defiant decision to turn his back on "new music" and start writing in a style that he regarded as authentic—from then on, he composed in a tonal idiom. An act of courage, no doubt.

I am eager to read what sort of associations the above will evoke in you.

---

10 The following story sheds light on János Viski's character, described by those who knew him as cowardly: he sat on the committee that was to decide whether György Kurtág's String Quartet op. 1 (1958) was to be allowed public performance. The work's daring modernity shocked him and he hastened to the Ministry of Culture to report on the emergence of a composition inimical to the people ("volksfeindlich"). In light of his cowardice, his decision to initiate Péter Eötvös into the music of Anton Webern is all the more to be appreciated.

PART ONE

COMPOSERS

CHAPTER ONE

HANS ABRAHAMSEN
(B . 1 9 5 2)

Danish composer

If you listen to Hans Abrahamsen's music, you enter a landscape—strangely familiar, yet oddly different from all other landscapes you have known. You are surrounded by shapes (melodies) you seem to have heard before but they are wholly new; you are aware of colors—timbres—likewise never experienced although somehow reassuringly familiar.

Particularly in his most recent pieces, such as let me tell you *for soprano and orchestra, which won him the Grawemeyer Award in 2016 or* Left, alone *for piano left hand and orchestra, which premiered in Cologne on January 29, 2016, you hear* music *that requires no adjective.[1] It is not new, and it is not postmodern, it does not look backward or forward. Hans Abrahamsen has created a world all his own.*

I told him as much when we met prior to the concert in his hotel and he seemed to agree—it was in any case something he was striving for.

We had had a fleeting encounter in Copenhagen in the early 1970s; I remembered a fragile young man with shoulder-length hair. That detail helped him date it to before 1974. I also remembered a smiling face and a limp. More than forty years later, the fragility, the smile, and an unembarrassed reference in our conversation to his not fully functioning right arm and leg

---

1 *let me tell you* (2013) to words by Paul Griffiths, was premiered on December 20, 2013, by Barbara Hannigan and the Berlin Philharmonic under Andris Nelsons. In *Left, alone*, the soloist was Alexandre Tharaud; the WDR Symphony Orchestra was conducted by Ilan Volkov.

are still there. Now that we had talked for nearly an hour, I was also struck by his quiet gentleness, his unassuming simplicity, and his utter dedication to his art. Like much of his music, he speaks softly, slowly, and with pauses for reflection.

You cannot but feel fondness and respect for Hans Abrahamsen—and genuine admiration for his music.

Cologne, January 29, 2016

The need for courage in your work appears to be something you take for granted. You have admitted that it took courage for you to overcome the fear of facing an empty page and to begin composing again after a decade of creative paralysis; it required courage to realize the simplicity you had planned for Schnee; *in our e-mail exchange where I congratulated you on* let me tell you *but wondered about the challenge you were bound to encounter in attempting another vocal work, you replied (on January 22), "I know the challenge of making something new, which is at the same time a continuation of a new way, but I dare to do it."[2]*

You remember the first song in *let me tell you*. It says:

> Let me tell you how it was.
> I know I can do this.
> I have the powers:
> I take them here.
> I have the right.[3]

I think writers tend to express such thoughts more frequently than composers. They feel the need to tell all the stories that emerge in their minds. Actually, composers feel much the same way. I remember when I started writing music and had my first public performances, I was sixteen years old. I was in a way very innocent, I did not think about courage consciously but in actual fact, I did need it to appear before an audience.

---

2 *Schnee* (2006–8), ten canons for nine instruments, was premiered by the ensemble recherche at the Witten Festival of New Chamber Music in 2008.

3 Paul Griffiths (1947) fashioned seven songs from his novel *let me tell you* (2008) to be set by Hans Abrahamsen.

I was composing freely, open to any outside influences, whether they came from music of the past or my contemporaries. Gradually, I found my language.

What really required courage was not to take the road in the middle but to try and find alternative paths. I was determined to do that even if it meant being on my own. There come moments when you feel you have ventured too far—but you dare to continue working. Even if it means falling silent. I composed nothing between 1988 and 1998. Or rather: I went on working but could not find my voice.

Courage also means for me to wait until I have something to say. And when I do have something to say, to fight for the right words. (*He laughs softly, shyly, with a slight hissing noise that reminds me, curiously enough, of Kurtág. There appears to be a kinship between the two composers in other ways as well.*) Finding the right words is not always easy, even in composing.

Does composing take you a long time?

Sometimes it does. I have to be patient. You have to have the courage to wait, and also to . . . to forget yourself . . . at the right moment and to listen to what is in the music I am working on and to listen to what emerges from the material. And then you must have the courage . . . where you have to . . . to do something! (*The exclamation mark should indicate the sudden vehemence of the last words, coming after several seconds of silence. The change of tone was quite striking—rather like a similar moment of unexpected eruption in* Left, alone, *a few hours later, at the Kölner Philharmonie.*) To know exactly when to do it (*the same brief, quiet, shy, hissing laugh*). And, in a way, to find out where you are. What to do.

Let me give you two examples. At the end of the first canon (Canon 1a, I think) in Schnee, *there appears out of nowhere just one tone that does not seem to belong there; you are not sure you have heard it right. It is a surrealistic moment. Is it something that comes as a surprise for you as well?*

That is something I heard coming out of the material. (*Abrahamsen makes a gesture with his hand, indicating almost physically the rise of that sound phenomenon out of the depth of his imagination, but for a split second also as if it had appeared from above.*) And I knew it had to be there.

Wonderful. Like a painter adding just a tiny spot of color at a particular place on the canvas.

Yes, that's right. Just a little spot of color—and I heard it emerge from the material.

The other question is this: Jörg Widmann told me in our interview how the tonal final chorus of his opera Babylon *had fallen afoul of some critics. Apparently they believed you were not supposed to write that kind of music nowadays. I was reminded of that by the third movement of your Double Concerto: it is wonderful tonal music.*[4]

Jörg Widmann's sister, Carolin, plays it so beautifully on the violin!

Did it take courage to write that tonal movement?

Oh, you know, tonal music has always been part of my language. When I started in the late 1960s, tonality was something very radical. You will remember Terry Riley's *In C*.[5] There were other pieces as well. Tonality for me had a kind of freshness. The Beatles also had it. It is like with painters—tonality is one color.

Do you know my early *Ten Preludes for String Quartet* of 1973? Four years ago, I also made an orchestral version of them.

The first nine preludes are in a contemporary idiom, the last one is joyful and innocent, rather like early Baroque music. It goes backward—or maybe forward, to C major.

I was very young at the time, twenty years old and I discussed the preludes with my good friend, Karl Aage Rasmussen, who is a bit older. I imagined the last movement played straight, just like Baroque music, but Karl Aage said you could not do that, the old music needs some sort of distance, it has to be put in inverted commas.

We composers, you know, have to be stubborn. Sometimes I am too stubborn. We discussed that piece for a long time. Eventually, I made two versions of it, just like painters do sometimes. So I did one to be played pianissimo, with sordinos. It sounded like old music played at a distance. It probably reflected the Zeitgeist more than my own version did—but in fact it was more radical. But at that time I did not dare to stand up for it, I did not dare to say what I really liked. In any case, the version I did under Karl Aage's influence was played only once. After that I withdrew it. Like Jörg Widmann, I ended up sticking to my own version—without excuses. Tonality was back—and it was fresh.

---

4   Double Concerto (2011) for violin, piano, and strings. Premiered on October 9, 2011.
5   Composed in 1964 for an indefinite number of performers.

That is where courage and taste—or ideology, or prejudice—overlap. You needed courage to go in the face of the taste of the time.

You are right. Composers have different tastes, different aesthetics. You have to follow your own aesthetic. You have to dare to do that, even if it means you are different.

I want to tell you another story from the seventies. *Winternacht* and *Walden* are very important pieces for me.[6] I also wrote *Canzone* for accordion solo, I think I wrote it after Winternacht.[7] This piece I have never been happy with. And then, in 2005, I wrote *Three Little Nocturnes* for accordion and string quartet, for a very good Norwegian accordionist.[8] He asked me what I thought of *Canzone*. He liked it but wondered if I would be interested in revising it. I said I would but did not have the time. Back home I looked at the score again. It is in a way two kinds of music. One is very innocent, and one seems to come from the outside world, very disturbing music—again, music of the Zeitgeist. When I wrote it, I did not dare to remove the disturbing part, I did not dare to reduce the piece to the quiet, innocent layer. I then wrote a new work called *Air*, which no longer had the modern bits.[9] Originally, I had thought the counterpoint between the two layers was interesting. But now, in reworking it, I stuck to the quiet part and the result is in a way timeless music. Originally, I had not dared to be as simple in that piece as it ought to have been.

Were you afraid of the reception?

No, it was something in myself.—I still quite like the first version, but it is far too bound up with the time in which it was written, whereas the new one is out of time. It is also better. The first version had too much small talk. I don't like small talk. There is a lot of new music which lacks concentration. In my own music, I notice that it can be very strict (like *Schnee*) or very free.

---

6 *Winternacht* (1978) for seven or more players. The title is derived from a poem by Georg Trakl to whom the first and fourth movements are dedicated. The second movement is dedicated to M. C. Escher and the third one to Stravinsky. The title of the wind quintet *Walden* (1978) is taken from Henry David Thoreau's novel of 1854. Abrahamsen composed a version for reed quintet in 1995.

7 *Canzone* was also composed in 1978.

8 The *Three Little Nocturnes* were written for Frode Haltli and the Cikada String Quartet.

9 *Air* (2006) for accordion solo is dedicated to Frode Haltli. In 2007, Abrahamsen wrote the following program note: "The work is a twin to my first work for accordion *Canzone* from 1978. The new work, *Air*, is different in that it retains the simplicity which makes room for more clear air, since the more restless parts of *Canzone* have not been included in the work."

I do find freedom also in Schnee, *though. In Canon 1a, the even beat in the background is overlaid by uneven beats on the piano in the foreground. It is wholly unpredictable in the way it will fall out of pulse, as if it were slightly tipsy.*

That's right. . . . How shall I put it? It started when I began to compose again. I mean the irregularity. I have this right hand and right leg, you know, and I have always tried to forget about them. Still, I am always aware of them—even now. It is part of me. You can hear it in my music most clearly in *let me tell you* where a piece of paper is rubbed against the surface of a drum. This kind of irregularity is also there in the first canon of *Schnee* where the first two beats are a little faster and the next two a little slower. The music limps. It could also be that now that I am older, I dare to show sides of myself that I did not dare to show when I was younger. Also, when I was young, my music was simple and innocent. As I grew older, it became more complicated. But I can still write simple music like in the *Ten Studies for Piano.*[10] I feel part of a family to which Kurtág belongs: he also dares to write simple music. Recently, I have once again had the courage to go back to the innocence of my early music, but in a different way. Somehow, one says the same things, but differently. I do not know if it has to do with courage.

What I am going to say has nothing to do with courage either. One of the things I love about your music is that you allow it plenty of time to unfold. It has a slow pace—and then it stops. Its silences are an important part of your music. I also admire the total freedom of your composing. The music broods over itself. Moreover, it breathes; the vocal lines—but also some instrumental ones—move in wide intervals, as if they were taking a deep breath. In let me tell you, *these wide intervals enhance the storytelling character of the voice; the soprano relates an ancient tale, perhaps a ballad. You have reached a stage where you no longer seem to care whether you are writing new music or old music or postmodern music—you just write* music. *Free of dogma, free of ideology—genuine music.*

You are right: as one becomes older, one is no longer interested in style, in ideology. There are so many of them today. When you are young, you are very much part of your time. I learned a lot from minimalism, I learned a lot from postmodernism. But now I no longer write in a style. I am creating my own world.

10 *Ten Studies for Piano* (1984–98).

That is important: creating your own world.

Yes, and I am telling my own stories. It is very interesting what you say about slowness, because I have been thinking about it a lot. You must take a great deal of time; the music moves at a slow pace. But then there are times when it moves very fast, like the second movement of my first piano concerto.[11] This music is actually derived from the second movement of *Märchenbilder.*[12] It is, like so much of my music, very strictly constructed. There comes a moment when the piano emerges out of the music. In the piano concerto, I lift it out and liberate it, so to speak, from that structure, I extend and shape it. But actually I could never have composed the music without that structure. That was the basis.

And now let me go back to your question about the slow movement of the Double Concerto. In November 1992, I learned meditation from a very good teacher by the name of Jes Bertelsen. I visited him in his "Vaekstcentret" which could mean "Center for Spiritual Growth" in English. To mark the center's tenth anniversary, I was asked to write a small piece and I composed *Efterårslied* (Autumn Lied) for soprano, harpsichord, clarinet, violin, and cello. They asked me to include a very beautiful melody in it. It is about the autumn; a bird sings about leaving the world: the time for leaving is approaching (*hums the melody*). I do not really regard it as a composition—it is more of a transcription. I realized that I could combine that tune with two themes from the *Kunst der Fuge* (*hums these too*). It is a kind of quodlibet.

It is very soft music, with the soloist singing a poem by Rilke, also about the autumn, and the falling leaves. That is why I call it *Autumn Lied.* When it came to embarking on the Double Concerto, I found I was frightened of the empty page. To help get started, I fell back on the *Autumn Lied.* In the concerto, I left the melody out and turned the regular beat of the Lied into an irregular one. There also comes some material with a regular beat. But beneath it all, if you listen very carefully, you can discern the shadow of the Danish melody (*sings it again*). Bach is also there. The music has to do with time and memory. It goes slower and slower and slower and slower. (*The last minutes of the interview—Hans Abrahamsen's monologue—had something of a confessional tone. His voice was soft, he spoke slowly, hesitantly. It was like some of his music.*)

---

11 Concerto for Piano and Orchestra (2000).
12 *Märchenbilder* (1984) for fourteen instruments.

CHAPTER TWO

JOHN ADAMS
(B . 1 9 4 7)

American composer and conductor

Vienna, March 13, 2015
Edited March 24, 2015

In his autobiography Hallelujah Junction *as well as during our interview at Vienna's Konzerthaus, John Adams struck me as a composer of acute public awareness.*[1] *It stems from his realization that he is devoting his life to an art form—"serious" music—that is condemned to a marginal existence both in the United States and the rest of the world. What appears to be his innate pessimism makes him overlook his spectacular success, which has turned him into a representative figure of American music. The questions that seem to exercise his mind concern the social relevance of his own output and that of his colleagues, in relation to popular culture. I think he feels responsible for the future of American music and strives to create works that should become part of the cultural heritage of the United States, a kind of humus for the seeds of music to be composed by future generations. John Adams is also keenly aware of the presence of American music—or its lack—on an international scale and his pride in its accomplishments is tinged with an inescapable inferiority complex in regard to European masters of the past and present with*

---

1 John Adams composed *Hallelujah Junction* for two pianos in 1996. His autobiography is titled *Hallelujah Junction: Composing an American Life* (New York: Farrar, Strauss and Giroux, 2008).

composers like Elliott Carter or Morton Feldman. I interviewed both of them decades ago: they were fiercely patriotic and simultaneously on the defensive.[2]

All this is apparent in our conversation, which took place after an intensive rehearsal with the Wiener Symphoniker at Vienna's Konzerthaus when John Adams was still suffering from jetlag and was not really fit or indeed inclined to give an interview. The text below is the result of careful editing for which he found the time in New York in the middle of a no less grueling rehearsal and conducting schedule.

With regard to his concert in Vienna: the very program was eloquent proof that John Adams's music fits seamlessly into the neighborhood of Beethoven and Stravinsky. One accepted it as part of that tradition without any need to make allowances. Of course, the reference to Beethoven in Absolute Jest *for string quartet and orchestra was deliberate, drawing its material from the late quartets (opp. 131, 135, and the* Große Fuge*). The piece found a natural niche right next to Beethoven's Fourth Symphony as it did to Stravinsky's Symphony in Three Movements. I am not sure if Adams also makes use of some distant Stravinsky quotes, but the program certainly made sense as a discourse on music history as well.*

The above is a record of my subjective impressions of John Adams, based on the hour or so we spent together in March 2015. I sent it to him for his approval and I am glad I did so, for it gave him a chance to correct two basic points: he is certainly not innately pessimistic, and he does not suffer from any inferiority complex with regard to European music. Here is his e-mail of November 24, 2015:

I was a bit alarmed to read that I appear to you to be "innately pessimistic" and have "an inescapable inferiority complex" about European music.

I think it's a bit more complicated than that.

Yes, I have time when I feel pessimistic about the relevance and the future of classical music, but I would never call that an "innate" part of my nature. In fact I think I share with many other American composers,

2   In 1982, I invited Elliott Carter to contribute to my book *Three Questions for 82 Composers*, which appeared in Hungarian in 1986, with the American and German editions published in 2011 and 2014, respectively. In his letter of March 17, 1985, Elliott Carter wrote: "It is courageous of you to include something about an American composer—for all of us have had a hard time penetrating European indifference to our work." Morton Feldman, whom I interviewed in 1983, seemed positively obsessed with the relationship between European and American composers and the relative merits of the music they wrote. "György, you are too gifted to write European music," he said to Ligeti. In our interview, he noted: "I think the tragedy of Ligeti is, in a sense, that his imagination is one place and his background and tradition are fighting both" (Varga, *Three Questions for Sixty-Five Composers*, 81).

including Ives and Copland, a fundamental optimism—if not always about classical music, but certainly about life in general. So, if I were your editor, I might suggest "occasional pessimism" or "mixed pessimism and optimism." If my pessimism were "innate" I wouldn't bother to work so hard to keep composing!

What is certainly true is that I feel a deep frustration about the dominance of pop culture in the United States. I recognize it as an essential ingredient in our American way of life, but I am constantly aware of how its omnipresence and commercial power tends to marginalize the kind of art that I care about.

About our "inferiority" complex: this a trope that I read often about Americans. You even read it about the great novelist Henry James, who supposedly suffered from feelings of inferiority and had to move to England to survive. I will surprise you when I tell you that I think we American composers actually feel LESS of an inferiority complex vis-à-vis the old European masters than most contemporary European composers. I have long wondered whether perhaps much of the disjointed, fractured musical language of postwar European music, beginning with Darmstadt, was the result of a sense of inferiority on the part of those composers, who were too aware of history. As John Cage put it (somewhere, in one of his lectures) we Americans are further away from the center of that great tradition and hence feel less of an obligation or obeisance to it. I don't think that something like *Absolute Jest* is the result of feeling inferiority—it's more an expression of love and, shall we say, an irresponsible freedom!

Of course I feel small and insignificant when I compare myself to Beethoven and Bach, but who doesn't? And I'm sure any good writer feels that way comparing himself or herself to Shakespeare. I don't think tagging us Americans with some sort of special "inferiority complex" is fair, nor is it correct.

I was going to ask you if courage played any role in the creative process. In preparing for this interview, I came across your conversation with Daniel Colvard where you say that when you compose you often need some kind of model.[3] In your reply you use an evocative image: that of a guardian angel holding your hand.

3   Thomas May, *The John Adams Reader: Essential Writings on an American Composer* (Pompton Plains, NJ: Amadeus Press, 2006), 197.

That's right. For example, a very unexpected model who came into my life when [I was] working on *Doctor Atomic*, my opera about the atomic bomb, was Edgard Varèse.[4] His music, particularly his later pieces such as *Déserts*, expresses that terrible Cold War angst of the 1950s. And it also typifies the fascination with science that creative artists, particularly composers, had during that particular historical epoch. I'm not necessarily a big fan of Varèse, but in this instance—when I was trying to summon up the psychic atmosphere of those years when atomic weapons were new and people genuinely thought that a nuclear war was imminent—the violence and tension of his language served as an excellent model.

I had a similar "guardian angel" experience when composing *On the Transmigration of Souls*, the piece that I was requested to write in 2002 as a memorial to the victims of the World Trade Center attacks. To be honest, I didn't want that commission. The event was so traumatic on a national scale and ultimately so overexposed in the media that making some sort of musical statement about it seemed a terrible idea. But then I thought about Charles Ives and how he might have approached the assignment. I thought about his character: his way of investing his spiritual philosophy in his music, his patriotism (not a false patriotism, but a genuine one) and his fundamental honesty and humility, and that model gave me courage to go forward with the project. Indeed, I ended up incorporating his *Unanswered Question* in my piece.

Well, that confession (if I may call it that) made it appear likely that you would answer my question in the affirmative. Ives and Varèse may well have played the role for you that Rauschenberg did for Cage or Maderna for Petrassi. You call it a "model."

I admire Varèse but as I said just now, I can't say truthfully that he is among my favorites. My identification with Ives is doubtless due to being from a small town in New England, just as he was. And also, like Ives, I learned music first from my father with whom I played in marching bands and learned to love "vernacular" music as much as the classics. In our home, when I was a boy, there were recordings of swing bands (Benny Goodman, Count Basie, Ella Fitzgerald, etc.) side by side with LPs of Mozart, Bach, and Sibelius. I think it's an essentially American trait to appreciate and love lofty "highbrow" art as well as the popular demotic kinds. Jazz and rock

---

4   World premiere, October 1, 2005, San Francisco Opera.

constitute America's folk music, and not being responsive to this expression seems to be a handicap to a composer.

But my personal history with Ives's music is very complicated. You know, Ives was virtually unknown in the classical music world until the mid-1960s. There were hardly any recordings of his music available, and he was never performed by our major orchestras. It was not until Leonard Bernstein with his glamorous telegenic personality was able to call attention to his music that the public became aware of Ives.

I have studied a lot of Ives and I have read his prose and have conducted a great deal of his music. I mention in my autobiography *Hallelujah Junction* that I was very frustrated with his work because I wished it were better. As an American composer I wanted to think I had a great godfather in the way that Europeans can cite Bach or Beethoven or Mahler. But Ives's pieces are to my mind compromised by the creative isolation he lived in. He almost never heard his orchestral music performed, so he lacked that essential "hands-on" professional experience that all the European masters had. As a result he often composed music with serious formal problems, not to mention containing endless insoluble issues with orchestration and balance. This is not to deny the fertility of his imagination.

In terms of rhythmic invention alone, Ives was many decades ahead of his time. Not until Conlon Nancarrow's player-piano music of the forties and fifties did anyone approach Ives's astonishing creativity in matters of rhythm. There are things inside the Fourth Symphony that are spectacularly original beyond anything done at that time in Europe—even by Stravinsky—but they are nested in a morass of competing material that ends up as self-canceling. And their orchestral treatment is often so murky and overloaded that the listener is pretty much unable to discern them. I think Ives was strangely ambivalent about his work, which may be why he left so much of it in a state of hopeless disarray. Nonetheless, I love him for his personal modesty, his generosity, and his visionary quest.

Who would be a model for you then?

I think I probably took the most courage from someone like Duke Ellington. Ellington had a great influence on me, largely because he has such deep and genuine feeling. It carries such impact because of its joyousness, its lyricism, its incredible physicality, and—I know this is a controversial term—its accessibility. Ellington always saw himself as an entertainer: a very consummate, highly skilled one, but an entertainer nevertheless. I suspect Mozart felt pretty much the same about himself. Isn't it wonderful to think that these two very great artists could give us the gift of their talent and imagination and also give us pure pleasure?

For me much of the trouble with Modernism is that it is extremely humorless. If there is any humor at all in a modernist piece, it must be ironic humor. It must be of the savage, embittered kind, like *Le Grand Macabre*. When we listen to Beethoven—I am just doing his Fourth Symphony this week here in Vienna—he is capable of such wonderful, buoyant humor.[5] The music is entertaining at the same time it is sublime. I feel Stravinsky had that quality as well—at least in many of his pieces such as *Petrushka*, *Les Noces*, Symphony in Three Movements, *Rake's Progress*, *L'Histoire du soldat*, and so on.

So did Haydn.

Yes, Haydn too. But Ellington also meant a great deal to me because he worked intimately with his musicians. He was a constantly practical musician, performing almost every night of his life. He would conceive an idea, then try it out with his players and then revise it or incorporate the peculiarities of a certain player into the final product. His was a collaborative working method, whereas Ives worked in a vaccuum. He wrote his pieces almost as philosophical propositions. Despite his radical stance, Ives still thought of himself as part of the "great composer" lineage, and that likely had a compromising effect on his creative life, especially when he found himself so profoundly ignored by his contemporaries.

But what did Ellington encourage you, a young composer growing up in the late sixties, to do?

You have to understand that I am younger than many of the people you mentioned—Bruno Maderna, Xenakis, Lutosławski. I am at least twenty to thirty years younger than them, so I came of age at a really strange time in the late 1960s when Modernism was prestigious, especially in the American university environment. But it was also beginning its decline. It had become fractured and sterile. As a young student composer, admittedly very impressionable, I looked around and saw on the one hand John Cage composing with chance operations and the I Ching, and on the

---

5   John Adams conducted two concerts with the Wiener Symphoniker on March 13 and 15, 2016. His program consisted of Stravinsky's Symphony in Three Movements (on March 15), his own *Absolute Jest* for string quartet (the Doric String Quartet) and orchestra, as well as Beethoven's Symphony No. 4.

other Boulez doing exceedingly obscure formal manipulations that only a handful of cognoscenti might be able to understand—not only could I not comprehend his music, I couldn't even understand his writing about it in *Penser la musique aujourd'hui* (I suspect no one else could, but most wouldn't admit it . . .).[6]

But at the exact same time—say around 1967—we had this phenomenal flowering of Dionysian music in the United States with the advent of rock and soul music. And jazz had reached a sort of emotional and formal cumulative point with John Coltrane and Miles Davis. I noticed that people, especially those of my generation responded to that with enormous enthusiasm. Rock and soul music—the Beatles, Aretha Franklin, the Rolling Stones, the Supremes, Jefferson Airplane, Bob Dylan—they all had huge audiences and exerted enormous cultural influence. When John Lennon spoke out against the Vietnam War, millions of young people paid attention because they already believed in him as a musician. Jazz, rock, and soul carried what I call the *anima*, that essential power to communicate feeling. To me, the serious modernist composers had abdicated it. It was not a promising time to be a young composer, believe me!

You have asked me in what way the composers I admired encouraged me. I can say that they gave me permission to not worry about the "evolution" of musical language. That's what Boulez and Darmstadt were all about, in a way also what Cage was concerned with—that the musical language MUST evolve and do so by increasing its complexity. This was sort of a fantasy that art must behave like biological organisms and obey some sort of imagined evolutionary law. In retrospect it really shows how dazzled, how blinded composers in the postwar period were by scientific models. And of course serialism was ideal for that kind of "scientific" approach to the act of composing.

It is interesting that you mentioned Cage and Boulez rather than Copland and Bernstein: they were also very much part of the music scene and their aesthetic may well have been much closer to you than what you describe as fractured Modernism. Their compositions are certainly accessible and have come to be regarded as representative of American music of a particular period.

---

6 Well, at least one composer did: in his interview with Ulrich Dibelius (1993), György Ligeti admitted that he had not been able to fathom Boulez's book (published in English under the title *Boulez on Music Today*), in French or in its German translation. In Ulrich Dibelius, *Ligeti: Eine Monographie in Essays* (Mainz: Schott, 1994), 260. See also Allen Shawn's comments at the end of the interview.

I met Copland several times. He was a lovely man and I love much of his music and continue to perform it. It means something very special to me, although I suspect his is a kind of art that only flourishes in its native land. I don't think that Copland is very popular for example in Germany or in Austria. What's wonderful about Copland's music is its simplicity of expression. He created an unmistakably personal voice, a mixture of Stravinskian harmonic language, American folk music flavored with a bit of 1920s hot jazz. It was a unique and immediately identifiable style, and over time it became emblematic of the "American" trait—you know, the prairies and *Billy the Kid* and *Appalachian Spring* and *Fanfare for the Common Man*. It would be easy to mock this if it weren't for the fact that he did it so well and one can't help being moved by its sincerity and directness. But maybe that's just an American thing—I can't expect, for example, a Russian or a Chinese listener to respond to it in the same way I do.

How about Bernstein's concert music, quite apart from West Side Story? *What I am getting at is that in thinking of contemporary classical music, you need not confine yourself to the avant-garde—there were very well others whose music appealed to the public at large. Nevertheless, you did not draw encouragement from them.*

Bernstein was a huge influence in the United States, and there has never been anybody like him since in classical music. He was an immensely popular figure; he was on television when television was new, and he was handsome and charming like a movie star. It's almost unfair that one person could be blessed with so many gifts. As famous as Toscanini and Stokowski might have been, they never approached the level of recognition that Bernstein did. He was highly educated, articulate and very smart, and with his televised Children's Concerts he was able to explain and communicate what he famously called "the joy of music" to several generations of young Americans. He also was responsible for establishing Mahler as one of the great composers at a time when very few people knew his music.

I was ten years old when I first saw him conduct, and he always fascinated me, even when I came to find problems with his "serious" music. Alas, his creative life was complicated—one could almost say "corrupted"—by his overwhelming public success. It was like Faust! The greater he became as a conductor, the more problematic his composing became. He ultimately lost touch with his true creative self because one simply cannot carry on such a frantic public life and still have the kind of intense internal focus necessary to produce truly important art. I know that is a harsh criticism for me to make, but I believe it's true.

Mahler was admittedly a very public figure and lived a difficult double life as conductor-administrator on the one hand and composer on the other. But despite how busy Mahler was, he kept an absolutely rigid schedule and nothing ever got in the way of his daily composing routine. Bernstein's later life was like that of a movie star. He had next to no private life, and that took its toll. I think Bernstein's grandiose "serious" music is largely embarrassing—works like the *Kaddish* Symphony or the Mass. His *Serenade* for violin, an earlier piece, although mostly a trope on Bartók's *Music for Strings, Percussion and Celesta*, is charming if lightweight. His symphonies I don't like at all. Bernstein's great genius was as a Broadway composer, and all of that was done while he was a very young man.[7]

To get back to the subject of courage: from what I have read, I gather you have become a representative figure in the United States: you stand for modern American music that has found its way to the public. It may require courage for you to compose new pieces without taking into account the public's expectations.

I think it takes courage to keep on going as a composer of "new music," especially in the United States, where popular culture is oppressive and inescapable. You must realize how little audience we composers have in the United States. All the major media, whether it is the Internet or television or the newspapers, are completely focused on popular culture whether it's movies, TV, pop music, or the Internet. A common cliché one hears is "classical music is dead." That comment is made in the press often as a challenge, as if to say "prove to me that it is NOT dead!" And of course one could provide endless lugubrious data to support that statement. But while it may not have the cultural relevance or "clout" that it did in Wagner's time or even Stravinsky's time, it still has a place. People will come up to me in the street and grab my hand and tell me how much my music means to them. It may be a small audience that I have (compared to a rock star), but it's enough to know that what I do is meaningful to someone.

On live recordings of performances of your music, one hears the audience's shouts of enthusiasm and delight. Your works are hugely successful in a way one rarely encounters at concerts of new music. There have been Adams

---

7   See Allen Shawn's comments at the end of the interview.

festivals. *The way one receives your music and the way it is commented on is highly emotional.*[8] *I know from your interviews how important feeling in music is for you—and quite obviously, the emotional charge of your compositions comes across.*

Your question was courage. I know that in the very small pool maybe I am a big fish but the courage is really not about music, it is about my art and my colleagues. Does what I write and what my colleagues are doing now have any use in the future, in the way Beethoven so strongly speaks to people? Or in a hundred years' time when people want to study the year 2005 or the year 1995, will they listen to John Adams or will they listen to Radiohead? Or some rap songs that have more social meaning?

I don't think people will know in a hundred years' time that Radiohead ever existed.

I am not so sure. I am not so sure. I often wonder whether two or three hundred years from now when people think of the 1960s which artists will best represent that era. I do suspect it will be someone like Bob Dylan and not Stockhausen.

Well, perhaps the same social layer will remember them. But another segment of society will know John Adams.

I hope so.

True: Lutosławski, for one, was worried about whether his music would be played after his death when he was no longer around to conduct it. And it seems to me that it has lost ground in the past ten years or so. Berio is also being performed less since he died. But I am sure they will come back due to the sheer quality of their music.

I hope so. The thing is: Wagner's operas had an immense impact on contemporary society. During the last decade of his life virtually every educated person had an opinion about him, whether they admired him or not. His thought and his art were profoundly important and debated at the highest levels of the intelligentsia. You can pick up any contemporary

---

8   Here is an example: "John Adams's Violin Concerto swept through the cheering Disney Hall crowd last weekend like the fingers of a perfect massage," Alan Rich, *LA Weekly*, November 9, 2004 (Adams, *Hallelujah Junction*, 343).

novel—I recently noted a mention in *Anna Karenina* of Wagner—and the characters are aware of him or on the way to Bayreuth or whatever. He was a major cultural phenomenon in the way that in today's world only a movie director or perhaps a very famous rock musician could be. When a performer like Bjørk releases a new album or a director such as Martin Scorsese or Woody Allen produces a major film it is "front page" news and widely discussed, as Wagner was in his time.

Are you really comparing Wagner with Woody Allen?

No, no, only in the sense of him being on the cultural radar, that's all. I am not saying that a Woody Allen movie equals *Götterdämmerung*. I'm just saying that Woody Allen or Bjørk or Bruce Springsteen are part of the larger cultural dialogue in a way that a composer like me is not. People will discuss him at dinner. Just as they did Fellini in the sixties. But very few people will talk about any contemporary composer, even a Boulez or a Steve Reich. Certainly not in the United States where "music" for most people, even the very educated, means popular music.

How can you say that? Your operas have been the subject of so much heated debate! And I don't mean just Klinghoffer *but your other music theater pieces as well. Those works make sure that you are very much on the public mind.*

I hope you are right. I don't see it that way. My audience is a very small one in comparison to Wagner's in his time or Stravinsky's in his.

I think it also took courage for you to comment on topical political phenomena, such as US-Chinese relations, the nuclear threat, or terrorism. I don't think any Hungarian composer has chosen the 1848/49 revolution as the subject for an opera, nor have they written one about the 1956 uprising. Of course, it would have been impossible to stage until the change in our political system in 1989, but our composers have stayed away from the subject in the decades since. I am sure that in a hundred years' time, your operas will come to represent a valid artistic statement on major political issues in the late twentieth and early twenty-first centuries. The very fact that they are there will merit at least a mention in any future history of music.
    Did it involve any courage for you to compose The Death of Klinghoffer?

It took more courage for the presenters! (*laughs*) You know what happened last fall [October 2014] in New York: when the production of *Klinghoffer* was condemned as "pro-terrorist" and "anti-Semitic" and hundreds of people mounted protests in front of the Metropolitan Opera. They even managed to briefly halt the opening night performance. I don't think composing that opera was a matter of "courage," as much as it was of daring to give voice, both musically and poetically, to points of view that were and continue to be violently controversial in the United States. An opera that begins with two choruses, one evoking the Palestinian narrative, and the other the Jewish one, was bound to elicit highly charged emotions. I knew this would be the case when I composed it twenty-five years ago, but I never imagined the hysteria it would provoke with some protesters holding placards comparing it to a terrorist beheading in Syria.

I think if opera is to have a future, it needs to speak about our lives. It needs to speak about things that we encounter every day and that deeply affect our unconscious psyche: terrorism (*Klinghoffer*) or communism versus capitalism (which is what *Nixon in China* is about), or the possibility that a nuclear bomb destroys our planet (*Doctor Atomic*), or poverty, capital punishment, and sexual abuse (*Other Mary*). It frustrates me when other composers write operas about trivial things or with characters that I don't care about and can't empathize with. Opera is a huge sensory experience: in addition to the music, there is the visual aspect, the scenery . . . there is dance, there is poetry—no other art form is capable of bringing all that together to produce an immensely powerful expression.

Of course, writing an opera is two years of very hard work—I think those were wonderful ideas by my incredibly gifted and imaginative colleagues, Peter Sellars and Alice Goodman. And *Doctor Atomic* was such a great idea for an opera—it was suggested by Pamela Rosenberg, who at the time was the administrator of the San Francisco Opera. Pamela wanted an "American Faust" opera; for her, Robert Oppenheimer was a kind of modern Faust.

And how about the courage (if that is the right word in this context) to devise singing lines that justify the fact that the characters sing rather than talk?

Well, what I try to do is to write a sort of vocal line that is very faithful to the way we speak.[9] I don't like it when the composer puts the emphasis on the wrong word. If I say to you "The cat jumped on the table"—ta*ta*-ta*ta*- ta*tata*—we'll both want the musical setting to mirror that internal rhythm. But there are composers who would lay the stress on the wrong

---

9 "He has always shown an unusual respect for language, keeping its everyday rhythms intact," Sarah Cahill, *East Bay Express*, May 19, 1995 (Adams, *Hallelujah Junction*, 346).

words—something like "*the* cat jumped *on* the tab*le*." It's incomprehensible to me that a sophisticated composer could be so tone-deaf to the natural spoken rhythm, but alas I see it all the time, which is why I often tell young composers not to listen to contemporary vocal music but rather to pay attention to the best popular songwriters, whether it's Joni Mitchell or John Lennon or Stevie Wonder.

It is interesting that at conservatories and universities, writing for voice is almost never taught. If you go to composition classes, it's almost de rigueur that the discussion will be about Ferneyhough or Cage, Ligeti, or Lachenmann. Students come out five or six years later and they still don't have a clue how to write for voice. And that was the case for me, too. It took me years of witnessing singers struggling with my awkward vocal lines to finally begin to understand that the human voice and the piano are in fact two very different instruments!

In your works, you not only draw on American vernacular music but, if I understand correctly, you also wish to create a genuine American musical idiom which future generations can draw on. Does that not take courage?

I don't know . . . I think we are very happy when we have an original idea. Courage simply means persistence. A lot of composers look at me and say "Oh, he is so successful!" But in fact I've just persisted. Not everything I've done has been as good as I've wished. But you just need to keep working. Every composer, I suspect, hopes that the NEXT piece is going to be the BEST piece. It likely will not be, but the impetus is to believe that it might is a good thing.

You can't get away from the jealousy of your colleagues. . . . It is part of the game.

Yes—and they don't know how I feel. I often feel that things are not going well for myself and my music. Where courage comes into play is just to believe in yourself and keep on going. In the Modernist experience, the idea of creating an "international style" was very prestigious, especially in the immediate postwar period when anything that smacked of nationalism or ethnic identity was viewed with understandable consternation. But for me, I've come to realize how much I love the "provincial," the "local." I love the earthy "ethnic" quality of Bartók; I love Duke Ellington whose music represents black American culture; I love what's Russian about Tolstoy or Tchaikovsky; or what is French about Debussy or Proust; or what's English about Elgar or Dickens. The international style is not very interesting for me. I find it quite sterile.

Bartók, of course, collected Hungarian (as well as Arab, Turkish, Romanian, Slovak, etc.) folk music and assimilated them in his own compositions. Do you make use of American folk music in your works?

No.

Why?

Because it does not fit my musical language. But what I do instead is to take the essence of the American vernacular and "sublimate" it so that its essence is there but not in the kind of obvious way that, for example, Gypsy music is obvious in Brahms or Russian folk songs in early Stravinsky.

The next opera I am doing is about the California Gold Rush—an unusual opera for me because it is set in the 1850s. I am using songs of that period, but only the texts. I will set the texts to my own melodies.

Of course, the text is also a source of inspiration.

The melodies of those old Gold Rush songs are really not very interesting (*laughs and sings a folk song. That short phrase was enough to convince me*). Of course, I'm just speculating at this point, as I've yet to begin work on the opera. It could happen that when I try to invent my own melodies for these 165-year-old texts, I may find it much more difficult than I expected! Often we discover that in the creative act, the simplest things are the hardest to accomplish.

Comments by Allen Shawn, August–September 2015

I am one year younger than John and was in at least one class with him when we were both students of Leon Kirchner at Harvard. He even played E-flat clarinet in an early composition of mine. It was a rather manic part, and I didn't give him enough space in which to breathe, but he was terrific. It is fun now to remember that at the concert I conducted him. (I believe I was nineteen and he was twenty.)

I also played rehearsal piano for an excellent college production he conducted of *Le Nozze di Figaro*. I believe that Mozart helped him discover his own identity as a man of the theater, and as someone with a gift for writing joyful music.

When he says to you that it was a strange time to study to become a composer, at least in America, he speaks the truth. Our teacher, Kirchner—who was a complete musician and played and conducted brilliantly—was quite exceptional in talking about music in a passionate and not always technical way, and in arguing that the unconscious played a crucial role in the composing process. This was very rare. Music classes were so arid!

I would say that John was blessed with the ability to come out from under the influence of that difficult musical period and rediscover his complete self and be the best possible John Adams, without apology. That is a kind of natural "courage" that many people in his generation lacked.

However, I disagree with his opinion of Bernstein's non-Broadway music. I think it holds up quite well. If you can accept its theatricality and broad gestures (and ignore some of the titles), it is very well-written and always musical in content, always written with love and precision. I know that the Symphonies are problematic in certain respects, but I think they are good music. The *Kaddish* Symphony has some marvelous passages, and its settings of Hebrew are lovely. Bernstein's own text in English is the problem there, in my opinion, and the music is at its best in the first half, where the English text is minimal. I believe that Mr. Berio would have come to Bernstein's defense, too. The fact that Bernstein's name couldn't be mentioned in a class on Contemporary Music when John and I were students is a sign of what a contentious time it was.

I keep thinking about our exchange about Boulez. It just seems to me that there is no one else like him. He is such a complex figure that there could be an entire book written simply about the nature of his influence and the various responses we all had to him. I belong to that group of composers who could assume that he would not find our music of any value or use, but who nevertheless deeply admired him and his music. (I never had a chance to test my assumption, but I believe that I am right.) He has been a very intimidating figure. At the same time he has created works that hint at a deeply sensitive, even vulnerable and delicate nature—even though there is a mask of control and objectivity in front of that nature. Although he ultimately rejected religion completely, he attended a rigidly disciplined Catholic School for eight years as a child.[10] It makes sense in terms of the adult he became and the music he made, which has something of the effect of a cathedral made of steel and glass. It seems to me that there is also some sense of his having created a cage for himself with his particular sense of

---

10 Between 1932 and 1940, Boulez was a pupil of the Institut Victor Laprade. With regard to religious practice there, he "expressed distaste for what he saw as the priests' 'mechanic attitude that had absolutely nothing to do with profound conviction'" (Roger Nichols, "Pierre Boulez Obituary: French Composer and Conductor Whose Influence Transformed the Musical World," *Guardian*, January 6, 2016, https://www.theguardian.com/music/2016/jan/06/pierre-boulez).

where music history was heading, and that he ended up conducting so much more than he composed. One feels that he was not exactly "free" to turn his back on previous ways of composing or to surprise himself with a completely atypical work, such as a transcription of a work by Bach, or a piece for children. The other important composers of his generation all seemed to flower and go in unexpected directions in a way that somehow he did not. But I think that his performances as conductor must have become a primary outlet for his unmatched ear and mind, since they are in their own category in terms of the balances, the clarity of detail, the pacing, and the illuminating of the structures of the scores. As a conductor he has elicited performances that are moving as well as luminous, going back to his *Wozzeck*, and his first Debussy recordings, and many others. Sometimes his restraint or even coldness creates a result that is amazingly tender. I love his conducting of Schoenberg's choral music, for example, and I have all of his Mahler recordings and prefer his versions to Bernstein's.

But going back to *Le Marteau* he has written music that has an awe-inspiring presence, stemming from his unmatched ear, and that mind that has command over seemingly every aspect of his vast designs. The way the percussion instruments are used in *Le Marteau*, for example, ending with the use of the gong in the last movement leaves an extraordinarily eloquent, ritualistic impression, as well as an amazingly balanced, almost mathematical one.

CHAPTER THREE

VYKINTAS BALTAKAS
(B . 1 9 7 2)

Lithuanian composer and conductor

Baltakas and I are both emigrants. We come from former socialist countries; until 1990 Lithuania was actually part of the Soviet Union.

I visited Vilnius as the representative of a Hungarian music publisher in the 1980s, to attend a festival of contemporary Lithuanian music. The few days I spent in the city, my encounters with composers and the leaders of their union, and the atmosphere of the concerts, have left lasting impressions.

Of course, it was all familiar: Hungary and Lithuania are both small countries and their musical life was defined by the same ideology. Figuratively speaking, the dominating color was red. During the course of those few days, I sensed a certain tension in the air, especially around the figure of the Lithuanian composer Osvaldas Balakauskas (b. 1937), whose music struck me as authentic and original, free of any ideology. From that point of view, it was unique among all the compositions programmed at the festival. I had the impression, instinctively rather than based on any tangible evidence, that he was rather isolated, actually ostracized by his colleagues. Impelled by a sense of solidarity, I demonstratively showed my sympathy and we became friends. We stayed in touch for several years afterward, and I succeeded in having one of his compositions published by Editio Musica Budapest.

Vykintas Baltakas experienced the final years of Soviet Lithuania as a young man. He was mature enough to realize that he would need to leave if he was to develop as an artist and was young enough to carry this out while still in his formative years: he studied composition with Wolfgang Rihm and conducting with Péter Eötvös in Karlsruhe.

He joined the stable of Universal Edition's composers around 2000 and it was my responsibility to promote his music until my retirement at the end of 2007. Promotion presupposes close personal contact. Beyond the compositions, one also has to fathom the composer. Baltakas was a young man marked by intensity, pride coupled with vulnerability, quite obviously free of any doubt regarding his calling and whatever he happened to be working on, and yet yearning for recognition and positive feedback.

The originality of his music fascinated me right from the start. It is new without aspiring to be so, it is far above ideologies, dogma, abstract concepts. It was perhaps his sound world that captivated me to begin with, with beauty of a kind that gives the listener a veritable physical pleasure. RiRo (1996–99) for soprano and trumpet—published by Aust in Cologne—was such a eureka experience; it recurred each time I listened to the piece. This sonorous fantasy made me simply happy—the imagination of this young man who produced such novel sounds for the human voice and the trumpet. In subsequent works I discovered traces of Lithuanian folk music that lent them a particular savor—more than that, an affirmative vitality. Equally important was the unpredictability of his compositions, so that the listener would be caught unawares in every moment.

The seven years of our collaboration produced a range of compositions that I look back on with pleasure—for music theater (Cantio, 2001-4), orchestra (Poussla, 2002-6, Scoria, 2001-10), ensemble (Ouroboros, 2004; [co]ro[na] 2005), and chamber music (b[ell tree], 2007, for string quartet).

I sent the above paragraphs to Vykintas Baltakas by way of information. His reply was a reminder that one ought to take one's own superficial impressions with a grain of salt. Rather than reword my text, I have decided to leave it unchanged but add the composer's comments.

December 18, 2015

There is just one thing I want to comment on, regarding the last years of Lithuania's Soviet occupation (ca. 1985–90).

You must clearly distinguish between the Union of Soviet Composers, which was still under strong political control and the national (Lithuanian) Composers' Association. In those years, we learned from poets, composers, and painters about freedom. The different artists' associations (especially in the Baltic states) found clever ways of escaping political dictates; they were frequently the springs of change that gave birth to revolutionary movements.

That is also true of the Lithuanian Composers' Association, dominated by such personalities as Vytautas Landsbergis.[1] If the festival and the music you heard made a conservative impression, it probably had to do with stylistic and creative limitations, the results of many years of isolation. The old school was still present but two new trends had also emerged, one represented by Bronius Kutavičius, rooted in authentic folk music, the other linked to Osvaldas Balakauskas, constructive and cosmopolitan in character.[2]

The years of change . . .

Did it take courage for you to become a composer in Lithuania, with your own ideas about music?

I grew up at a time of change, when the old system was no longer functioning and the new one had not yet established itself. It resulted in a great deal of freedom in the arts. Sometimes I think that composers in Lithuania around 1990 were freer and keener to experiment than they are today.

Culture played a special role: since one was not allowed to talk about politics and the difficulties the country was facing, we could only do so indirectly, in literature, in music, and the theater. Those media proved harder to control through censorship. As a result, the arts in those years were strongly pervaded by extraneous ideas. For a foreign listener who knows nothing about the political and historical context, they surely appear odd and difficult to grasp.

Do you mean that prior to 1990, new music was a mouthpiece for the opposition?

Yes, no doubt about it. Never before was new music so popular as then! The arts played a very strong and positive role in Lithuania's political life before the change of system.

---

1   Vytautas Landsbergis (b. 1932), Lithuanian musicologist and politician. He was his country's first president after it gained independence.
2   Bronius Kutavičius (b. 1932), Lithuanian composer and professor.

What kind of music did you compose at the time?

I studied with Vytautas Barkauskas and was influenced by Bronius Kutavičius (who had taught me at school), later also by Osvaldas Balakauskas. I think highly of those composers up to this day and perform their works with my LENsemble.

Did you have access to music from the West?

Yes, certainly from the 1990s onward. To begin with, I was greatly impressed by the music of Luciano Berio; I heard it on Radio Free Europe, as far as jamming made it possible. Later, with the political thaw, when the Ensemble Modern appeared in Vilnius, they had Ligeti on their program. That was a revelation! I left the hall with my head swimming and decided to find out all I could about Ligeti.

And I was thirsty for music all the time. I was saturated with Lithuanian music and wanted to hear something different. I went to Karlsruhe to study with Wolfgang Rihm and spent hours in the music library of the academy to discover music that was new for me.

Do you regard your decision to leave Lithuania to have been courageous?

I do not think so. I was twenty-one at the time and acted without thinking about it. Of course, I had no money at all. The economic situation in Lithuania was wholly different from today; I could not expect any financial support. But in any case, a young man acts on an impulse, and as I said the thirst for the new was overwhelming. I felt no anxiety, or courage, I just did it.

Revised March 2016

Back to the point . . .

We recorded that conversation in December 2015. Reading the transcript has brought home to me that we discussed courage/anxiety/freedom solely from a political aspect.

The question goes far deeper than that. It is linked to human psychology and is not as closely dependant on outside factors as one would think. Outside factors can of course narrow the boundaries of freedom, or indeed, expand them. In fact, totalitarian regimes, such as National Socialism or Soviet Communism can impose such debilitating limits as to stifle any creative work. But the tension created by anxiety/courage/freedom remains even if outside factors have become more favorable. Why?

Composers are affected by the times they live in. They cannot choose them, nor can they evade the historical period they are born into. That also determines the social, cultural, and economic relationships they face. Artists are social beings and those relationships are necessary for them to survive. They strive for communication, they want to be understood. A storyteller must tell his story in a language that will be grasped by his listeners and use images that will evoke familiar associations for them. Otherwise, his story would make no sense, it would be just an acoustic experience. He may experiment to the extent that he does not lose contact with his listeners. If he goes too far, he will lose his relevance; indeed, he will stop being a storyteller. With all its social and economic consequences.

That means that a story-teller's freedom is constrained by the limitations of his listeners. The expansion of those limitations should occur simultaneously with the artist and the consumers of his art; in any case, the distance between them should keep "visibility" intact. That explains why the history of art can only proceed step by step.

That is also the reason why the storyteller feels a tension between his longing for total artistic freedom and the uncertainty produced by his creativity. I am consciously avoiding the word *anxiety*, for this is all about the fundamental human need to communicate, and to be understood. Anxiety, on the other hand, is a negative motivation: if one is afraid of certain consequences, one acts differently than one would normally do. That is why you can regard the need to communicate as a positive effort to adapt oneself to the environment. If, on the other hand, you act out of anxiety, you restrict yourself in a negative fashion. The new music world often regards the need to communicate as a kind of populism. That is, however, not always the case: without the necessary communication between the artist and his "customers," there would probably be no art. The boundary between populism, the need to communicate, and self-restriction is narrower than one would assume; all artists are forced to make difficult decisions.

If this dialectic regarding the storyteller and his listeners is projected onto society, we can observe a similar process in cultural milieus. Whether they be in Germany, France, Scandinavia, or Central Europe—artists seek access to a cultural circle and—at the same time!—an escape from it. Those circles stake out their aesthetic and ideological terrains, with their boundaries binding on artists. In other words, they provide artists with the raison d'être and recognition they need but at the same time impose on them aesthetic and ideological limits. A comparison with totalitarian systems offers itself at this point. The difference lies in the word *total*: totalitarian regimes apply their ideology and aesthetic on the entire territory under their control, whereas cultural circles in democracies determine solely their own sphere of influence; several such cultural circles can exist side by side—peacefully or otherwise—within the same country.

It is thrilling to observe how hard the different cultural circles have to fight with one another to legitimize their existence: Darmstadt versus Henze and his circle, the group around Boulez versus the advocates of Dutilleux, and so forth.[3] But the relationship of cultural circles to society is similar to that of artists to cultural circles. A circle seeks contact with society to establish its own relevance: political, economic, or ideological. Frequently, concepts are put forward in the field of politics, economy, and ideology that are generally accessible and easily digestible—such as "we safeguard our cultural heritage," "we care for the young generation," "we are the visionaries," and so forth.

The Darmstadt school after the war is a good example. A radical break with musical tradition was covered up by the principle of "ideology-free," "objective" music (as against ideology-saturated music in the Third Reich). That worked very well, the Darmstadt composers gained social legitimacy and were able to devote themselves to unprecedented radical experiments. It is important to note, however, that in order to communicate the ideology of Darmstadt (a movement that had no truck with populism) it was necessary to use an-easy-to grasp (that is, in a way, popular) element to secure social support for their experiments. "Objective" music, "free of ideology" was understandable for anyone, they fitted into postwar thinking and they sufficed for New Music to be left alone, in other words, to be free.

The same is happening in the music of the individual composers. To expand the limits of one musical aspect, composers are intuitively compelled to treat another aspect in a traditional manner, in order to maintain

---

3   Baltakas is referring to a heated debate between Helmut Lachenmann and Hans Werner Henze on October 13, 1982, in Stuttgart. In the decades since, their dispute has become symbolic of the fundamental difference between two compositional stances: Henze representing those who turn without any compunction to tradition and make use of its means of expression in an avowed attempt to be understood and, indeed, loved by the public. Lachenmann, on the other hand, stands for the pioneers, the innovators, who accuse traditionalists of serving a false utopia that has nothing to do with reality. The debate between the two composers lives on vividly in the minds of the younger generation of composers, as borne out by references to it in this book, in the interviews with Enno Poppe and Johannes Maria Staud. For details, see Helmut Lachenmann, *Musik als existentielle Erfahrung* (Wiesbaden: Breitkopf und Härtel, 1996/2015), 331–33, 408–10.

communication with their listeners. John Cage, for instance, needed to place his *4'33"* in a traditional concert situation, with a musician and his instrument. Karlheinz Stockhausen saw it advisable to embed the abstract music of his operas in a simple, accessible mythology. Luigi Nono incorporated topical political themes in his music and Lachenmann uses the most traditional group of instruments—that of a string quartet—to produce his *musique concrète instrumentale*, even though other means would also be perfectly feasible.

That is no criticism. I simply want to call attention to the fact that both aspects—the progressive and the traditional—are necessary; they support each other. The dimension of the amplitude between the two, and the extent to which the unity of both elements is realized serve as yardsticks for the greatness of an artist.

An art that repeats itself, that no longer strives for the new and has as a result degenerated into mere "production" is at the extreme end of that amplitude. It hardly deserves to be called art. At the other extreme you will find art that has grown so distant as to have lost its ability to communicate. It has turned into a private language, without any social relevance.

Great art, on the other hand, is capable of assuming new forms all the time, but has retained a sufficient link to the outside world so that it can still communicate its message.

The movement of art in time can therefore be seen as that of a millipede. The way it moves its feet is a metaphor for the endeavors of artists. They are not synchronized, the direction is open. However asynchronous the movements of the little feet may be, they need one another to be able to stay in motion at all. It is not until the end of an epoch that we can see where the millipede has got to. At that point, a new millipede will be born—perhaps bigger or smaller than its predecessor—that will continue to move on the leaf of art.

And how about the question of courage?

The millipede needs neither too big nor too small feet. . . . The feet feel that intuitively and adapt themselves. That usually marks the border of an epoch. However, one has to have the courage to step with one foot forward, whether it is too big or too small, taking the risk of being rejected by the millipede.

CHAPTER FOUR

GEORGE BENJAMIN
(B . 1 9 6 0)

British composer and conductor

Intuitively, I associate George Benjamin with Witold Lutosławski. I do not mean that their music has anything in common. It is rather the fastidious care with which they approach(ed) a new score, each detail crafted with utmost attention and in no undue rush to meet a deadline, with the result that each premiere became (and for Benjamin still becomes) a much anticipated musical event.

I actually knew the Polish composer better than I do George Benjamin. I succeeded in getting the older man invited to conduct in Budapest a number of times, and he and his wife Danuta came to my place, where we had long conversations over meals. None of this has been the case with George, but our few meetings, telephone conversations, and e-mail exchanges over many years have created in me the impression that Benjamin—like Lutosławski— views his work with an almost religious awe. The phrase "my music," when uttered by George sounds as if he were talking of a being independent of him, with an existence all its own, whether it has been written, is in gestation, or being planned for the future.

All this is terribly subjective, of course. What counts—apart from the music itself—is the confession that George Benjamin has contributed to this book. It may be rather brief but it does reveal some very important aspects of his goals as a composer: new concepts, independent path, never-heard combinations. As far as I can judge, he has achieved them all.

June 2015

Courage? Surely "courage" isn't the right word. Obstinacy and patience—
they are more suitable terms related to the act of composing. After all, no
musician has ever had life or limb threatened by writing a simple dot on
manuscript paper—unless that musician has the great misfortune to live in
an insane totalitarian state.

And yet the empty page does hold its terrors—for, particularly with
large-scale works, the first marks on a virgin sheet herald a long personal
journey for its owner, pursuing an isolated path into the unknown that will
inevitably have its fair share of dead-ends, blockages, and traumas until
the final bar is reached. A spirit of adventure is also essential in order to
explore new concepts in terms of structure or never-heard combinations
on the smaller scale, while determination will also be crucial in surmount-
ing the technical challenges that will certainly be encountered en route.
Optimism also plays its role, in the stubborn belief that eventually the work
will be complete—and might be of some worth. Finally, a degree or two of
intransigence is essential in order to pursue an independent path, ignore
the fashions of the day, and remain true to oneself.

And as for the wider world and public reception—the happiest state
for a creator, musical or otherwise, is to be oblivious of them altogether,
in the hope that the all-consuming challenge and excitement of the task in
hand will cocoon one from such considerations.

CHAPTER FIVE

FRIEDRICH CERHA
(B . 1 9 2 6)

Austrian composer and conductor

Vienna, March 13, 2015
Revised September 2015

I know Friedrich Cerha better than most of the composers in this book. I was responsible for the promotion of his music during my time with his publisher, Universal Edition, and that has meant knowing his wife, Traude Cerha, just as closely. They are a modern reincarnation of Philemon and Baucis, very much like György and Márta Kurtág.

Friedrich Cerha is one of those rare personalities whose very presence in a society establishes a standard the rest of us regard with awe and aspire to be worthy of. That is what teachers should ideally be like—and he was for many years a professor of composition at Vienna's music academy. Friedrich Cerha is a poeta doctus. *I admire his music with all its various facets—perhaps most of all its lyricism with its touch of melancholy and pain—but also his (often self-deprecating) sense of humor in private intercourse as well as in his hilariously witty pieces based on Viennese popular music.*

I have often experienced Cerha as a conductor—sparing in his gestures, steering the orchestras and ensembles rather than impressing them with spectacular flourishes—and sometimes also in preconcert talks where in his quiet voice he gave us fascinating insights into his music and his private world that feeds it.

Your wife has very nearly discouraged me from confronting you with my question regarding the role of courage in the creative process: she says courage is so much part of your makeup that its presence or absence simply does not arise as a problem.

Indeed, I cannot make much of the notion of "courage." It is rather like "happiness." You may perhaps hear people say, "I am so happy," but they are more likely to say, "That was a happy time." And I think no one would declare, "I am courageous"; they would rather say, "It was quite courageous of me at the time." Courage is a quality you simply have—or you do not have.

I have never felt "courageous." Twice I deserted the German Wehrmacht. It could have cost me my life but I never considered it an act of courage; it was the most natural thing to do, once the chance had presented itself. The same goes for programming Cage's piano concerto in 1959 in my concert series with the ensemble "die reihe."[1] In retrospect one might well say that it was a courageous thing to do but I did not see it in that light at the time. It was natural for me to want to inform the Viennese public of the existence of this highly remarkable musical phenomenon as represented by Cage's Concert for Piano and Orchestra.

Courage could be part of your inborn need to be free—from constraints and the like.

As a matter of fact, I developed early on, as a child, a strong resistance to any kind of constraint, perhaps as a reaction against the demands of my dominant mother. As a young man, I obeyed the same urge in resisting the Nazi regime, and later on, it also influenced my activities in the field of culture.

I remember how in the 1970s when I started the international promotion of contemporary Hungarian music, composers would pilgrimage to Warsaw to hear what their colleagues in the West had been up to. The Warsaw Autumn was the only festival behind the Iron Curtain where they had a chance to do so. They would then try to draw their own conclusions in writing their new works. It must have taken courage for a composer not to jump on the bandwagon. Perhaps most composers do have a need to belong somewhere.

---

1   Founded by Friedrich Cerha and Kurt Schwertsik in Vienna in 1958, "die reihe" was a forum for acquainting audiences with new music by Austrian composers and their colleagues worldwide. Friedrich Cerha conducted the second European performance of the Concert for Piano and Orchestra, with David Tudor as soloist.

I have never felt part of a group or a trend. But once again, that had nothing to do with courage; it was a stance that came naturally to me. Courage is always a question of deciding between two possibilities, provided both are feasible; one musters courage to choose one. That is what happens when I decide in October to spring yet again into the cold water of my pool. Essentially, however, I have never faced a quandary of that sort. Whatever I have done sprang from a natural necessity.

You never felt part of a group or a trend. Were you not tempted in 1956 to join the composers of the Darmstadt Summer Courses or to let yourself be influenced by the novelty of their ideas?

I found the atmosphere incredibly stimulating. My exposure to the ideas of the Darmstadt avant-garde inspired me to make the leap onto uncharted territory as far as the musical idiom was concerned. Still, in the pieces that came about as a result (to begin with surely in an instinctive manner, I should say) I reacted straight away critically to an essential danger inherent in orthodox serialism: that of losing your bearings aurally, something you cannot avoid if you start with creating single elements and thereby totally fragment connections. Already in my *Deux éclats en réflexion* (1956) and in *Formation et solution* (1956–57) I worked with groups of tones, primarily with rhythmic groups, with which I succeeded—for all the fragmentation—in creating connections, developments once again. The titles go to show that this had in fact been my conscious goal.

In 1958, Ivan Eröd and I played those pieces in Darmstadt,[2] with Nono in the audience. He criticized me for using new means to make old music. I carried on all the same. Naturally, I noticed how the ideologically charged atmosphere exerted pressure on some composers and I analyzed this in my writings, but it never affected my work in any way.

In the 1970s you nevertheless reverted to traditional qualities.

It was in the 1960s that I started to rediscover and exploit the qualities offered by tradition. It all began very slowly in *Exercises* (1962–67/1987) and initially remained unnoticed. I made very extensive use of it for a short time from 1969 or so. *Sinfonie* (1975) is a case in point. When it was premiered that year at the Royan Festival (it was a prominent festival of new music at the time), the piece created something of a shock. Those who were

---

2   Born in 1936, Ivan Eröd is an Austrian composer of Hungarian birth.

familiar with *Spiegel* (1960–61), thought I had gone mad. Antoine Goléa, who did not know my music at all, declared that I was a Saint-Saëns well-versed in Webern.

More importantly, I was regarded from then on as a renegade, a traitor to the cause of new music. That performance was to have disastrous consequences for my so-called career in the world of new music. All the same, I ignored all that in my work.

To return to your large-scale orchestral cycle Spiegel: *were you aware that you were entering a hitherto unmapped territory?*

Yes, of course. After *Mouvements* (1959–60) it was perfectly clear to me that with *Fasce* (1959–74) and *Spiegel* I was following a novel course of development. And I fully expected never to hear the piece in my lifetime.

It was apparently not a matter of courage for you to carry on but—how shall I put it—one of determination. After all, it was a tremendous effort; it took a great deal of time and energy to complete the cycle.

It was a fundamental need, just like any other necessities of life. You do not decide whether to breathe or not to breathe—you just do it. The birth of the cycle was a similar process.

It was in my opera *Baal* (1984–87) that I succeeded for the first time, I think, to seamlessly integrate all my experiences into a musical organism. How many of the ideas of the *Spiegel* cycle survive in it and in later pieces, such as the orchestral work *Nacht* (2011–13), is only being grasped gradually.[3]

If you conceive of a new idea, do you ever wonder if it is worth following up? Were you always absolutely sure in your mind that what you were doing, the way you were doing it, was right, to the exclusion of any other path? Is doubt as much foreign to you as courage is?

I have always regarded my decisions to be necessary for me there and then. It does not mean that I never had any doubt concerning certain elements or steps in my development. But there was no doubt in my mind as to the necessity of doing a particular thing at a particular time.

---

3 World premiere, October 17, 2014, Donaueschingen, with Emilio Pomàrico conducting the SWR-SO Baden-Baden and Freiburg.

Since you have mentioned the *Spiegel*: I have never given any thought to the scale of work facing me in notating a composition. But now, at the age of eighty-nine, I seem to have fallen into my own trap, so to speak: I am writing a highly complex piece for fifty solo strings . . .

So I have heard, yes . . .

And I failed to foresee just how much work it would involve. Terrible! For the first time in my life I am thinking—if only I had known, I would not have . . .

But you are carrying on.

Yes.

Did you have any doubt about embarking on the completion of the third act of Lulu? *After all, it meant renouncing your own work for a very long stretch of time.*

I did have a great deal of doubt. I had studied the material for a whole year or perhaps longer to decide whether one may or should or must undertake it. After all, I am no friend of arrangements or encroaching on somebody else's work. But then it became clear to me that this difficult and lengthy job could and had to be done, as a service to the composition. I was not required, you see, to produce anything new as far as composing was concerned—more or less everything had been left behind by Berg. However, I had to establish, to establish scrupulously, what remained to be done and then decide if it could and should be done. It was then that I resolved to undertake it—a resolution that had nothing to do with courage. And so I set about doing it.

There ends the interview recorded in Friedrich Cerha's home in March 2015, edited and supplemented by the composer in September of that year. A few months earlier, I had sent him the paragraph from Karl Aage Rasmussen's contribution that gave me the idea to add "the tyranny of taste" to the title and the subject of the book. Rather than take up the interview, Professor Cerha sent me the following text:

To begin with something fundamental and at the same time personal: I am against wrenching notions out of their original context and transferring them to other domains. For me, taste applies to our senses; it has to do with eating and drinking. And I see no reason why it should not be left that way.

As a matter of fact, taste has become a questionable notion. I avoid using it because it covers so many things. In this particular case, we cannot even begin to fathom all its connotations. I find it remarkable that in the title you have chosen for your interviews, a word that denotes sensory and aesthetic perception stands next to the word *tyranny*.

Beyond the role played by man's herd instinct and the imitation instinct in what we like and value, what we accept and what we reject, the need to belong to a leading group and the fear of failing to do so constitute an essential motif in the emergence of what one calls taste, what leads to fashions and finally perhaps to what you name "the tyranny of taste."

With regard to the situation of new music in the 1950s, your combination of the two notions has a provocative aspect to it in that no one at the time spoke of "taste." The genuinely exciting new ideas were based on ideologically motivated theses, expounded with imposing confidence by intellectually and verbally potent artists and fervently defended by a quickly emerging camp of followers. That it turned just as quickly into a doctrine, even a dictate, as to what new music should be like could in my opinion only happen in the kind of authoritarian society that existed primarily in Germany at that time, in contrast to British society, for instance. This becomes evident if you remember that aleatoric music, diametrically opposed to serialism, in its most extreme manifestation—for instance, John Cage's piano concerto—could become just as quickly the same kind of ideologically grounded and defended doctrine.

Ideologically motivated debates steered the market and thereby perception. As we can establish with hindsight, the actual compositional work of major composers happened in any case ab ovo in a different manner from the way propagated (to a certain extent right up to this day) by the ideological superstructure. How much it did influence the paths of composers is one of the questions to be clarified, perhaps, by the replies you will receive to your questions.

As pointed out above, I found the ideas that I first encountered in Darmstadt in 1956 highly stimulating and they surely influenced my work, but I never felt "tyrannized" by the dominant ideological requirements. In the beginning, I perceived them marginally and later, more than anything, as an interesting phenomenon.

The notion of "taste" has a peculiar history in connection with composing. Mozart's father expressly admonished him to bear the "popular" in mind—that is, to heed the taste of the time. Ideas and conventions of composition at a particular period as well as their transformation allow us to observe a succession of styles that are, as far as we can judge, bound up with the dominating spirit and taste of the time. Of interest is the question of when and how this word, in connection with art, acquired a particular, negative "haut goût." Possibly, it happened in connection with the vociferous emergence of the "avant-garde" at the beginning of the previous century that strongly opposed the status quo and was indeed seen as its alternative.

Ideological standards turn into "taste" when one no longer knows where they come from and what happens if they are transgressed. This applies not so much to composers, I think, as to the public that—influenced by the ideological superstructure referred to earlier—has grown used to particular sound events and has eventually come to like them. Over the past decades, I have observed that those who did not flee from the concert hall right at the start, ended up as enthusiastic supporters and later—when the music failed to match certain newly established expectations—tended to be irritated rather than reject the music altogether. Apparently, a taste had developed that one wanted to see served.

Indeed, the public of "new music" concerts seems to take whatever is offered to them without any differentiation—something I find irritating. The wide range of styles that now marks current-day music makes for fundamentally different works on offer. Even former centers of what is known as the "Darmstadt aesthetic" are showing signs of change, while continuing to cling to what was initiated there. It has not entirely lost its influence on the market.

What of the "tyranny of taste" today? The audience for "new music"— amazingly large in Vienna—has grown used to visiting certain concerts and festivals. Whether these events meet their taste or to what extent their taste has changed or whether it has retained any willingness to apply judgment in their taste is difficult to assess. Hopefully, music sociologists are aware of these questions.

Composers may have in the meantime reflected more thoroughly on any link between ideological concepts and questions of taste; and the concomitant pressure, provided it ever existed, has in any case lost much of its impact.

CHAPTER SIX

UNSUK CHIN
(B . 1 9 6 1)

South Korean composer

I have never met the South Korean composer in person but have seen many of her photographs. In looking at her pictures one day, there loomed in the background the deeply furrowed face of Isang Yun (1917–95) whom I had visited at his Berlin home some decades before. Yun's face, the expression of his eyes, his stooping figure, the slowness of his gestures bore traces of the hardships he had undergone: both he and his wife had been kidnapped by the South Korean authorities in 1967—together with fifteen other Korean nationals living in the Federal Republic. He was imprisoned and sentenced to death.

There was a universal outcry, with Igor Stravinsky, Otto Klemperer, Herbert von Karajan, and Luigi Dallapiccola among those signing a petition for his release. Eventually, Yun was able to return to Germany; he obtained West German citizenship and never returned to his native country.

If you read Unsuk Chin's interview about her life with Stefan Drees, you are spared Yun's horror story but do get a very graphic picture of the thorny path that has eventually led her to world fame as one of the major composers living today.[1] It is a veritable fairy tale and one cannot but bow one's head in honor and appreciation of her achievement.

In preparing the German edition of my Three Questions *book, I listened to a great many works by Unsuk Chin (one of the new contributors to the*

---

1 Stefan Drees, ed., *Im Spiegel der Zeit: Die Komponistin Unsuk Chin* (Mainz: Schott, 2011), 13–26.

*volume) and in my introduction, I rendered my impressions in some detail.[2]
In 2014, the Lucerne Festival featured her music and premiered a new work
commissioned by the Roche pharmaceutical company. A book was also published and at Unsuk Chin's request, my introduction was included, both in the
original German and the English translation by Thomas May.*

*To give you an idea of the way I hear Chin's music, here are a few excerpts
from that text:*

> Unsuk Chin's works have afforded me a completely new experience of mu-
> sic; never before have I encountered a contemporary composer, male or fe-
> male, who has had as much to say to me as she does that is new, unusual,
> unsettling, fascinating, and at times terrifying.

> Unsuk Chin has created a world that is uniquely hers: a bright, glittering,
> at times metallic sound, produced by instruments that must very often play
> in the high register, and very fast. What this creates is a tapestry of sound
> with several layers that seem to be infinitely deep. Short motifs flash by,
> often far "below" (you sense a physical distance between the layers of this
> music), very gentle, yet clearly perceptible—like a hallucination. The musi-
> cal continuity is interrupted by sharp, occasionally savage blows.[3]

December 2015
Revised January 2016

I am not quite sure whether courage is quintessential for composing.
What, however, seems crucial is a certain stubbornness and faith (the
latter hopefully coupled with skepticism). After all, the process of composing is a highly unpredictable undertaking, featuring symptoms of a
bipolar disorder—including weeks of staring at an empty piece of paper
and several setbacks—but also sudden breakthroughs, none of which can
really be foreseen. The composing process always used to be complicated,
but seems even more so today, when no binding "grammar" exists anymore (a "grammar" such as—to name but one of the most evolutionary
"fit" ones—functional tonality used to be for about three hundred years).
What has never changed, however, is the very nature of the process of
composing, which resembles a tightrope act between success and failure—no risk, no gain. Picasso certainly was right when he declared that
style is an enemy of art and that the only way to progress is to attempt

---

2   Bálint András Varga, *Drei Fragen an 73 Komponisten* (Regensburg: ConBrio, 2014), 79–81.
3   Roche Commissions, *Unsuk Chin 2014* (Lucerne Festival, Lucerne Festival Academy: Roche, 2014),
    119.

something one hasn't attempted before; it is by passing through chaotic zones that the new arises. Hence, the future of new music depends on whether the eccentricities and unpredictabilities of the composing process can continue to be tolerated. Without such trust in the long-term value of experimentation, the music of the *Ars subtilior*, Beethoven's late quartets, or Webern's music, to name but three superlative examples of many, would not have come into existence.

"Courage" as an attitude is dangerous, but music can provide courage. I was born in the remote South Korea of the 1960s, during a period after decades of occupation and the Korean War, a period marked by poverty and repressive structures. When I was four years old, my father, a Presbyterian clergyman, taught me some rudiments of music and a bit of score reading. Roughly from second grade onward, I was expected to accompany his services on a small organ, thanks to which I learned the basics of harmony (and also acquired practice in prima-vista transposition: as the parishioners' singing grew louder, the pitch rose with it, so that I needed to transpose the music half a tone higher. Later, as they once again sang more softly, the pitch slid downward, and so on).

My dream career was to be concert pianist, but that was impossible due to a lack of money and, hence, a lack of indispensable early formal training. But my middle school music teacher, a composer, encouraged me to pursue composition, and he gave me the key to the school's music room, which allowed me to encounter the gamut of the canon of Western classical music from Bach to Stravinsky in the form of records: an overwhelming experience given the general scarcity back then. Besides, I taught myself by copying out symphonic scores, by listening to recordings, and studying occasional music theory textbooks. Music certainly gave me strength and courage during that time, not as a form of escapism, but as a powerful, transcending means to grapple with reality. When I entered university after two failed attempts (due to lack of private tuition and that I wasn't aware it was forbidden to use a ballpoint pen and that only a very particular type of harmonization was allowed), I entered the composition class of Sukhi Kang, a pioneering figure of contemporary music in Asia who had lived and worked for a decade in Europe. Kang nourished us with the newest avant-garde scores and recordings from Europe, a musical world unheard of in Korea back then. It was not a question of whether this music was "beautiful" or "right"—it was simply fascinating to throw oneself into these new experiences. Listening to Iannis Xenakis, I learned that music could be about defiance and individuality, an important lesson for someone living in a dictatorial country—a lesson learned also, albeit in a *rather* different way, by listening to British pop music. For me, a covertly rebellious youngster growing up in a strictly Confucian country, it was also encouraging to learn that the postwar avant-garde had almost been a youth movement and that Boulez, to name but one example, had been only twenty-one when he composed his iconoclastic First Piano Sonata. My crush on the avant-garde notwithstanding, I didn't, however, abandon my love for, say, Brahms's chamber music, Chopin's piano music, or Stravinsky's ballets.

The next courage-providing experience that was to shape my musical life was when I studied with György Ligeti in Hamburg in the mid-1980s. Paradoxically, its impact was highly dispiriting—not to say devastating—at first. At that time, Ligeti had just overcome a major compositional block by composing his Horn Trio and the first book of his Piano Etudes. In doing so, he had turned his back on the Western avant-garde, renouncing his former faith, as it were. The avant-garde thus became—after fashionable neo-tonality—one of the main objectives of Ligeti's criticism (and he, in turn, became a target of fiery attacks from the German avant-garde camp). It was an interesting time . . . As for Ligeti's teaching approach, it was absolutely unconventional and undogmatic: for instance, he used to play and analyze recordings of all kinds of music, ranging from Sub-Saharan music to Conlon Nancarrow and from Miles Davis to Guillaume Dufay. We rarely listened to music of the avant-garde (for example, I learned about Gérard Grisey's remarkable music only later and on my own initiative). Ligeti could be sarcastic to the bone and he was very exacting: from himself and from fellow composers, he expected the craftsmanship of Stravinsky combined with the maverick originality of Harry Partch, and he was perhaps no less demanding of pupils—a call for perfection that, as one can imagine, resulted in mutual frustration between teacher and students (I recall that a wastepaper basket played an active part in the weekly group lessons). No wonder he dismissed my early prizewinning works as carbon copies of the European avant-garde, reinforcing my own doubts about composing in a post-serial vein and driving me into a deep crisis. In a total stylistic U-turn, I composed the first version of my cantata *Troerinnen*, turning my back on post-serialism, but after that was unable to compose for nearly three years. I found a way out of this block only when I moved to Berlin and started to work at the Electronic Music Studio of the Technical University. Working with computers and electronics back then, in 1988, wasn't the relatively straightforward experience that it is today. For me, it was a totally new, intimidating terrain and I thought that if I should manage to master these apparatuses I would also be able to actively compose again. Looking back, the crucial thing was that by working in the studio I was able to greatly expand my notion of music: for in an electronic music studio one can research—as if with a microscope—the inner life of sounds, on the molecular level, as it were, and make myriads of discoveries. Even though I don't use a computer or other aids when composing acoustical music, these findings have had a great influence on many of my nonelectronic works and on my musical language in general. Working at the electronic music studio back then required of oneself a certain dose of masochism: for example, several hours of computing time were needed to prolong a single note. But just because of this effort one was forced to *reflect*. Today, everything has become so much easier, the technical possibilities are virtually unlimited . . . but the work with electroacoustics has lost much of its charm for me. There's a lot of technical input but comparatively little creative output, and electroacoustic music has not infrequently become more impoverished—a strange phenomenon, but characteristic of many fields. As for the composition process in general, I feel that, paradoxically, it is often through self-imposed limitations that new realms of freedom and creativity can emerge, as ways of escaping one's capriciousness. Or, in Auden's words: "Blessed be all metrical rules that forbid automatic responses, force us to have second thoughts, free from the fetters of Self."[4] It is important, however, that these rules are not preset but that they can and must be discarded anytime if the mind's ear, the final deciding instance, chooses otherwise.

The next groundbreaking experience for me was ten years later, when during a sojourn in Bali, I occupied myself with gamelan music, hearing a number of excellent performances and also studying it for a short time. The encounter with a highly developed and refined musical culture with a long tradition and a fascinating dialectic between very high complexity and simplicity was a liberating experience and it has remotely influenced a number of my works—most notably my Double Concerto for prepared piano, percussion and ensemble—even though I have not imitated any stylistic traits of the gamelan. Non-European traditional musical cultures and other influences from beyond the traditional and contemporary canon of Western classical music remain an important source of inspiration for me. In fact, I have written a concerto for a non-European traditional instrument, the Chinese mouth organ *sheng*, not because I would have

---

4   W. H. Auden, *The Critical Heritage*, ed. John Haffenden (Abingdon, Oxon: Routeldge, 2002), 474.

been interested in pursuing any so-called synthesis of East and West (one should be wary of mixing things that have completely different heritage lines), but because I had been fascinated by this instrument since my childhood, because I feel this highly versatile instrument lends itself to such an undertaking and, especially, since I met the brilliant sheng virtuoso Wu Wei, who had greatly expanded the possibilities of the instrument. Such experiences can broaden one's notion of music. In recent times, I have ventured to write more and more gestural, "unpure" (i.e., less abstract) music, in works such as *Graffiti, Gougalon—Scenes from a Street Theatre, Cantatrix sopranica, cosmigimmicks—a musical pantomime,* and *Mannequin—Tableaux vivants* (or, in a completely different manner, in my opera *Alice in Wonderland,* whose musical style is meant to resemble a funhouse mirror). Paradoxically, it is by trying something new and pushing the limits of one's possibilities—without knowing whether it will work out—that one gains the courage to go on. Of course, as a composer, one has a certain craft, certain methods, prefers certain materials, and draws on compositional techniques that have been acquired through the years—but still, each new work should, ideally, have a unique shape. It's a long and awkward process from the first ideas appearing and ripening in one's head, writing them down in sketches, and finally beginning to flesh out the piece: as a rule, I discard up to 98 percent of my initial ideas and inspirations, but it is not a straightforward process—often one suddenly moves away from a certain idea and looks for an alternative, radically different, possibility before one perhaps comes back to it in a roundabout way. This learning from mistakes and admitting them, the openness to alternative solutions, is quite a difficult thing and requires courage (or, shall we better say, a certain distance from oneself)—and it is a complex emotional process. How can one find out what has succeeded and what has not? In music there is no right or wrong in the strictly logical sense, but one can compare a new piece with masterpieces spanning a thousand years and originating from different cultures and thus develop criteria: on the one hand there is the question as to whether the new work makes sense within the respective cultural convention, while on the other the question is whether it is original. But in speaking about musical "values," language reaches its limits: the devil is in the details and the "how" is infinitely more important than the "what." Why is Mozart's music so fresh and unique although the means were far from original? Or what makes Messiaen's *Turangalîla*-Symphonie, a sublime experience even though it often verges dangerously close to kitsch? The difference is only a thin red line, thinner than paper. How futile would it be to devise rules out

of such subtle (but crucial) differences! But this is what frequently happens amid the bewildering variety of music today, it is always the easiest
solution to categorize composers and compositions by means of clear-cut
dogma and other generalizations, many of which are merely based on
prejudices. It is exactly this kind of pseudo-rational security, this tyranny
of "taste," this self-immunization (by excluding any error) that is deadly
for creativity. And creativity, after all, is known to arise in the most unexpected places.

CHAPTER SEVEN

GEORGE CRUMB
(B . 1 9 2 9)

American composer

As a European not really familiar with musical life in the United States, I have no means of establishing the extent to which the music of George Crumb forms part of the standard concert repertoire today. I do remember that his music—primarily the chamber pieces—were de rigueur at concerts of new music, certainly in Hungary. One could rattle off their titles without a moment's hesitation: Night of the Four Moons *(1969),* Ancient Voices of Children *(1970),* Black Angels *(1970). They had a sound world all their own and were pleasant to listen to, reinforced by the comforting knowledge that in enjoying Crumb one was being ahead of the times. If I remember correctly, no Feldman, Brown, or Cage were programmed at the same concerts; Crumb comfortably stood for new American music.*

In his reply to my first question in my 1983 interview, Crumb listed his sources of influence with remarkable clarity.[1] He was quite obviously perfectly aware of whom he had learned from (Mahler and Debussy, as well as Bartók and Webern) and what exactly he had taken over from them. Oddly enough, what he failed to comment on was what inspired him to use direct quotations from composers of the past. As Paul Griffiths cites the composer in his Modern Music and After, *Crumb had "an urge to fuse unrelated elements and juxtapose the seemingly incongruous."[2]*

1   Varga, *Three Questions for Sixty-Five Composers*, 50–51.
2   Note from Nonesuch H 71255, quoted in Paul Griffiths, *Modern Music and After*, 3rd ed. (Oxford: Oxford University Press, 2010), 179.

If you want to find out just what lies behind Crumb's initial attraction and his relative disappearance from concert programs (certainly in Europe), you need go no further than Richard Steinitz, also quoted by Paul Griffiths, combined with Griffiths's subsequent explanatory notes: "The direct quotations from Bach, Schubert, or Chopin, heard through Crumb's strange and unworldly soundscape, acquire an amazing aura of distance both cultural and temporal. Surrealist museum exhibits, their mummified beauty seems utterly remote, like a childhood memory of warm, homely security."[3]

Griffiths goes on to explain: "It worked. But it worked only as long as tonal and atonal were strictly separate categories, implying a similarly strict separation between ancient and modern. Once composers began to re-establish tonality, and working again in traditional genres (and Davies was doing both from the mid-1970s), such quotations as Crumb's lost the shock, the inadmissibility, on which their effect depended." That may be true, but even with the shock gone, Crumb's music seems to have retained its fascination for record companies, musicologists, and music students. The list of recordings of his music is impressive (Naxos and the Swedish label BIS being in the lead), both portrait CDs—for instance the four books of the Madrigals *together with* Music for a Summer Evening—*and on mixed programs, such as the* Five Pieces for Piano, *coupled with works by Copland, Carter, and Cage.*

The number of doctoral theses concentrating on aspects of George Crumb's music as well as books and articles focused on it further indicate that the American composer has maintained a lively presence in the musical consciousness. This is also borne out by the number of times his works are listened to on YouTube.

I seem to have found cogent counterarguments to my own, admittedly unreliable, impression that George Crumb's oeuvre may have lost its previous impact of a few decades ago. Whatever the truth may be, its future lies in the hands of generations yet to be born.

April 24, 2015

I am sorry for this very belated response to your inquiry. I needed some time to ask myself if I had experienced anything as a composer related to the "courage motif" that interested you and might eventually result in a book.

As you may know, my own musical language is very much involved in the exploitation of *timbre* as an important expressive element. The obsessive use of this element first appeared in my Five Pieces for Piano (1962)

---

3   Richard Steinitz, "The Music of George Crumb," *Contact* 11 (1975): 14–22, quoted in ibid.

and led to my experimenting with many extended effects such as the production of harmonics, glissandos over the strings, muted tones, pizzicato, and so forth. I later pursued the enlargement of coloristic possibilities for percussion, string, and wind instruments, and the human voice. I began to refer to my scores as "danger music" because of a performer's difficulty in mastering totally new techniques of sound production. And I encountered much resistance from instrument makers and piano tuners who feared that playing my music would harm their instruments (which of course it would *not*). If there was a personal "courage motif," it consisted in my determination to follow my ear and write the kind of music I was destined to write!

CHAPTER EIGHT

CHAYA CZERNOWIN
(B . 1 9 5 7)

Israeli composer

The State of Israel is a tiny country with a population of some eight and a half million people. It has produced proportionally many outstanding instrumentalists and singers who have made international careers. On the other hand, for whatever combination of reasons, there seem to be few Israeli composers who have had international success. I used to maintain a short-lived correspondence with Dan Yuhas (b. 1947), whose surname has obvious Hungarian roots (juhász means shepherd). In Donaueschingen especially, I would come across the name and the music of Dror Feiler (b. 1951). Most important, perhaps, I met Josef Tal (1910–2008) on my only visit to the country of my ancestors; I met him in his home overlooking the old city of Jerusalem. A few years later, he had a world premiere played by the Berlin Philharmonic, which brought him to Germany.

But there is no doubt in my mind that the one Israeli composer whose name has a familiar ring to it is Chaya Czernowin. She is the first one who comes to mind when one thinks of Israeli composers; her presence in our musical life is a simple fact of life.

We met on her visit to Vienna in the lobby of her hotel and I was struck by the depths in her dark brown eyes—the eyes of someone who has experienced much in life, the eyes of a thinker and perhaps, I hardly dare write this, the eyes of someone who knows more unhappiness than she does happiness. (How far one is allowed to go in making public one's subjective impressions,

I do not know. But I am trying to write in these introductions the truth—my truth).

I was very happy with our interview, for her replies never failed to surprise me. How right she is, for example, that it is extremely difficult to reach a state of genuine loneliness—that it is something to aspire to rather than dread—to dispel the specters of all one's former influences, whose opinions might prove stultifying once one has developed a world of one's own. I used to imagine that the loneliness of a creator sitting at a desk might equal the earsplitting silence of a vacuum. How wrong I was—I now know that, thanks to Chaya Czernowin.

Vienna, November 19, 2015
Revised November 22, 2015

I feel very strongly about the loneliness of creative people in the face of their own creativity. They are solely responsible for their decisions, for the choices they have to make—the act of creation is an act of daring.

This is very interesting because actually, to reach a degree of real loneliness is not easy. As a young composer, you are surrounded by the voices of your colleagues and the voices of your teachers. All those voices are with you when you are composing. Physically, you may appear to be alone in your room, but actually you are not alone. You hear your friends and know what they would be saying, you hear your teachers' comments on this or that move you have made. Also, you have in your head all the pieces you have heard in the past. In other words, you have to work hard to reach genuine loneliness.

Is it something you are consciously trying to achieve?

Yes, this is something you have to do, consciously—perhaps not when you are young, because then you need all those voices. They are external but your internalize them. You need them, because they help you to navigate. It is like in life—in life, you also make a lot of moves and you have to make your decisions by yourself. You are alone, even if you have good friends you can consult. But making a decision is an act of loneliness—if you deserve it! Because if you let yourself be influenced by what your environment, your friends, or the authoritative forces in your life are saying, it is not your own decision. You have to make a distinction between what others expect of you and what you want to do. This distinction is not to be taken for granted.

Is the making of that distinction an act of courage?

I want to understand to begin with what you mean by courage.

I believe it was courageous for Cage to come forward and present his silent piece 4'33"—but for him to take that step, he needed the encouragement he drew from Robert Rauschenberg's white paintings.

To my mind, to call that courage carries a great deal of pathos. False pathos. I would never say I am courageous—even though I am. But it is not about courage. This is something dependent on your psychological makeup. It is not about embarking on something that nobody has done before (*she makes fun of the theatricality of heroic gestures by raising her fist high, rather like a socialist-realist statue*).

Much rather, it is about the uncompromising existential need to leave a dent in the world. You want to leave something behind. You feel you have a mission. It is not a matter of choice—it is what you are here to do.

You write what you have to write.

You have to write because if you don't, you do not exist. This is not courage—this is compulsion. I think courage is a Romantic notion, you do not think in those terms anymore.

We have talked about Israel. If you live in a certain political climate and you go against it, you have courage. If you hear people making a racist remark and you say: excuse me, this is not the right way to talk about that person, then you have courage. I believe in courage in small things, when a person goes against a group, or against a climate.

Let us say—because you are obviously concerned about what is going on in Israel . . .

. . . and the world . . .

. . . and the world. If you were to write a vocal work—an opera or oratorio, any setting of a text—criticizing the Israeli far right, would that take courage?

That is again a problem, when it comes to artistic expression. The question is: is the music strong, is it fulfilling for you as music? Or do you take music and enslave it to serve something that is very important for you, for your philosophy?

My two operas are actually very political. *Pnima* (2000) is about the necessity, even in the face of failure, to communicate a trauma. In this particular case, autobiographically, the trauma of the Holocaust. The second opera, written as a counterpoint to Mozart's *Zaide*, is about the oppression that the reality of war in the Middle East, with its authoritative extremist voices, has on a mixed couple who fall in and out of love because of the war situation.[1]

In both cases, the position that I wish to articulate is not a simplistic one-dimensional political position. It states: stop! Stop and think, and don't be an automaton. A message for the right wing, for the left wing, for everybody: stop for a moment. Think about individual people and not about groups.

We talked about invention in connection with Cage. There are two sides to invention: either you go to a place that has yet to be discovered, or you follow something that exists and let it guide you. I have written about this subject—"The Art of Risk Taking: Experimentation, Invention and Discovery."[2] And that is, perhaps, what we are talking about. If you talk about risk taking, that is something that I really believe in. It has none of the Romantic connotation that courage has. It is perhaps smaller but more precise as to what I feel creativity is about.

Have you ever experienced the negative influence of other people's taste in judging your music?

If you go to YouTube and see what people say about your music, it is enough to put you in a bad mood. Or in a good mood. It is not so important. I do not write to get a reaction in that sense. Reaction is something deeper and it actually takes much longer. I do not write in a certain style. Actually, I am anti-style. Over the years, my writing has been a study in how to peel away style, preconceptions, and prejudices of my own and try to get to a place where my soul (a Romantic notion but I will use it) can speak—clearly, and with its own voice. This is not easy to do. It is actually very difficult to bring off. Because of what I said about loneliness: it is never absolute. There is always what has been done before. It is not that I want to invent myself. But maybe I want to believe that there is something small, ten centimeters by

---

1   *Zaide Adama.* Fragments. Composed in 2004/5, the world premiere took place in Salzburg in 2006.
2   The text was written as a keynote speech for a symposium at the Orpheus Institute in 2012. The symposium was called "Composition–Experiment–Tradition."

ten centimeters, that is my island to which I was born to contribute. This island grows on everything that has been done in the past. It is not new. It is in a river of knowledge, a river of creation. And I can contribute one drop to that river. But that one drop, if I want to contribute it, it has to be mine. Otherwise, I did not contribute.

CHAPTER NINE

PAUL - HEINZ DITTRICH (B . 1 9 3 0)

German composer

This is a sad, indeed, a tragic story.

When I first met the German composer in Berlin, capital of the German Democratic Republic (GDR), probably in 1983, my job was to do a radio program on music in the GDR. We met in the lobby of a hotel with Georg Katzer, Friedrich Goldmann, and Friedrich Schenker also present to be interviewed.

I sensed a distance that appeared to separate Dittrich from his colleagues. Even after an interval of more than three decades, I cannot forget a head turned in another direction when Dittrich was speaking, I can hear the silence that followed before another composer broached a subject that did not seem to have anything to do with the one discussed by Dittrich.

The reason for his apparent isolation was that, of all the East German composers, Paul-Heinz Dittrich had a publisher in the West: Universal Edition (UE) had signed him on, thanks to the interest taken in his music by UE's director, Alfred Schlee. That made Dittrich's position unique: he received commissions, his works were performed beyond the East German borders—he could step across the Iron Curtain.

And suddenly, it all came to an end. By the time I joined Universal Edition in 1992, Paul-Heinz Dittrich had vanished, if not from the catalog, certainly from the list of composers actively promoted by the publisher. I do not know the reason and, faced with having to master such a huge catalog, I am ashamed to admit that I failed to make inquiries.

You can read the whole story in the following page or so, told by the composer himself, who is physically still here with us but who will leave us one day, with his music filling shelves rather than concert halls. By the way, the "political change" to which he refers was the shift from communism to capitalism, beginning with the fall of the Berlin Wall in 1989.

> Zwischen Hochmut
> und Demut,
> steht ein drittes,
> dem das Leben
> gehört, und das ist
> der Mut.[1]

May 19, 2015

In my long life as a composer, that motto by Theodor Fontane has proved itself time and again, in many regards. I am thinking therefore not only of the past, the time when I was living in the German Democratic Republic. Also in the years following the change of regime (1989), many people were enthusiastic and welcomed the new times, which turned out to be disappointments. The thorny path of the past continued, albeit in a different direction. Courage often became a test of courage.

But let me begin with an objective chronology of events. After my studies at the Leipzig Music Academy, I had no other choice but to become a composer. Subsequently, I became a pupil of Professor Wagner-Régeny at the Academy of Arts in East Berlin and I realized that I was facing a future of never-ending difficulties. The musical materials I was using exposed me to criticism and censorship by the socialist state of the GDR. I was even personally attacked and offended even though I was a professor at the Hanns Eisler Music Academy in Berlin. Eventually, I was dismissed without notice in 1976.

The consistency of my position meant that I was left without a publisher and consequently any performances. It was only later, thanks to Alfred Schlee's invitation for me to join the stable of composers of Universal

---

1   It is difficult to render the quote from Theodor Fontane (1819–98) in English, based as it is on the common root of the words Hoch*mut*, De*mut*, and *Mut*, with their wholly different meanings: arrogance, humility, and courage. Fontane points out that it is courage that makes life worth living, and it occupies a place between arrogance and humility. Theodor Fontane, *Romane und Erzählungen*, ed. Peter Goldammer, Gotthard Erler, Anita Golz, and Jürgen Jahn, 8 vols. (Berlin: Aufbau, 1973), 4:438.

Edition, Vienna, that I had some international success, even though I was never allowed to go to Austria.[2]

For financial reasons, my works published in Vienna were never played in the GDR. Until 1990, I led a precarious existence without a job—I lived as a freelance composer. It was humiliating in the extreme, with no hope for any change.

After the death of Rudolf Wagner-Régeny, it was primarily Paul Dessau who helped me as a colleague in many ways.[3] He helped me submit exit visa applications so that I could attend world premieres of my works in West Germany, France, or the United States.

After the change of regime, I was confronted with difficulties of a different kind. The political and artistic censorship was replaced by economic and existential problems. I was now without a publisher and once again had no performances. I became wholly isolated. It took a great deal of courage and survival strategies to stick to my consistent path.

Despite the greatest difficulties, I have produced more than 150 works that have remained unpublished since the political change. Many of them can be examined in the archives of the Berlin Academy of Arts. A hopeful/ hopeless thought?

> Courage stands at the beginning
> Of action,
> Happiness at the end.[4]

---

2 Alfred Schlee (1901–99) joined Universal Edition in 1927 and soon became a figure of key significance not only for the publisher but also for the history of twentieth-century music.

3 Paul Dessau (1894–1979) played a positive role in the stifling cultural life of the German Democratic Republic. He used his influence with the communist party (Socialist Unity Party of Germany) to help his fellow composers when they fell foul of the authorities.

4 Democritus, *Fragmente zur Ethik* (Stuttgart: Reclam, 1996), 77.

CHAPTER TEN

PASCAL DUSAPIN
(B . 1 9 5 5)

French composer

I believe you have to read Dusapin's short text much the way you listen to a piece of music or look at a painting: you have to absorb its message at your own pace, read it again, and reflect on it.

Born in 1955, Pascal Dusapin can look back on decades of writing music and he is in a position to summarize his experiences in these few lines. Of course, he has much in common with the experiences of his colleagues. When he talks of the need to "unlearn," he probably means the same thing as Chaya Czernowin when she talks of the need to achieve genuine loneliness. Dusapin puts three dots after "History is something we live with" indicating, I suppose, much the same thing that Iannis Xenakis did when he said he wished to sever his contacts with the past so that each new work would be a wholly novel departure.[1] (He of course was aware of the hopelessness of his undertaking.)

"I knew nothing of jealousy"—with once again followed by three dots to indicate that so much underlies those words. Does he mean jealousy he has felt or has encountered? Perhaps he means both, although he does say he has never fought against others, merely against himself. That again is intriguingly

---

1 I have checked this bold statement of mine against the actual interview with the composer and found that he was rather less adamant than I remembered. However, he did say this: "It has the precondition that I free myself of any ties or conditioning that prevent me from being free. One has to shed the fetters of the past. Therefore one has to think, to feel, to work." Bálint András Varga, *Conversations with Iannis Xenakis* (London: Faber and Faber, 1996), 50–51.

rich in implications. Artists in whatever domain will surely understand just what Dusapin has gone through in creating his own world in music.

Fighting against your own virtuosity—what a graphic description of the danger inherent in allowing ideas to flow all too easily from your pen. Your brain has developed certain patterns, they wait ready-made to be summoned. Once you have banished history, the next step for you is to banish your own . . . (if I may use my own three dots).

October 31, 2015

Dear Bálint,

Courage comes principally from unlearning; to never again speak of the past, not even the beginning. History is something we live with . . . Never again say it takes courage (very presumptuous . . .), and that it was so hard to begin. Obviously it was not easy, but I was joyful and I still am fighting to keep that feeling today. No: whatever it was, it was not courage. That's just the way it was. I started my life as an innocent composer (I knew nothing), and I was naive (it was a must . . .), and even something of an idealist (I knew nothing of jealousy . . .) and I fought, I fought, not against others or against history (such vanity . . .), but against myself. I showed courage against myself. And no, as people often try to make me say, serialism in music did not prevent me from writing, not even the spectralists who knew all about the future and even less the critics or anyone (including some composers) who know everything before you and against you. I hardly thought about all of that.

So courage would be to advance, unlearn, undo, turn what we know inside out, fight against our own virtuosity (the *experience*, that strategy adopted by professionals when they do not know what to say . . .), have less knowledge, forget everything, return to the right path . . . yes, it would be something like that. Courage is looking and listening to what is around you, questioning, having fun too, never judging or thinking the world is sinking into darkness, but keeping your head held high, staying alert, looking straight ahead, and staying hopeful.

CHAPTER ELEVEN

LORENZO FERRERO
(B . 1 9 5 1)

Italian composer

It surely takes tremendous daring to leave the ship you are sailing on, in good and supportive company, and change midcourse to another vessel headed in a different direction. The ship was showing no signs of sinking by any means, its passengers clearly convinced that "fair stood the wind for the future" (to misquote the title of H. E. Bates's war novel).[1]

Lorenzo Ferrero is not the only composer to have decided that he needed to turn his back on his former musical convictions. The most notable—or notorious—example is perhaps the Slovak avant-gardist Ladislav Kupkovic (b. 1936) who went as far back as Robert Schumann to find a new point of reference. In a way, I also count Alexander von Zemlinsky among these stubborn musicians, even though he had never jumped on the dodecaphonic bandwagon but defied his brother-in-law Schoenberg in keeping to his own special brand of late Romanticism.

I think I need not add anything to the above: the first few paragraphs of Lorenzo Ferrero's recollection provide a graphic description of the situation into which he had maneuvered himself. Those paragraphs also tell you of the downright harmful role some music critics have played in their dogmatic ef- fort to get the stray sheep to return to the flock. A clear case of the tyranny

---

1   Bates's novel, *Fair Stood the Wind for France*, was originally published in 1944.

of taste! You need all your conviction and strength of character to stay away from the pen and graze on fields you can call your own.

April 30/May 13, 2015

For me, the word *courage* is related to a specific moment in my career. I grew up as if the avant-garde were the natural language of music. Very early on, I received admiration, recognition, commissions . . . Except that at some point I realized there was something wrong in that, the musical language I mean. A few hints of different directions, cautiously included as quotations in some works, immediately caused critics to suspect me of betrayal. I remember one of them, a former admirer, who went all the way down a corridor with his face to the wall in order to avoid meeting me. We were in the late seventies of course . . .

So the courage was to deliberately and even provocatively abandon what looked like a promising career and write the music that I felt not only as mine, but also somehow as the real music of my time that could speak at least to my generation. It meant starting my career all over again. But this was not the worst part. The worst part was the compositional effort to translate into notes what I felt my music should be and to abandon the old, too easy habits. Nearly three years of aphasia . . .

I think that Luciano Berio, and others of his stature (including Boulez and Cage; I do not mean their far too many epigones), considered my music so "far away" from theirs that they just accepted it as inevitable without any discussion and even some respect (Luciano [said]: "The problem is that I cannot say it's not well written . . .").

In the western European situation, during the seventies and early eighties, there was (coincidentally with the Cold War?) a kind of upside-down Zhdanovism. In other words if in Soviet-controlled societies music had to be optimistic, in capitalistic society it had to be pessimistic. I remember a friend saying: "You know what the problem is? We are not allowed to write an Allegro."

It is certainly true that many intellectuals of the time were rather left-oriented, so this form of reverse Zhdanovism was not imposed by any threat (except maybe of being accused of lacking any "sense of history"). It was rather an evolution of the immediate post–world war attitude. One can read the success of integral serialism of the earlier decades in many ways (or the Cagean alea that led to the same results according to the well-known essay by Ligeti), but to me the most important of them is the "obliteration of the subject."[2] If the strong and willing "subject" led to such immense inhumanity and destruction, it was better to control it with severe constraints. Something similar happened with the anti-Romantic reaction and Neoclassicism after World War I, but that is another story. Anyway, the strict obliteration of the subject could not last too long, and in fact we actually have very few instances of fully integral serialism or full alea. Somehow the subject emerged again, but could not forget what happened so recently and could not suddenly turn itself into a hymn to the consumer society. So it turned into a form of "unglückliches Bewußtsein" which is the appropriate counterpart to the Zhdanovist optimism.[3]

I guess the reference to Hegel is self-explanatory. After all Adorno (for whom I have the greatest respect) and his Frankfurt friends were the last Mohicans of the Hegelian left . . .

The description by Karl Rasmussen is vivid and very close to the truth. In Italy, as far as I can remember, Strauss was less of an issue (except that one pretended to forget the composition date of the *Vier Letzte Lieder*. . .). But certainly Prokofiev, Shostakovich, not to mention Poulenc, or Bernstein, well, the list would be long, were to be kept out of any serious discussion on new music. And what is more important, to be kept out of your *mind*.

Let me say a word about poor Adorno. As I studied philosophy I can claim, contrary to many, that I actually read his books. You cannot understand what he really thought by reading just his books on music. Also, he had a much broader vision—this is now being recognized by younger scholars who are rediscovering him. For instance, the concept of "musical material" is not just the Lego brick to which many have reduced the concept.

His thought was fully dialectical, always looking for something contradicting a statement rather than confirming it. If this is not kept in mind,

---

2   György *Ligeti*, "Kompositorische Tendenzen heute," first published in *Nutida musik*, no. 3 (1960): 116.

3   "Unhappy consciousness," from Hegel's *Phänomenologie des Geistes* [Phenomenology of Spirit], published in 1807.

the book on Schoenberg and Stravinsky (*The Philosophy of Modern Music*) can be seen as praising the one and condemning the other,[4] whereas in fact they are both necessary to each other in order to complete the dialectic duality that describes the state of modern music at the time.

On the other hand, Adorno did not like what he saw and heard at Darmstadt. He wrote the essay, "The Aging of New Music," where he observes, in a nutshell, that it promulgated a "one-directional" thought, excluding dialectical contradiction from the language of music.[5]

Seen from another perspective, Karl Rasmussen's story tells another of the many similar stories at the time. Up to and including Schoenberg, every generation wanted to do something new, but never through a tabula rasa of the past. Schoenberg's effort to show that even Brahms was "modernist" was at the same time titanic and pathetic. And here I have to go back to a consideration I wrote to you a while ago: they didn't invent the tabula rasa, it was already there, accomplished by the bombs of World War II. If I belonged to that generation I would probably feel the same. Beauty could exist only through its denial (paraphrase from Adorno).

But the next generation, fed on American powdered milk, did not see the ruins (quickly rebuilt) and started wondering if music could not revert to an expression of the self, an expression denied by all dictatorships, including the dictatorship of taste.

---

4   Theodor Adorno, *Philosophie der neuen Musik* (Tübingen: J. C. B. Mohr, 1949).

5   Theodor Adorno, "Das Altern der Neuen Musik," in *Dissonanzen: Musik in der verwalteten Welt*, 2nd ed. (Göttingen: Vandenhoeck und Ruprecht 1958), 120–43.

CHAPTER TWELVE

MICHAEL GIELEN
(B . 1 9 2 7)

German-Austrian composer
and conductor

I owe Michael Gielen three of my basic musical experiences: his interpreta-
tion of Mahler's Third Symphony in Vienna's Konzerthaus, a concert devoted
entirely to compositions by Webern at the same venue, and a performance of
Kurtág's Stele *in Donaueschingen.*

It is difficult to render in words what made the Mahler symphony such
a unique experience. It was a journey of discovery, with an extraordinary
creative and re-creative musician of analytical bent as my guide. Just how
analytical becomes apparent if you read Gielen's essay on a short passage of
the symphony. It makes an astounding, well-nigh frightening read: you are
invited to witness the dissection of the composition's body—the joints, the
sinews—with relentless objectivity.

At the concert, Gielen allowed the soul to take over and fill the dissected
body with life once again; he also showed aspects of the music I had never no-
ticed before. It was a new Mahler, richer, more "modern," more adventurous
than any of the interpretations I had heard. It was immensely exciting and,
thank goodness, has been made available on CD.

Gielen had clearly also dissected Webern in the same manner, but what
struck me at that concert was the rehabilitation of the music as music in the
Mahlerian sense of the word. I have a vague memory of Peter Stadlen, a pupil
of Webern, remembering the composer's admonition that his music was very

well charged with emotion, it was anything but a cold, objective structure of tones.[1] *Gielen demonstrated what Stadlen, that is, Webern had in mind.*

The story of Kurtág's Stele *in Donaueschingen was an object lesson in the fundamental significance of authentic interpretation for the future destiny of a composition. Completed in 1994 for Claudio Abbado and the Berlin Philharmonic, Kurtág's Opus 33 proved a hard nut for the noted conductor to crack. In fact, he never managed to crack it—a failure that misrepresented the music and had a devastating effect on the composer. He told me that after a performance in Valencia, Spain, he had been ready, figuratively, to jump out of the window.*

I heard Abbado's interpretation of the music with mixed feelings, wondering if Kurtág had perhaps not succeeded in mastering the orchestral medium that he had avoided for so many decades. Michael Gielen proved that the opposite was true. I heard an entirely different piece of music in Donaueschingen, which made me believe that Kurtág had revised it. He reassured me there and then that it was the very same score that Abbado had attempted to conduct.

Gielen revealed for all to hear that Stele *is a masterpiece—and thereby saved it for the future. Thanks to him, it has become a part of the international repertoire, a status few contemporary orchestral works have achieved.*

In our interview at Gielen's house on a hill overlooking the Mondsee, a lovely lake in Austria's Salzkammergut region, we concentrated on his work as a composer. Unavoidably, however, his conducting career also came up. We were sitting in his library, surrounded by books as well as giant scores, many of them manuscript copies: works of the twentieth and twenty-first centuries, to which he had devoted his life. I was moved as I looked at them: they leaned against one another, apparently untouched for some time. Michael Gielen had announced that he would end his conducting career in 2014.

Innerschwand/Mondsee, May 26, 2015
Revised June 2, 2015

You use the word courage *in the second sentence of the chapter "My Compositions" of your book* Unbedingt Musik.[2] *You write: "He [Vinko*

---

1   Peter Stadlen (1910–96), Austrian composer, pianist, and musicologist. In 1937, he played the world premiere of Webern's Variations for Piano Solo, op. 27. His performance of Schoenberg's piano concerto on April 12, 1946, in Brussels with Franz André conducting, may have been the work's European premiere. According to Therese Muxeneder of the Arnold Schoenberg Center, Vienna, Stadlen had asked for the right of European premiere in 1944 and may have played the work in England. There are, however, no details of any performance prior to the one in Belgium.

2   Michael Gielen, *Unbedingt Musik: Erinnerungen* (Frankfurt am Main: Insel Verlag, 2005), 309. The title of Gielen's memoirs translates roughly to "By All Means Music."

Globokar] *is the only one who has ever encouraged me to compose." Why did you need encouragement?*

Because the examples are so great and my talent is so small. What God has given me does not suffice to secure me a place among the best composers. I have decided, however, that I *must* nevertheless write music as a means of personal expression, a document of who I am—and to leave it as a testament of my personality, even though it bears the influence of Berg and others. I have composed very little but believe that with the passage of time, the influences have grown less marked.

It takes courage, to begin with, to assume one is so important as to want to leave something behind. My uncle Eduard Steuermann, after a day or week in Salzburg where we showed each other our works (we read the scores, we had no means of performing them) said: "You know, Michael, we both of us know that we are not Beethoven but it should not hinder us from expressing ourselves."

In your book, you say that for you, composing is the most beautiful and the most personal activity. Even if you are "no Beethoven," composing has been particularly close to your heart.

It was indeed the most important of my musical expressions. I became a conductor because I am not good enough as a composer. As a conductor, I have made quite a name for myself. But in my heart, to strike a sentimental tone, in my innermost self, in my consciousness, composing has been more important than anything else. I rarely managed to get down to work, have written very little, and I have allowed even less to see the light of day. There are a few pieces that I regard as personal enough to endure. But, as I have said, they are not Beethoven, or indeed Schoenberg. They are not even Steuermann, if you know his compositions (there is hardly anyone who knows Eduard's pieces, but even fewer who know mine [*laughs*]).

There is my string quartet of 1983 that was premiered by LaSalle and has been released on a DGG compact disc, together with Schnabel's Third (a coupling I regard as an honor).[3]

He was a remarkable composer.

---

3 Michael Gielen, String Quartet, *Un vieux souvenir*. With texts from Baudelaire's *Les Fleurs du Mal* (1983). The world premiere took place in 1985 in Cincinnati, at a concert of the LaSalle Quartet. Arthur Schnabel, Third String Quartet (1922).

A highly original one but not particularly pleasant to listen to. It was nevertheless a privilege for my music to be paired with his, for it showed that it is a valid document of someone who lived at that time.

Originally, I had the idea of having the second of the five movements performed with *Sprechstimme* in the way of Schoenberg's *Ode*, and the fourth one sung (second movement: Une charogne, fifth movement: Le Cygne, both from Baudelaire's *Les Fleurs du Mal*). Walter Levin strongly advised against it, for financial and organizational reasons. I gave in, and now have the musicians say and call out particular words or sentences in a language to be chosen by them (French, German, or English).

I find it interesting that as a conductor, you worked almost exclusively with orchestras (I do remember an all-Webern program at the Wiener Konzerthaus where you conducted an ensemble); as a composer, however, you never wrote for orchestra—because, as you say in your book, its hierarchic setup is alien to you.

Yes, that's right. I am against the hierarchy of instruments: the first violins play always, or nearly so, the melody, the flutes invariably the upper part, the brass in the background supplies the harmony, and the trumpet the solo—the function of the instruments in the orchestra is so rigid that I have never had the courage to transgress it while nevertheless keeping it as a reference. The orchestra is after all equal to the tradition of the orchestra. But the world is not any the poorer for the lack of an orchestral piece by me. I do have a composition for forty players.[4] Is that big enough? (*laughs*)

In your book, you write of your Piano Piece in Seven Movements: *"The music is in addition 'evocative' in the old Romantic sense. I will leave it open whether this is of advantage or disadvantage."[5] That reads almost like an apology for writing music that might appear to have a Romantic tinge. Does a contemporary composer need courage to compose music with some sort of a link to tradition?*

That is a rather ambiguous question. For one thing, I regard it as absurd that quite a few people nowadays have reverted to tonal composition. I believe that the relationship of new music, of twelve-tone composition, to tonality was determined by late Schoenberg as well as, in particular, by Berg. It was apparently important for Berg not to let the past vanish without a

---

4 Variationen für vierzig Instrumente (1959).
5 Michael Gielen, *Unbedingt Musik: Erinnerungen* (Frankfurt am Main: Insel Verlag, 2005), 324.

trace—instead, he wished to integrate it into the new technique of composition with twelve tones.

Yes, the question is if one is to integrate the past in one's life, whether one wishes to distance oneself quite consciously from it. That would surely apply to some of Schoenberg's atonal works, but in his Third and Fourth Quartets, the relationship to tonality is quite obvious and audible, even for people who are not musically educated. You can forget about the quote of a Bach Chorale in Berg's Violin Concerto: it is a case of stylistic incongruity. The audience is bound to say "At last, some real music!"

May I repeat the question: did you need courage to write a piano piece with a Romantic tinge?

I would not call it Romantic; rather, it evokes moods. On the other hand, the technique with which that work was composed makes no sense, as it were. It was not meant to be a self-standing work for piano; in actual fact, it is the piano part of the fifth movement of *die glocken sind auf falscher spur* that I turned into a composition in its own right.[6] Since its tempo and dynamic differ from those of the original work, moods emerge and, depending on the interpretation by the soloist, this can exude a range of different atmospheres (the description Romantic would be out of place) and can be personal in nature. However, it may also be played in a way that it is just a succession of highly abstract chords. The thirty-two six-part chords that occur twice make for the exact opposite of expressive music. It is marked by a degree of monotony: one chord is followed by another over a long period of time, each equally dissonant, devoid of any interconnection. In other words, it is "modern" music in quotation marks. I believe the fact that it can be evocative or abstract, without any reference to the individual, is a trait of this piece that justifies its existence. Also, it has not been composed as such but has been drawn from an already existing work, and it is an elaboration of material from one piece into another, with the same approach and the same basic material—that is quite original.

Xenakis with whom I conducted two extended interviews, felt isolated in a music world dominated by serialism. He said he was at a disadvantage in that he received no commissions in Germany and his Paris institute, CEMAMu, eked out a precarious existence while IRCAM was provided with lavish state

6   Commissioned by Saarland Radio for the New Music Days of 1970, it is scored for soprano (Joan Carrol), violoncello (Siegfried Palm), piano (Aloys Kontarsky), percussion (Christoph Caskel), and guitar (Wilhelm Bruck).

subsidies.[7] *As a composer, did you also find that it took courage not to join any trend but to go your own way?*

It took a great deal of courage! I admire Xenakis for that, even though I do not particularly appreciate his music. I think highly of his determination to rely solely on himself. I find it remarkable that he should have complained to you, for he was a proud man. But he was the only representative of his own school. It would have been wrong to advise him to choose more conventional means in order to have more performances.

When he does get played, one is lost for words, for one is stunned by something that has so little to do with music—with the traditional concept of music that is always bound up with expression. He renounces that completely, in what I know of his work. I can only express assumptions.

In our conversations, Xenakis and I discussed compositions like Aïs *for baritone, percussion, and orchestra. I heard this moving piece of music as a requiem for his mother, but he would have none of it. He also denied any intention of expression in* Nekuia *for chorus and orchestra, whereas I had been overwhelmed by its sheer emotional charge when we listened to a recording in his studio at the rue Victor-Massé. (Because of his impaired hearing, he turned up the volume very loud so that the music made an additional impact.) For Xenakis, expression was a remnant of tradition and he wished to have no truck with it.*

I conducted the world premiere of his *Ata*.[8] That was not much fun. It was hard work, for there are no transitions, just blocks. It took a great deal of time for the orchestra to master it—the fact that a new tempo, a new situation have to be grasped with a single beat, without any subsidiary beats. It is not easy for the conductor either.

Did you write twelve-tone music because it was your mother tongue, so to speak?

I had no choice, I was brought up with it. The fact that I am a nephew of Steuermann and he was committed to Schoenberg to such an extent that even the vilest private experiences failed to cut his allegiance to him—it

---

7 CEMAMu stands for Centre d'Etudes de Mathématique et Automatic Musicales. *IRCAM* stands for *Institut de Recherche et Coordination Acoustique/Musique.*

8 Composed in 1987, *Ata* was premiered on May 3, 1988, by the Symphony Orchestra of Southwest German Radio, Baden-Baden, under the baton of Michael Gielen.

seemed to me a matter of course to try to carry on along the same path. Although there is a book on Schoenberg's Third String Quartet and as I read it, I thought to myself: for God's sake, I know absolutely nothing about this technique, I have merely made use of it at my own discretion, according to my abilities. Looking back at it now when I have stopped composing, it was not particularly professional. If you examine the Third String Quartet, you will be struck by the flexibility with which he applied the technique. The same may well be true of the Fourth Quartet, I have never looked at it, but the Third seems to me to be a high point in the entire history of twentieth-century music and also a high point in the application of twelve-tone technique.

You have conducted the world premieres of so many compositions and have kept many of them in your repertoire. What role do you think courage may have played in writing them? How much courage might Stockhausen have needed to compose a work for three orchestras and three conductors?

For a composer with his incredible talent for organization, it was original but not particularly courageous. His piano pieces are surely more daring than *Gruppen*. Nono's *Canto sospeso* is far too much of a masterpiece to have required much courage. Nono had been a member of the resistance, he was acquainted with many people; *Canto sospeso* called for talent and compassion and such things, but no courage.

Composers were supported and protected, big radio stations furthered and performed their works; they did not need all that much courage.

If I may compliment myself, I needed a great deal of courage to ensure that Zimmermann's *Soldaten* was eventually premiered, in the face of a hostile orchestra.[9] The musicians had all been brought up in the Third Reich and learned too late and too little about what went beyond the doctrine. Zimmermann was very courageous, although he took up a position behind Stockhausen's in the opinion of critics and musicologists. *Die Soldaten* is possibly more courageous than *Gruppen* because it sets out to do something wholly different and also because of its humanity. You can detect no ideology in *Gruppen*.

I attended so many of your concerts in Donaueschingen, where you appeared on the rostrum as an authentic personality with a unique authority and aura. Whenever you were standing onstage, one had the reassuring feeling that

---

9   Bernd Alois Zimmermann, *Die Soldaten*, world premiere, Cologne Opera House, February 15, 1965.

one was in safe hands, one would be hearing the music in the best possible interpretation. Did it occasionally take courage to present compositions you saw little future for?

On the contrary, it was cowardice. The artistic director of the festival had a particular taste and entertained particular friendships, which meant that pieces were programmed that did not deserve to be presented.[10] Some of the pieces that I premiered I hated, I regarded them as worthless but as chief conductor I felt it my duty to defer to the program director of the festival and not to create a scandal by refusing to conduct a work. The audience will have noticed without a doubt when I identified with a piece and when I was merely doing my duty. I did not share the taste of his successor either.[11] I gave up my position largely because I no longer wanted to premiere music I did not believe in. I refused to go on pretending.

---

10 Josef Häusler (1926–2010) led the Donauschinger Musiktage in 1975–91.
11 Armin Köhler (1952–2014) was program director in Donaueschingen in 1992–2014.

CHAPTER THIRTEEN

DETLEV GLANERT
(B . 1 9 6 0)

German composer

What follows is a moving document, a no-holds-barred confession by a composer who writes music even if it puts him at a considerable disadvantage compared to some of his colleagues of the international avant-garde.

In preparing the German edition of my Three Questions *book, I invited Detlev Glanert to contribute to the project and asked for a selection of recordings. I was impressed by his music and described it in my introduction in my own subjective manner, relying on the associations it had evoked. Natural images emerged in my mind, trees, clouds, birds, and the wind.*

Glanert asked me to delete those references, for he feared they would reinforce the misconceptions his aesthetic sometimes evoked, that might cause his music to be falsely seen as program music. I complied and rewrote the entire introduction.

Detlev Glanert would be the ideal composer to interview about courage and the tyranny of taste, I thought, and his contribution has confirmed my assumption. Taste and prejudice can obviously still exercise a tyranny of their own and a composer like Glanert needs courage—obsession—to go on composing the way he is convinced is his own.

February 2016

In view of what is happening in the world today, it appears frivolous to describe aesthetic decisions by composers with the word *courage*. Rather, it takes obstinacy to overcome resistance, to face controversy, and to embark on a path that may turn out to be lonesome. Also, to ignore opposition and detractors.

Most composers—indeed, most people in general—are not particularly courageous and are beset by all kinds of anxieties, especially about pain, failure, humiliation. Courage (obstinacy) means perhaps to go on composing regardless of such uninviting prospects.

Naturally, one works in the face of expectations and prejudices. Nowadays, you need as much—or as little—courage to set up taboos as you did in the past to break them. What really is remarkable, to my mind, is that one should stick to one's way nevertheless: that is, create new music that will only appeal to a very small group of people; music that requires a great deal of effort and expense to be performed and will in most cases not make enough money for the composer to live on. For all that, what I do and many of my colleagues do, is of existential significance, of paramount importance in our daily lives. For some, in their entire lives.

If you forget about music written purely for entertainment, any music composed today will be pilloried, as it were: criticized by musicologists, dramaturgs, administrators, conductors, musicians, and the public. No composer today manages to gather a Mozartian majority behind him. That is why it takes a bit of inner stability to stick to what one has decided is the right thing to do, unaffected by critics, blogs, statements, and shitstorms. Also by genuine or spurious applause.

Of course, it will all become very difficult when one's own path leads to such a degree of loneliness that commissions no longer come one's way, with the result that what one has imagined will have no chance of getting a hearing. After all, unlike writers, composers need interpreters, groups, and institutions to realize their work—all the abundance and magnificence of an apparatus based, in essence, on handiwork.

One is more or less aware of that before taking the plunge, and basically, composing requires as much or as little optimism as other professions do. There is, however, a big difference: a high degree of obsessiveness that would be well worth exploring. Scores after scores are being produced in an almost maniacal manner, even by colleagues who have no hopes whatever of getting performances; I note in my own case a certain desk-fanaticism that sometimes approaches a compulsive state.

"There again, he has lost control over his ink," a critic would say about something that failed to appeal to him. That is not nice for the composer and it does take a degree of stubbornness for him to present another work that is bound to provoke the same sentence. For the conflict between "my" position and "theirs" is surely rooted in divergent tastes and divergent convictions. But far more importantly, the thing about one's ink is not a question of failing control but of a positive obsession, ready to banish the outside world so that one can try to enter a risky way toward something new, unconcerned about tastes and comments.

Does one need courage to express oneself in a musical idiom that some people regard as "wrong"? Does one need courage to write in a style that will displease people in leading positions, so that they will not give commissions and decide against programming particular pieces? Perhaps yes, a bit, the same way one needs courage in life in other respects as well. What you really need, however, is a readiness to ignore your own anxieties, to overcome your own pettiness, to make the way free for your obsession and to reinvent the world with your own tones.

CHAPTER FOURTEEN

SOFIA GUBAIDULINA
(B . 1 9 3 1)

Russian composer

In the "plurologue" that emerges among composers in this book, each individual tells his or her story—stories that add up to an aspect of the history of
music in the last decades of the twentieth and the first years of the twenty-first
centuries.

Sofia Gubaidulina was five years old when the Stalinist purges began to
wreak havoc in the Soviet Union and eight when they ebbed away. To what
extent her birthplace, Chistopol, in the Republic of Tatarstan was affected, I
do not know. Did she grow up in an atmosphere of fear?

She was twenty-two when Stalin died; the year after, she graduated from
the Kazan Conservatory. During her subsequent studies in Moscow, her music was deemed irresponsible because of her experiments with alternative
tunings. Roughly at the same time, György Ligeti fell afoul of the authorities
in Hungary because of some unorthodox aspects of a movement of his Six
Bagatelles for wind quintet; János Viski suffered a fatal heart attack after a
confrontation with the Budapest Music Academy's director over a dangerously Webernian student composition by Péter Eötvös. Siegfried Matthus and
Paul-Heinz Dittrich supply their own reminiscences about their experiences
in communist East Germany. Their luckier colleagues in the West, such as
Wolfgang Rihm or Manfred Trojahn, comment on those years from their own
vantage points.

Gubaidulina was to face further difficulties over her experimentations with improvisation; she was bound to be condemned by the all-powerful general secretary of the Union of Soviet Composers, Tikhon Khrennikov. She found support from Dmitri Shostakovich—and several of her colleagues represented in this book confirm their need of a father—or mother—figure at some point in their lives: such as Günter Bialas was for Jörg Widmann, Marianne Stein for György Kurtág, or Elfriede Jelinek for Olga Neuwirth.

For all these aspects that Sofia Gubaidulina may have in common with some of her colleagues, she is very much a personality all her own. On the only occasion I met her for a couple of minutes in person, she struck me as extremely shy. Her contribution to this book explains why: I saw her in a concert hall prior to the performance of one of her compositions. She was about to have a highly personal, intimate manifestation of her innermost thoughts relentlessly exposed to hundreds of people. I think she must have been feeling extremely vulnerable, torn between wishing to keep the music for herself and wanting to share it with others. This dilemma is, as far as I can judge, unique to her.

Gubaidulina's mystical spiritualism may not be her exclusive trait but it is a feature that needs to be mentioned even in a short text like this. Her music is imbued with a transcendental air, as if the composer were turning her face toward a light emanating from above and communicating with it.

To begin with, she wrote her text below in Russian and subsequently translated it herself into German. In other words, she went to great lengths in her effort to explain in her shy, quiet, and rather resigned manner just what her life has taught her to understand by the word courage.

October 2015

On the Notion of Courage

Surely, everyone must demonstrate courage in their lifetime, if they are to defend their way of life, their opinion, their own system of values. And to stand up for their own personality.

For in life, we are always confronted by attitudes that are opposed to our own inner convictions. And on occasion, they are even aimed at our personality.

One rarely succeeds in putting up wholesale resistance without outside help. Even if there are examples every now and again where people prove to be genuinely courageous. That is admirable.

Alas, I cannot count myself among such people. Each time that I was forced "to swim against the tide," I turned for help to the words of Dmitri Shostakovich, who had once advised me to stick to my "false" path. But for such powerful support, I might very well have been unable to follow my own way. It would have been difficult.

But even if I had been able to overcome those difficulties, had one been able to describe it as "courage"?

It seems to me that in the life of a composer it is no less important to possess a trait that one could describe as "humility."[1] For it is extremely important for every composer to confess to themselves right at the start, that every now and again they are bound to find themselves in a tragic situation of total helplessness.

What does this helplessness consist in? It is particularly apparent in the case of John Cage. When he was composing his piece *4' 33"*, he was immersed in an inner experience. He imagined a major transformation of the sound event from one state into another. He imagined the sounding drama of an infinite reality and its great transformation into lasting stillness.

But fate has foreseen a trying condition for composers: each work must pass from the realm of an *inner idea* to the realm of *presentation*.

Is it really necessary to expose this great experience of transcendental being to presentation? In front of an audience? That is really horrifying, the horror of our fate.

Basically, each composition lands in a situation like that—perhaps not always in such a radical manner.

This fact cannot be changed. There is nothing for it but to resign oneself to it in all humility, for the sake of the aural experience.

The realization will always be imperfect. Perfection is unattainable, it will never be reached.

Realization is the greatest happiness and at the same time—the greatest torment.

Therein lies the paradox of all existence.

And two contrary notions are applicable to one and the same psychological condition: "courage" and "humility."

---

1   Gubaidulina uses the word *Demut* (humility) related to *Mut* (courage).

CHAPTER FIFTEEN

GEORG FRIEDRICH HAAS (B . 1 9 5 3)

Austrian composer

In his poignant text, Georg Friedrich Haas reveals what determined—and oppressed—his life and his music for several decades. For me, his confession comes as a revelation: after all, I have known him for decades and we worked together closely for fifteen years. It provides the key to many things I experienced, which I accepted as part of his personality and his music, without having an inkling of the actual causes.

His desperate battle with himself and the past of his family inspire his music. He may have suffered a great deal, but this gave birth to something positive: his incomparable art. His music may have been enveloped in darkness, in a figurative sense as in his chamber opera Nacht, *or in concrete terms, with the lights turned off, as in a scene of his opera* Die schöne Wunde *(one of the most beautiful scores he has ever written) or in his String Quartet No. 3 "In iij. Noct.," which is to be performed from beginning to end in darkness, but it nevertheless radiated a powerful creative expression.[1] Light first appeared in the chamber work* Sayaka *(2006), which indicated in its title (Japanese for "light") that a change had occurred in his outlook, to do with the birth of his daughter from his third marriage. Soon afterward, he composed the*

---

1 *Die schöne Wunde* (2002–3), an opera in two parts, world premiere at the Bregenz Festival on August 14, 2003. The third string quartet was composed in 2001.

piano trio "Ins Licht"—Into the Light—(2007), for the concert that Universal Edition organised for my retirement at the end of that year.

On learning of my Jewish heritage, Haas told me of his family's involvement in some of the crimes of the Third Reich. Observing his painful awareness of their guilt and, through theirs, of his own, I tried to reassure him, but sadly to no avail, that his age and also his total rejection of his family's past absolved him of any guilt whatsoever. During those exchanges, we would both be quite upset and we grew even closer to each other.

I have read his text with a confusion of feelings (to quote the title of a novel by Stefan Zweig),[2] of which joy and relief have dominated. Thanks to his fulfilling relationship with his wife and also, perhaps, to a new life away from Europe, in New York, Georg Friedrich Haas has now been able to reach peace with himself. His considerable success as a composer will also have played a role. I am happy that his contribution to this book on the courage of composers has given him a chance to take stock.

April 2016

COURAGE

For Bálint Varga

When the *New York Times* published a big article on me, in which my private life, my sexual orientation, and my everyday existence with my submissive wife were described, many of my acquaintances from the BDSM-scene congratulated me on my "courage" to go public.[3]

I was surprised to be called "courageous" in this particular context. Half a year earlier, my wife and I had appeared jointly at a small kink meeting in Toronto where we openly discussed our relationship in front of people who had made a conscious decision to live out their unusual sexuality in a loving way. I accepted that our interview would be documented on video and I did not protest against it being posted on the Internet, on YouTube.

I then gave an interview to a small German Internet magazine. I had been informed that the entire issue would be devoted to the subject of "sexuality."

The article was translated into English for the Internet and a few days later, I was approached by the *New York Times* for an interview. It gave me

---

2   Stefan Zweig, *Verwirrung der Gefühle* (Berlin: S. Fischer Verlag, 1927). The novel is known in English under the title *Confusion*.

3   Zachary Woolfe, "A Composer and His Wife: Creativity Through Kink," *New York Times*, February 23, 2016.

a chance to talk openly and honestly about the miracle of my relationship with my wife.

I did not feel I was being particularly courageous. After all, what would have been the alternative? To try to conceal the truth about my life?

If you give my wife's first name in the search engine, you will end up with the intentionally provocative title of her Internet site, "perverted negress." Ought she to change her name? Assume a pseudonym? Should I live in permanent fear that our "secret" might come to light?

I am not doing anything wrong. I have nothing to hide. Why should I waste time and energy in an attempt to conceal my life the way I live it?

My coming out was a reasonable and clear decision. If any courage was involved, it consisted in standing by it and, if it should come to that, being ready to live with the consequences.

Just as over forty years ago, it was an absolutely clear and reasonable decision to opt for the language of "new music" as a composer.

We were initiated into new music at secondary school by my music teacher Gerold Amann.[4] Yes, it was courageous of him to perform with our school choir Penderecki's *Lukas-Passion*—after all, we were living in a conservative little town, Bludenz, where the greatest place of interest was the chocolate factory near the railway station.[5] It was courageous of him to perform this radical piece of new music at a school with old Nazis among the professors. It was courageous of him to acquaint us with brand new music by Ligeti, Berio, and Stockhausen. But his courage was no end in itself. He was a teacher conscious of his pedagogical responsibility on the highest level. He understood art as an existential challenge—and wanted to inculcate us with it.

I do not think it was courage that made me engage with new music. Ligeti's Requiem and Cerha's *Spiegel* were strong pieces.[6] Incomparably stronger than the conservatives' pathetic late tonal efforts. For me it was obvious: this is the way forward. Not that one. True, some professors frowned when they saw my music ("So you are one of *them* . . . !") But it did not take much courage to provoke them.

Right after passing my final exams, I was called up to serve in the Austrian federal army. I still believed at the time that I had to do my "duty." I was demobilized after six months and during my years as a student I was

---

4   Gerold Amann (b. 1937), Austrian composer.

5   The town of Bludenz is situated in Austria's westernmost province, Vorarlberg, with a population of some fourteen thousand.

6   György Ligeti (1923–2006) composed his Requiem in 1965. *Spiegel* is the title of seven orchestral pieces of pivotal significance in postwar Austrian music, composed by Friedrich Cerha (1926).

called upon to do what they termed "military exercises"; I did my best to survive them unscathed.

There were also shooting exercises. I loaded my weapon, descended into the shooting range—and discovered that I was supposed to fire at the outlines of a human figure, with its belly as the target. I spontaneously realized that I could not very well do that. I had not been prepared for a situation like that. All I knew was: no. I could not ever do it. I climbed out of the ditch and told the officer on duty that I could not shoot at the dummy of a human being. A dialogue unfolded that ended with him giving me a formal command and my replying that I was not in a position to obey, just as I could not obey if he were to tell me to fly like a bird onto a tree. He informed me that in case of my refusal, I would have to face punitive measures that could lead, among other things, to being forever banned from practicing the profession of a teacher. Panic-stricken, I descended back into the shooting range and fired in quick succession the entire magazine into the air. Trembling all over, I climbed out and said: "I have obeyed your command." The situation had visibly become unpleasant for the officer as well—he let it go. A few months later I was informed that I had been released from the military on account of being "unfit."

No, in that instance I was not courageous. I ought to have refused to carry out the command and accept the consequences, right up to legal proceedings, which in the last instance I might even have won. That would have been a courageous thing to do. I find it remarkable that I never thought of the simplest and slyest solution: to calmly take the weapon and aim off target.

Also as a composer, I am not "courageous" enough to go to the lengths of demanding the extreme. Of course, if particular aspects of a piece were to make it absolutely necessary (for instance, in a concerto, setting six pianos tuned in distances of 12th of tones against a large orchestra), I have no other choice but to do it.[7] It would be out of the question for me to resort to the shrewd solution of simply using electronically detuned instrumental sonorities: the sound quality would suffer.

My music has been described as sombre. Depressive. For decades, I could not bring myself to talk about the two reasons underlying the darkness: for one thing, there was my sexual orientation that I had rejected and attempted to repress—something that made me fear I would never be able to live in a really fulfilling relationship. I am now finding it easy to talk about it. And my music has turned lighter.

---

7 The composer is referring to his *Limited Approximations* (2010), premiered in Donaueschingen on October 17, 2010. For all its unusual demands, the work has since received numerous performances.

But there was something else as well: I was born into a Nazi family. My parents and grandparents had been Nazis and brought me up to become one as well. It was not until I turned twenty that I woke up to my heritage and endeavored to digest it. Later I felt doubly guilty: for one thing, I sensed I was carrying on my shoulders the guilt I had inherited through the crimes of my family. For another, I was aware that I myself had been part of the brown morass for two decades (as a child and an adolescent).

For decades I was unable to talk about all that. I did drop hints. I informed the encyclopedia *Komponisten der Gegenwart* (Composers of the Present), among other things, that my grandfather had been an architect. But no one had ever asked me for his first name. Just by supplying that piece of information (he was Fritz Haas), I would have disclosed our dark family history.[8]

My compositions contain several encrypted hints. For instance, my cello concerto (dedicated to Bálint Varga) begins with a mighty outcry in the orchestra, followed by a desperate Lamento on the solo cello.[9] And a quote from Schreker's opera *The Distant Sound*: "O Father, your sad heritage." Although I made a reference to that in the program book, I was not asked at the time what I actually had in mind. And no one went to the

---

8   I found no indication on the Internet that the Austrian architect Fritz Haas (1890–1968) had been involved in any way in the crimes of the Third Reich. Having told the composer so, I received the following e-mail from him on April 14, 2016:

> *Dear Mr. Varga,*
> *yes, encyclopedias provide no details. The same is true of others as well.*
> *He was one of those responsible for Kaprun.* [Kaprun is a resort in Salzburg province. The suffering of Jewish prisoners during the building of a power station there was the subject of a play by Nobel Prize winning writer Elfriede Jelinek, 2003.] *There, prisoners of war were made to work under inhuman conditions—their possible "death by accident" was part and parcel of architectural planning.*
> *There were Jewish families in Vienna who tried to survive by staying in the streets during the day and begging for shelter at night. One of those families committed the mistake of ringing the bell of my grandfather. He called the Gestapo.*
> *As Rektor, he was responsible for the university's personnel policy. He determined what research should focus on in time of war.*
> *And that is merely what I know for certain. There lies behind it a gray zone of whatever else happened in addition.*
> *Right up to his death, he remained a major figure among former Nazis. The "great architect." The "professor." The "decent one."*
>
> *Kind regards,*
> *Yours*
> *Georg Friedrich Haas*

9   The Cello Concerto was composed in 2003–4 and premiered in Munich on July 9, 2004.

trouble of taking a closer look at my father's biography (he had been a functionary in a neo-Nazi students' organization).

My opera *Nacht* interweaves a number of different elements.[10] Not only does the libretto have many hidden layers, so do the artistic messages they serve to convey. I have referred to the fact a number of times that the opera has to do with the loss of utopia. Also with the inability to love. With hopelessness. But there is an additional plane of meaning as well: my feelings of guilt. Scene 13 has been composed as the quiet, inward-turned culmination of the opera. The music comes to an abrupt calm, a simple overtone chord dominating the sound space and the baritone, the opera's "I," sings "All is over, Diotima. Our people have murdered . . . Our brethren have also been struck dead."

This text is repeated at the end of the opera, and then it continues. The baritone, the "I," takes the guilt upon himself "I stood at their head, I, I, I, I, I." There follows a veritable apocalypse of sound.

It was the courage of despair that had induced me to supply a clear expression in the music of what I had in mind. I would never have been able at the time to talk about it in words.

Only now can I do so.

And that is perfectly all right with me.

It is not "courageous." But necessary.

---

10 *Nacht* (1995–96/1998), chamber opera in twenty-four scenes. Concertante premiere at the Bregenz Festival on August 7, 1996, stage premiere at the Bregenz Festival on August 7, 1998.

CHAPTER SIXTEEN

GIYA KANCHELI
(B . 1 9 3 5)

Georgian composer

*My go-between for composers published by Sikorski in Hamburg has been
its selfless and helpful director, Hans Ulrich Duffek. He was kind enough to
establish contact on my behalf with the Georgian composer Giya Kancheli as
well as with Sofia Gubaidulina, gently reminding them once in a while of my
request for a contribution to this book.*

*Kancheli was particularly hesitant about whether he was up to bringing
pen to paper: he was ill and had just completed a new orchestral work that
had exhausted him.*

*The short text he did eventually send me is moving in its simplicity and
humility. At the end of one's life one realizes one knows little in comparison
with the masters of the past—but one goes on writing music nevertheless,
with this nagging question in one's mind: am I any good? I find something
oriental in this attitude: the master, pen in hand, crouching over a sheet of
paper, bowing his head in honor of his predecessors.*

May 2015

I have recently completed a work and have called it *Nu.Mu.Zu.*[1] In the language of the ancient Sumerians, the three words mean "I do not know."

---

1   *Nu.Mu.Zu* premiered in Brussels on October 16, 2015. The Belgian National Orchestra was con-
    ducted by Andrey Boreyko. The first US performance took place in Seattle on November 5, 2015.
    The Seattle Symphony Orchestra played under the baton of Ludovic Morlot.

And indeed, the longer I live (I shall turn eighty this year), the more frequently I am confronted with questions to which I do not know the answers. For instance, I do not know how a normal human being who has heard Bach's B-minor Mass, Mozart's Requiem, or Stravinsky's *Le Sacre du printemps* can muster the courage to compose music. *Nu.Mu.Zu* (that is, I do not know).

CHAPTER SEVENTEEN

GYÖRGY KURTÁG
(B . 1 9 2 6)

Hungarian composer

The following conversation took place on February 17, 2016, in Budapest, two days before György Kurtág's ninetieth birthday.

Concerts of his music were mounted daily between February 14 and 21—a grueling week for the composer and his wife. I was very lucky indeed to catch half an hour or so with him right in the middle of it where Kurtág agreed to answer my questions. Of course, it was anything but an undisturbed thirty minutes. Telephone calls would interrupt the interview: musicians were calling to wish him many happy returns. Kurtág would support himself on his cane and my arm and walk ever so slowly to take the receiver. Also, the door would open at regular intervals; Márta did her best to keep the visitors away and eventually left the room to act as temporary Cerberus.

I do not think I had ever felt so tense and anxious during an interview. I was fully aware that I would probably never have another chance and felt bad about taking Kurtág's time when he was obviously exhausted. No wonder I would forget what we had been talking about when he had finished a call and I turned on the recorder again.

When Márta returned, we had just finished the interview. She asked: "Well, how was it?" Kurtág replied: "I did not say anything of interest." He repeated the same thing a few weeks later when I had rung him to ask if he had received the transcript of our conversation. It is far too short, he said, full of mistakes; it is really not worth publishing. He was nevertheless willing to answer the questions I had put to him in my accompanying letter and to clarify the mistakes. I took it as a sign of his tacit agreement that I might include the text in this book. I was lucky after all.

Budapest, February 17, 2016

Over thirty years ago, you told me it had taken you a long time to accept that you had the makings of a composer. Márta played some of your compositions for Szervánszky, and . . .[1]

She did not play them for Szervánszky. Márta appeared at a concert of the academy's student composers and performed four of my silly little pieces. (Only the third one survives to this day: I have touched it up a bit and it should appear in *Játékok IX* under the title . . . *apple blossom* . . .). I played at the concert Ligeti's Sonatina. It was really his *Capriccio I*. I could not make head or tail of it, nor could I understand his chromatic *Invenció* (Invention). For some reason, he had not coached me beforehand. His *Weöres-Lieder* were performed at the same concert and were immediately recognized as masterpieces, although the singer, Edit Gáncs, still had a small voice at the time and sang the Lieder pretty poorly. (In later years she was to become a well-known artist.)[2] [See exx. 1 and 2.]

When did the concert take place?

Some time in 1948.[3]

Did Szervánszky attend?

---

1 Endre Szervánszky (1911–77) was a Hungarian composer and professor of composition at the Budapest Academy of Music. During World War II, he saved the lives of people persecuted by the Nazis and was posthumously included in the list of Righteous among the Nations. Between 1945 and 1949 he worked as a music critic for the daily newspaper *Szabad Nép*. He was the first Hungarian composer to apply the dodecaphonic method of composition (Six Orchestral Pieces, 1959). His String Serenade (1947–48) is quoted in Kurtág's string quartet *Officium breve in memoriam Andreae Szervánszky*, op. 28 (1989).

2 Edit Gáncs (1927–2012) married the conductor István Kertész and appeared under the name of Edith Gábry at the Cologne Opera House.

3 Louise Duchesneau, the longtime assistant of György Ligeti, has kindly helped me to find out the details of that concert. It took place on May 22, 1948. Ligeti dedicated his *Capriccio I* (1947) and *Invenció* (1948) to György and Márta Kurtág.

Example 1. György Kurtág, "Almavirág" [Apple blossom], *Games*, vol. 9, p. 3. ©
2013 by Editio Musica Budapest.

... almavirág ...

... Apfelblüte ...
... apple blossom ...

Example 2. György Ligeti, Capriccio I, p. 1. © 1991 by Schott Music—Mainz, Germany.

für Márta Kurtág

Capriccio Nr. 1
(1947)

György Ligeti
1923–2006

Szervánszky was in the audience as music critic of *Szabad Nép* and wrote an article in which he deplored the fact that Ligeti had written such abstract music. But it had made that impression mainly because I had no idea what I was playing. Márta, on the other hand, gave a masterful rendering of my own pieces and they impressed Szervánszky. As a result, I became a well-known figure in musical circles and was later even given a kind of grant.

Could it be that Szervánszky's favorable review of your music encouraged you to think of yourself as a composer?

(*laughs*) I do not think of myself as a composer to this day.

What I am really getting at is do you need courage to compose?

Yes, very much so. A great deal of courage.

Is it courage toward yourself?

Mainly.

Basically, what I lack is moral courage. Márta is displeased that I am often downright cowardly. Nor am I disinclined to make compromises. No way.

And as regards composing?

The same applies. To everything.

The ruling taste was always very important for me. For a long time, I wanted to write music that reflected current fashions. I went to Paris really to get to know the latest musical trends, from Boulez and others. When I realized that it required mathematical aptitude, I gave it up. For all that, I wanted to write such music. Then . . .

Then you wrote a string quartet that proved to be a tremendous challenge for musicians; András Mihály needed countless rehearsals to achieve a decent performance.[4] *You also composed the* Bornemisza Concerto, *which*

---

4   Kurtág composed his String Quartet op. 1 on his return from Paris, in 1959. The world premiere could only take place thanks to the tireless efforts of András Mihály (1917–93). Mihály was a composer, a conductor, and a professor of chamber music.

continues to be extremely difficult to do justice to.[5] You cannot really say that your goal was to serve the general taste.

No—but I always strove to be equal to something. I wanted to be a "good pupil." Marianne would admonish me to seek who I was, and praised the *Ariel-Lieder* in the accidental music to *The Tempest*: in her view, I was on the right track.[6]

(The interview had to be interrupted at this point: the telephone was ringing. When I switched the equipment back on, we returned to the string quartet and the Bornemisza Concerto.*)*

It went on like that for quite a long time. In recent years, I have reached the stage where I actually break basic rules. For instance, I use octaves.

That had already happened in your birthday piece for Boulez; you worked with octaves even though you were aware that Boulez could not stand them.[7]

Of course. More recently, I am attempting to break elementary rules. That is why I say that now I dare to do almost everything.

Whom are you defying in "daring" to transgress barriers? Are they barriers that you have erected in yourself?

They were part of my education. I have developed some rules around Schoenberg and Webern that are valid for me and that I observe more or less. With regard to prosody, I obey very strictly what Bárdos taught me.[8] It works with any language.

---

5   *The Sayings of Péter Bornemisza*, Concerto for Soprano and Piano, op. 7 (1963–68).
6   The Hungarian psychologist Marianne Stein (1913–94) played a pivotal role in Kurtág's life. During the year he spent in Paris, she helped him find the way back to composing. In later years, too, she would give him important advice. Kurtág composed incidental music for Shakespeare's *The Tempest* in 1961, at the request of the Hungarian theater director László Vámos (1928–96) who was working in Budapest's Madách Theater at the time.
7   "Octave" is the title of a poem by Samuel Beckett in the volume *Mirlitonnades* (1978). Kurtág set it to music, together with other poems by Beckett in his *... pas à pas–nulle part ... poèmes de Samuel Beckett*, op. 36 (1993–96), for baritone solo, string trio, and percussion. The version of *Octave: Message à Pierre Boulez* for baritone solo was premiered on Boulez's seventieth birthday, May 26, 1995, in Berlin (duration: 34").
8   Lajos Bárdos (1899–1986) Hungarian composer, mainly of choral pieces. He was also an important musicologist and a professor at the Budapest Academy of Music.

What you have said about Schoenberg and Webern is interesting. In a concert interval at the Berlin Philharmonie, in March 1999, I remarked that you had never mentioned the name of Alban Berg. You replied, rather as if you were ashamed, the following (according to my diary): "May God forgive me—because it is almost like that" (you were referring to Elgar's Violin Concerto that we had heard in the first half). You added that you did not like Schoenberg, although his astringency was a saving grace. You did not like Berg either, for you feared your music had too much in common with his. You only admired Webern: his was music at its purest.

Yes, that is correct. But it was Schoenberg who laid down the rules of twelve-tone music—and they include the octave ban.

In other words, you no longer wish to be a good pupil and dare to consciously break the rules.

That's right. But there is also something else. It is only very recently that I have started writing my own music.

Composing for you has been a struggle against your self-erected barriers.

Barriers that are still there.

Were they implanted through your education at the academy?

That is surely true. Ferenc Farkas is with me, to this day, all the time.[9]

Will you elaborate?

Compositions must have order in them. He was right, too.

That is all very interesting: the many barriers that you are now trying to dismantle have not prevented you from creating a world all your own that is immediately recognizable; it is different from Schoenberg's or Webern's. Your struggle has been successful.

---

9 Ferenc Farkas (1905–2000), Hungarian composer, a notable professor of composition at the Budapest Academy of Music. His pupils included György Ligeti and György Kurtág.

I do not know. *Bornemisza* is still replete with such ... Webern's *Five Canons* exerted a very strong influence, especially the first one.[10] The *Mattocks* section of *Bornemisza* was the first one to be composed; it is a type of canon that stems from Webern. Of course, I borrow patterns that I need. [See exx. 3 and 4.]

What is the difference between the borrowing of patterns and what you call "stealing"—from Stravinsky or Wagner?

If I take over something literally, without processing it, I call it stealing. They are mostly turns. I cannot bring myself to listen to *Troussova* any more, it is so full of clichés.[11] Nothing but major sevenths, minor ninths, or minor seconds.

   Of course, this is not quite true, for *Liubi menia* is different.[12] [See ex. 5.]

Or Autumn flowers fading ...

You can find countless things like that with Schoenberg. *Autumn flowers fading* has reminiscences of *Pierrot*. Heaven knows. *Pierrot* was a required piece on the program of Péter Eötvös's course for conductors. It is very very strong music.

Was it an act of courage for you to embark on your opera? In our conversation of 2007, you were still doubtful whether Beckett could be set to music, because, you said, he himself had so many musical ideas about his plays. You said you would only need to fill in a crossword puzzle. Incidentally, Márta mentioned three short plays: Footfalls, Play, *and* Rockeby.

Yes, at the time Pereira commissioned me to write an opera, I still had those three little plays in mind.[13] Since I had started out from *Endgame* to begin with, I decided at one point to try my hand at it. I had very little idea of the actual challenge I was facing. It took me five years of work to have some sort of glimmer. I spent the first two years on the first two big monologues—and they are still not finished. They are next on the agenda.

---

10 Anton Webern, Five Canons, op. 16 (1924) for high soprano, clarinet, and bass clarinet.

11 *Messages of the Late R. V. Troussova*, op. 17, for soprano and chamber ensemble (1976–80).

12 Люби меня (Love me) is the tenth movement in part 3 of *Troussova*.

13 Alexander Pereira (1947) was administrator of the Zurich Opera House in 1991–2012, led the Salzburg Festival in the same capacity in 2012–14 and has been administrator of the Milan Scala since 2014.

Example 3. Anton Webern, "5 Canons für hohen Sopran, Klarinette und Bassklarinette," op. 16/1, p. 1. © 1928, 1956 by Universal Edition A.G., Wien / UE 9522.

Example 4. György Kurtág, "Die Sprüche des Péter Bornemisza. Concerto für Sopran und Klavier," op. 7, p. 30. © 1973 by Universal Edition A.G., Wien / UE 14493.

10

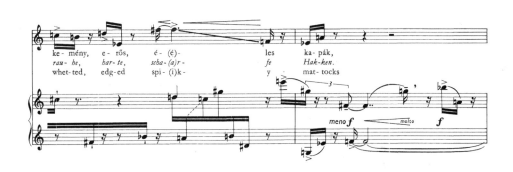

Example 5. György Kurtág, "Liubi menia" [Love me], *Messages of the Late Miss R. V. Troussova*, pp. 107–8. © by Editio Musica Budapest.

10

Люби меня...

Example 5.—*(concluded)*

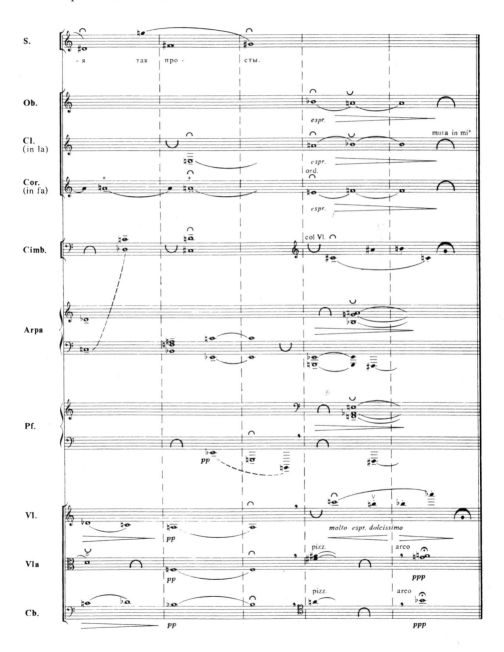

The Finale is nearly ready. I have the whole of the ashbin monologue, have already rehearsed it with the singers. The protagonists who will be playing Hamm and Clov visited me a week ago. Hamm will do very well indeed—he was Astramadors in *Le grand Macabre*—a quite excellent bass.[14] I am rather doubtful about Clov, he is far too steeped in operatic clichés. He lives in Berlin at a stone's throw from the répétiteur's house; I hope they will work together all right.

Rather like Boulez, you clearly aspire to create something absolutely new that has nothing to do with traditional music theater.

I am not sure. *Pelléas* and *Poppea* are closest to me. Especially Monteverdi: I do not omit a single word. It is probably silly, it could render the piece boring.

If the music is good . . .

But the spoken sentence is something in between that cannot transmit musical information. It is in any case a decent attempt—let it then fail.

---

14 *Le grand Macabre* (1974–77, rev. 1996), opera by György Ligeti.

CHAPTER EIGHTEEN

HELMUT LACHENMANN

(B . 1 9 3 5)

German composer

Ever since I joined the staff of Universal Edition in 1992 and became a regular visitor to Donaueschingen and other new music festivals, works by Helmut Lachenmann featured on the programs as a matter of course. I experienced him as a revered figure whose authority lent unquestioned significance to his support of younger colleagues—gestures that he makes generously whenever his judgement inspires him to do so.

Performances of his compositions, whether he was present or not, were always greeted with applause—without the slightest hint that not everyone in the audience appreciated his instantly recognizable, highly individual musical language.

I took it for granted that it had required quite a bit of courage for him to develop an idiom that he himself characterizes in our e-mail exchange (below) as "a consistent application of noise" and "the alienation of instrumental sound." The significance and background of the rest of the sentence ("to be played by musicians at their own 'peril'") escaped me at the time.

Lachenmann's firm rejection of the very idea of courage led to my tongue-in-cheek (and, admittedly, cheeky) remark that he was apparently a composer whose path had been smooth, free of thorns and potholes.

That in turn provoked his protest: "Are you making fun of me?" which was followed—as you will see—by his impassioned admission that his path had been anything but smooth—indeed, doubt had accompanied him throughout his career and he had had to overcome it time and time again. Nor was his reception as unanimously positive as my own experience had misled me to believe. Indeed, from the very beginning, Lachenmann's music has had a hard time gaining acceptance, in the face of the animosity of musicians, critics, and the public. Scandal has been a recurring feature of his performances.

If only I had known, I would not have provoked him with my irresponsible remark.

We resumed our correspondence in July 2016. Helmut Lachenmann was impelled to expand on his statements of the previous year. I am truly overwhelmed by the beauty of his words:

> Courage which presupposes strength of resolve founded on hope, has been replaced—as I wrote you—by "creative obsession." Mahler said: "I do not compose, I am composed." A composer who has something to give cannot do otherwise. He has no other choice but to create what has been waiting in him. And a lack of alternative like that is the impulse that helps, indeed, forces one to overcome one's doubts.

Those ideas are true of artistic activity in any domain provided it has left the well-trodden path of tradition.

Contact with Helmut Lachenmann via our exchange of e-mails in 2015 and 2016, has been an enriching experience. I am happy to be sharing it with readers of this book.

July 28, 2015

Dear Mr. Lachenmann,

We agreed in May that I might contact you again in August. You said you would be spending the month in Italy, with more leisure to consider my two questions.

It would be a great pleasure if you could indeed contribute to the book; if you happen to be at Donaueschingen in October, we might do an interview.

In my introduction to the text you prepared for the Three Questions *book, I wrote:[1] "He also refers to a phenomenon that would justify a book*

---

1   Varga, *Three Questions for Sixty-Five Composers*, 146.

all by itself: the moment of courage which it evidently requires for a creator to make an artistic decision."

The time has now come to get down to the book. In the attachment, please see some examples I have collected from other composers, so that you know what I have in mind.

As far as the "tyranny of taste" (also of ideologies and prejudices) is concerned, the idea occurred to me on reading the following paragraph from the contribution by the Danish composer Karl Aage Rasmussen:

> *As an artist, however, you are unlikely to totally avoid a sense of pressure from whatever artistic lingua franca is surrounding you, and the fear of becoming a pariah is deeply rooted in most people. As a student of composition in the late sixties, among not particularly academic modernists, I was nonetheless acutely aware that openly admiring—just as an example— the late Strauss of the* Metamorphosen *required an assurance that I did not posses at the time. And speaking fondly of, say, Prokofiev's music was inconceivable, so you kept your fascination secret. Some of Adorno's one-liners ("you can hardly hear a note without having to hide a smile") was an ongoing slap on the wrist, creating an anxiety about always attempting "the right thing"—or nothing at all. A mind model that enveloped my every artistic viewpoint during my early years.*

"Courage" and the "tyranny of taste" are of course closely bound up with each other (it takes courage, for instance, to stand by one's own taste . . .). In my life as promotion manager of music publishers, taste and the problems that it entailed played a major role. I would be keen to have your comments! Much looking forward to hearing from you,

Yours sincerely,
Bálint András Varga

July 30, 2015

Dear Mr. Varga,

I hesitate to confirm my participation in your projected book.

The notions "courage" and "taste" are not part of my vocabulary when pondering my own composition or the composition of others. I would assign them both, not without contempt, to the culture columns of newspapers.

The notion "courage" implies danger—of what? What did Ligeti risk in writing his Horn Concerto? Composers like Cage were actually more "daring" in involving chance, or "others" in their consistent application of noise or of the alienation of instrumental sound, to be played by musicians at their own "peril," or yet others in their shameless return to tonally poled consonance.

As for the notion of "taste," it implies a reception that has more to do with decorative, indeed, with gastronomic aspects of experiencing music than with the, forgive me, "existential," sensuous contact between spirit and structure. I doubt that in coming upon a planet—and what else is the genuine experience of art?—or in confronting a "friendly" or "eerie" or even "menacing" landscape, whether it is a desert or an arctic space, a jungle or a barren mountain, or in watching a sunset or witnessing an earthquake, "taste" can conceivably be a criterion, just as it is out of place when I receive news that will change my life in whatever direction.

I do not suffer under the tyranny of taste, except, perhaps, when I am looking at the totally standardized entertainment on offer: it makes use, among other things, of the aesthetic achievements of art—but then it has done so at all times in the past. (Mozart's *A Little Night Music* in a Salzburg taxi might appear tasteless but that is the world of business and I am no moralizer.) The notion of good or bad taste that reigns "tyrannically" over art presupposes a mannered and obsolescent idea of reception. To put it another way: the very discussion of the "tyranny of taste" in connection with art is in bad taste.

The same is true of pondering "courage" in art. When the young organist J. S. Bach distorted the good old Lutheran chorales in the ears of the Arnstadt parishioners through his unusual harmonization, risking his dismissal, he was not being courageous, he was being J. S. Bach. And Schoenberg's leap into atonality, just as the serially organized structuralism of those composers after World War II who attempted to define the notion of music anew, ignoring reactionary expectations, that is, the "taste" of a "mankind intoxicated in the dullness of its mind" (as Thomas Mann put it in 1955, in his lecture on Schiller)—that was no proof of their "courage," but a sign of their innocent creative obsession, in other words, of creative bliss.[2]

"Courage" implies the possibility of choosing between balking at danger or consciously defying it. Nobody but an epigone has that choice. The

---

2　Friedrich Schiller died in Weimar on May 9, 1805. On the occasion of the 150th anniversary of his death, Thomas Mann wrote an essay titled "Versuch über Schiller" ("Versuch" means "attempt" and also, in a way, "essay"). He turned the text into a speech he presented at official celebrations of the anniversary on May 8, 1955, in Stuttgart (West Germany) and on May 14, 1955, in Weimar (East Germany).

authentic creator of art "cannot do otherwise." Clearly, he cannot breathe in a totalitarian social system that represses the free spirit, he cannot realize himself, he can, at the most, "spit into a crater," to cite Karl Kraus.[3] But I am not challenged to do that.

It requires no "courage" for the creator of art to follow his own path in defiance of the "ruling taste," and in doing so, risking ostracism by society, slight as well as inner and outer crises—such fabrication of false heroism is, if I may say so, part of the ruling tastelessness of a society oblivious of the spiritual, a society that abuses art. If a creator of art is to be credible, he must a priori be defenseless. Courage and taste in the sense of incorruptible adventurousness, based on competence, are the requisites of cultural managers—they ought to possess those abilities. But that is a vast subject and you do not need to ask composers about it just as you need not ask rabbits about the use and indispensability of rabbit fur.

Once again: "courage" and the "tyranny of taste"—you will have no moralizing by me . . . They damage the image of "New Music" rather than serve it.

July 30, 2015

Dear Mr. Lachenmann,

Thank you very much for explaining in detail why you decline to contribute to my project. May I nevertheless use your reply as your contribution? I am bowled over by your fantasy and the passionate formulation of your argument.

Obviously—and luckily for you—you need no courage to embark on a new work. You are not dogged by doubt, neither are you a composer whose work has had a hard time gaining recognition.

I have been corresponding with composers in the United States who were required to compose serially to be employed at a university, or indeed, who were only taken on if they were not serialists. "Change your style"—was the advice offered to a young and talented composer if she was to have a chance to get on. That is of course more than taste—it is ideology. And for me, ideology is something like institutionalized taste.

Here is an extract from a new book of conversations between Péter Eötvös and the Portuguese composer-conductor Pedro Amaral.[4] It demonstrates how

---

3   The quote is taken from the journal written and published by Karl Kraus, *Die Fackel*, 1 vol. no. 890–905, Vienna, July 1934.

4   Eötvös and Amaral, *Parlando-Rubato*, 216–19.

ideological differences in Hungary in the late 1950s and early 1960s could have lethal consequences.[5]

The same was of course true of the Soviet Union, the GDR, and so on, as well as the Third Reich. The Austrian composer Gerhard Wimberger relates a similar episode in Vienna: thanks to his professor, he was allowed secret access to the music of Schoenberg and Webern during the years of Austria's Nazi occupation.

Xenakis deplored his isolation in postwar Europe because he refused to join the serialist circle of composers. That was once again no longer a question of taste, it was an extreme form of it, an ideology bordering on religion.

I do not know how I should define Boulez's supposed rejection of the octave—in any case, György Kurtág consciously made use of it in a birthday piece dedicated to the composer.

Taste—"I like it," "I don't like it"—can have damaging consequences, when it concerns people in powerful positions. I mean festival directors, conductors but also music critics who are doubtless capable of influencing public taste, of creating an atmosphere around an artist. That is why I have decided to interview some of them for this book.

Dear Mr. Lachenmann, once again thank you very much indeed for taking time to reply.

All best wishes,
Bálint András Varga

August 5, 2015

Dear Bálint Varga,

Thank you for your reply and your understanding even if the latter appears to misconstrue my reservation: whether the composer Helmut Lachenmann is not one "dogged by doubt" and whether I am *no* creator who "has had a hard time to gain recognition for his work" . . . are you making fun of me?

No "courage" has helped me to overcome the recurring doubt that God knows has dogged me time and again, it has not helped me even against "anxiety." It was only my survival instinct as a composer—to be exact, my patience, diligence, perseverance, indeed, my breathing.

And as for the "ruling taste"—where does it rule and who is ruled by it? Angela Merkel? Franz Beckenbauer? Thomas Gottschalk? Or Joachim

---

5   Please see the quote in "Prompts."

Kaiser?[6] My work has hardly "gained recognition" any more than the music of Schoenberg or Webern. It has earned a certain respect among a group of insiders; it is now being performed with increased frequency and has indeed found some enthusiastic listeners almost everywhere. I was lucky, probably thanks to my moving *Mädchen* opera.[7] However, the "ruling taste" is unlikely to be influenced by my music with its niche-like presence—after all, it embodies the overall unstoppable decline of our civilization into superficiality and dullness—a politically most dangerous process.

---

6   Angela Merkel (b. 1954), chancellor of Germany since 2005. Franz Beckenbauer (b. 1945), German soccer player. Thomas Gottschalk (b. 1950), German radio and television anchorman. Joachim Kaiser (b. 1928) is an influential German music-, literary-, and theater critic.

7   *Das Mädchen mit den Schwefelhölzern*, 1988–95, based on Hans Christian Andersen's tale *The Little Match Girl* (published in 1845).

CHAPTER NINETEEN

LIBBY LARSEN
(B . 1 9 5 0)

American composer

One lesson I have drawn from compiling this book is the extent to which popular music and jazz have influenced classical composers, both in the United States and Europe. Libby Larsen freely admits to the role Chuck Berry, James Brown, and Big Mama Thornton have played in her development, in addition to Bach, Berlioz, and others.

If you listen to her music, as a European not really well-versed in the American tradition, you cannot fail to discern an underlying streak of what one identifies as coming from the United States, without being able to define just what it is. Of course, the presence of ragtime is obvious in pieces like Mephisto Rag—*one does not need the title to help one place the music—but in* Holy Roller *for alto saxophone and piano, the uninitiated cannot trace the influence to what the composer describes as "classical revival preaching." One hears a mixture of influences that, to this listener, include, jazz, Debussy, and even, at one point in the piano, Beethoven—but it is of course altogether subjective and probably wrong. More importantly:* Holy Roller *is a colorful, multifaceted piece of music, ideal for a good saxophone player, that cannot fail to appeal to an unprejudiced audience.*

Interestingly enough, the vocal music that I have heard sounds more English than American to my ears, with The Peculiar Case of H. H. Holmes *at the top of my own private list. It is a wonderful psychogram of a tortured soul that comes across with irresistible power even before one finds out that*

Holmes was a serial killer in Chicago who found ingenious ways to torture his victims. Any baritone with psychological insight, and a background not just in Lieder but also in opera, will welcome this unique challenge.

I have heard Libby Larsen's one piece for young performers, Hambone, which is great fun for the children to play (having to slap their thighs and shout, in addition to playing instruments) and also for the audience. It is the wind parts that help place the music as coming from the United States.

November 9, 2015

I have never equated courage with my creative process. For me it's the opposite. It would take a great deal of courage to silence myself and *not* compose. Composing is like breathing to me. Why would I suffocate myself?

Music exists in an infinity of sound. I think of all music as existing in the substance of the air itself. All gestures, sounds, rhythms, pitches, colors, textures, shapes—they all exist in the air. It doesn't take courage to breathe in or breathe out a piece of music.

I think of the Muse as ceteris paribus, the place where all thoughts are equal; as yet without shape, sound, motion, and emotion. This place is pure and is my font of creativity. If my process is true and I am vigilant with my relationship with the Muse, then I know my music comes from itself and is authentic to itself. The question becomes, "Who can listen to what I have to say in my music?" I suppose taste may have some credence here, but authenticity is detectable and permanent. Taste is a matter of transient perception.

CHAPTER TWENTY

L I Z A   L I M
(B .   1 9 6 6)

Australian   composer

Unlike so many Australian composers whose names may be familiar in Europe but whose music has failed to penetrate through the geographical distance (I am thinking of Peter Sculthorpe and Richard Meale in particular), Liza Lim has achieved a remarkable presence in Europe and the United States, while also remaining active in the musical life of her native country.

Lim's initial contact with Europe might have come about thanks to her studies in Amsterdam with Ton de Leeuw. In any case, invitations have followed for her to write works for major European ensembles and festivals, also to compose an opera for Berlin, where she was artist-in-residence of the German Academic Exchange Service DAAD in 2007–8. Liza Lim has also accepted major commissions from orchestras in the United States such as the Los Angeles Philharmonic and has lectured at several universities. In 2008, she was appointed professor of composition at the University of Huddersfield.

Her contribution to this book mirrors her devotion to her art, her striving for authenticity, and, perhaps most important, her sensitivity to even minute stirrings in the outside world. Similarly to Robert Morris and Luca Lombardi, she values artistic freedom, which enables her to produce works no one else is capable of giving as a gift to lovers of music.

May 2, 2015

Dear Bálint,

Thanks for the invitation to contribute something to the conversation about "courage." For me, the word in relation to artistic practice, could perhaps be substituted with "authenticity"—to be true to one's inner spirit without being swayed by pressures to conform to external voices as to what constitutes success in art. This pressure might be about being accessible and commercially productive or in equal measure about being "cool" and reflecting the latest intellectual and technological trends. These kinds of pressures are often about meeting expectations about some kind of image or branding. I'm amazed at how many ways there are of creating zones of inclusion and exclusion in the politics of art.

I'm not saying that an artist shouldn't be in dialogue with the world and all its trends—not at all since I feel that I am rather transparent to my environment and often very much influenced by some subtle thing occurring in my field of consciousness that registers on my antenna. I also understand the craving for recognition, for love and acceptance and to be understood by a community—I feel these things too.

Yet I do think the project of "authenticity," whatever that might mean for an artist (it might very well be commercially enriching or an austere refusal of communication, the content itself is not the point) is the most important thing an artist can give to the world. I think one can sense this gift through a kind of sparkle of wonder—a sense of opening to freedom created by the uniqueness of *this* voice or act in *this* time and space that will not be produced by any other. This is a romantic attitude I know in an age of reproducibility driven by consumer culture . . .

An example of art that I've found incredibly comforting and inspiring in relation to my own pursuit of authenticity is the work of numerous Australian Aboriginal artists. There's a phenomenon in Australia of these Aboriginal women in their seventies or even eighties taking up painting—after a lifetime of immersion in ritual lore, performance, and body painting, they transfer their knowledge to canvas with acrylic paint and the work has a bold, raw power, a heady sensuality and feeling of spiritual revelation that is absolutely authentic in its expression. This is "no-holds-barred," unwavering work that can be stark in its colors and designs or incredibly sophisticated in its patterns but is answering to an inner vision without question of compromise. I have some paintings by Eubena Nampitjin and they take me to another world governed by spiritual laws that are unknown to me and yet the work speaks with an unbelievably direct power that shakes me at my foundations. I also love the fact that these women are working at the height of their creative powers at an age where Western society has often consigned people to irrelevance and neglect—the age of people stuck in nursing homes—yet these artists are fully immersed in their art and one can see the life force in their work. I really do hold up these artists as role models.

I hope these comments add something to your collection.

Kind regards,
Liza

CHAPTER TWENTY-ONE

LUCA LOMBARDI
(B .   1 9 4 5)

Italian-Israeli composer

Luca Lombardi was born in the year that World War II ended. This puts him at a considerable advantage over composers born in the 1920s—Nono, Berio, Boulez—who were cut off in their formative years from music that, in fascist regimes, was considered degenerate, primarily music of the Second Viennese School. Even the slightly older generation, such as Henri Dutilleux, had had a hard time catching up and digesting the experience of encountering for the first time in their lives an idiom that was radically different from what they had grown up with.

One is struck by the tone—and of course the corresponding content—of Luca Lombardi's recollections. Carefree might be an apt way of describing it. He himself uses the word "freedom" at one point, and that could be the key to his attitude to his art. He realized at a young age that writing music was his natural way of expressing himself. What tools he might hit upon and how those tools may be received by the outside world do not seem to worry him in the least. An admirable and enviable philosophy of art and life.

Luca Lombardi is one of those composers for whom personal style is not something to strive for. Like Heinz Holliger or Péter Eötvös, he is perfectly happy with the apparent fact that each new piece turns out to be different from the previous ones—that there is no instantly recognizable Lombardi profile in music.

He is like a mussel—the pearls he produces are musical compositions.
Each is an object in its own right, and whether it was born in hard labor is
something he does not reveal. The beauty of the pearl is what counts.

Tel Aviv-Yafo, September 1, 2015

A few years ago, a colleague asked for a "motto" about my work, to be included in a publication she edited.[1] I sent her the following text:

> I wrote my first composition on the day I turned ten years old. I have
> known ever since that I am a composer. I never asked myself why—it was
> simply like that. And that is how it has been up to this day. Later, mainly
> around 1968, I did pose the question according to the fashion of the time,
> why and, above all, for whom I composed in the first place? I found a
> range of more or less convincing answers at the time, but of course, deep
> down, a composer is unaware of his motivation. The making of music is
> an expression of my will to live and my vitality, it is my way of experi-
> encing and digesting life and of taking a stance. It is for me a chance to
> achieve and to "construct" freedom. I am my own first listener and my
> first critic. If others derive pleasure from what I do, it makes me happy.

That more or less says everything there is to say: since my tenth year,
composing has been a necessity of life and expressing myself through music has become my second nature. For nearly sixty years now, I have been
doing what I set out to do. It has frequently found acceptance, frequently
it has not. Everyone wants to be loved by all, that is natural, but what differentiates the consciousness of an adult from that of a child is that one
gradually perceives that one cannot be loved by all. Willy-nilly one has to
accept it . . .

If I think back, some episodes come to my mind where the making of
music gave occasion for me to demonstrate my will, indeed, my obstinacy:

In 1958, I was not yet thirteen years old, I entered the composition
class of Gianluca Tocchi (1901–92). I had been composing after a fashion
for nearly three years by then and was very proud indeed of my, in part,
rather amateurish efforts. On one occasion, for instance, I showed Tocchi a
Sonatina in stile classico for the harpsichord. I had performed it myself at a
celebration of the German School at the Santa Maria dell'Anima (the church

1   Violeta Dinescu, ed., *Begegnungen mit Musik unserer Zeit: Komponisten-Colloquium der Carl von
    Ossietzky Universität Oldenburg 1996–2011* (Saarbrücken: Pfau Verlag, 2011), 195.

of the German-speaking Catholic community in Rome). Incidentally, my mother, who was basically not particularly bourgeois-minded, insisted that I wear a tie . . . I would have none of it, it was far too posh and middle-class for me. I remember I was already onstage, waiting for my turn, when a German friend of our family appeared with a tie in his hand and tried to make me change my mind. . . . That gives an idea of the customs prior to the decisive turn of the years around 1968 and how they have changed since then. . . . But also of my will to be different. End of bracket. Back to my first teacher of composition. I showed him my little piece and, with pencil in hand, he was about to make some corrections. God forbid! I instantly began to suffer intensely and would not allow Tocchi to destroy my work, of which I was rightly or wrongly so proud. I asked him to put his corrections in parentheses. "What, parentheses? Well, I never! Out!" And with that, I was kicked out of class.

Fifteen years later, in 1973 (I was spending some months in East Berlin), I was a master's student of Paul Dessau. We would meet at his house at irregular intervals at Lake Zeuthen and on one occasion, I showed him the beginning of a piece I was working on: *Non Requiescat: Musica in memoria di Hanns Eisler*.[2] He knitted his brows: "Well, you are making the trumpeter's job very difficult indeed! Why don't you assign the part to two trumpeters?" That was precisely what I would not do, for that particular section was supposed to render the player's gasping for breath. I had Godard/Truffaut's film *À bout de souffle* (*Breathless*) in mind, but more important, I was thinking of a sentence of Eisler's: "I am only the messenger who arrives out of breath and has to deliver just one more thing. . . . To do something useful, something one can deliver."[3] Apparently, I was able to get my message across to Dessau, for—whether he accepted my reasoning or not—he did not ask me to leave his house.

From 1978, I lived for ten years in Milan, teaching composition at the Conservatorio Giuseppe Verdi. My music was published by Ricordi and I worked closely with Luciana Abbado Pestalozza who was responsible for the production of my scores.[4] She had her preferences among the composers—there is nothing wrong with that—her favorite being my respected colleague, Salvatore Sciarrino. Anyone who knows new music is aware that Sciarrino's work, apart from its many other qualities, is characterized by

---

2   Originally published by Moeck, the work was acquired by Ricordi when it purchased the entire Moeck catalog.
3   Hanns Eisler, *Gespräche mit Hans Bunge; Fragen Sie mehr über Brecht* (Leipzig: BDV, 1975), 214.
4   Luciana Abbado Pestalozza (1929–2012), a sister of Claudio Abbado, was a publisher and festival director.

its instant recognizability. From the very beginning, his compositions are marked by certain recurring features of sonority. Perhaps that is one reason for the success of his work. Also, for its numerous imitators, there are indeed dozens of composers who—especially in those years—absorbed a great deal from Sciarrino, so much so that in the 1980s one could speak of a veritable Sciarrino school—or Sciarrino epigones—in Italian music.

As far as I am concerned, I have never bothered about having a personal style. On the contrary: I have endeavored not to repeat myself (whether I have succeeded, is a different matter). For me, composing is a journey of discovery. It is not so much about new sounds and playing techniques, but about new insights into myself and my relationship to reality. (I once wrote an essay titled "Comporre come conoscenza e autoconoscenza" [Composing as perception and self-perception], where, on the basis of two compositions, I explain what I mean by them, in other words how it works with me concretely—not always, but every now and then—that composing takes the form of a learning process. At the end of a "journey of composition," I know—if I am in luck—more about myself than before.)

However, my good friend Luciana Pestalozza did not see eye to eye with me. She was appalled by the difference between one piece and the next, for when she heard a work, then another and yet another, she could not recognize the same composer. . . . That was not the case with Sciarrino whose music she could immediately identify. In her view, it was a shortcoming. Today, after decades of working this way, with a highly diverse stylistic range of compositions, often written at one and the same time, listeners to my music tell me that, for all the difference between the individual pieces, the music has a color all its own. That gives me pleasure, for it is an aspect to which I have not devoted any attention, yet it shows that I may have many faces but just one soul—or perhaps one face and many souls. Which reminds me: in the mid-1980s, I got down to writing my first opera, *Faust: Un travestimento* (to words by Edoardo Sanguineti, after Goethe's *Faust I*). It is marked by a particularly great variety of stylistic elements, for reasons of content and also due to the virtuosic abundance of masks in Sanguineti's adaptation. The last (fourth) scene of act 2 is set for soprano (Greta) and string quartet onstage. I had all along meant that scene to be an autonomous concert work as well, with the title *La canzone di Greta*. One day, my colleague and friend Armando Gentilucci dropped in on me, noticed the score on the piano and began to turn its pages.[5] The piece uses material from Schubert's *Gretchen am Spinnrade* and is a kind

---

5   Armando Gentilucci (1939–89), composer, teacher, and lector with Ricordi.

of journey to different and contrary landscapes of mood of the simple girl Greta who has just fallen in love with the youthful Faust.

Armando commented: "Are you out of your mind to write something like that?" I did not have the impression that I had gone crazy. Nevertheless, it was probably not "musically politically correct to compose something that smacked of minimalist music (a playful outcome of the repetition of a piano figure in the Schubert Lied that was iterative in nature anyway), not to speak of the use of consonances or—God forbid!—even of tonal passages . . . In the 1980s—and partly up to this day, although to a lesser degree—the "Cold War" was still lingering, causing havoc in music, in a wholly different way, of course, from politics. In music, too, you had (and have) the "Good Ones" and the "Evil Ones."

You need not even hear a piece to decide whether it has to do with one or the other; it suffices to know its technique and musical idiom and whether it has been "accepted"—by whom? Well yes, by some radio producers, concert organizers, interpreters, and critics, who set great store by conformity with the Zeitgeist, or whatever they regard as such. Sometimes you need not even take the trouble of ascertaining the style of a composition, you only need to know its genre. A musicologist informed me once that he ignored composers of symphonies. Shostakovich, Hartmann, Pettersson, Henze, Schnittke, Rihm . . . they are all implicated, to hell with them!

Sanguineti himself was altogether different. He was an experimental writer and poet, well-versed in contemporary music (not only because he worked closely with several composers, Berio in particular). He was no conformist but an open-minded artist. *La canzone di Greta* was the first bit of music he heard from the opera then in the making, and he wrote a text about it that tells something of the way he went about translating and disguising Goethe. That was what I tried to set to music, with wholly different means, of course.

A "Travesty" is neither a translation, nor is it a parody but a "ricreazione" that carries in Italian, as in English, at least a double meaning. It is no *à la manière de* but a *d'après* [in the case of my *Faust* a "d'après Goethe," of course, a "*secundum* Goethe"—L.L.]. One undertakes an orbiting maneuver, so to speak. One attempts to touch concrete reality, the hard present, in that one surprises it from behind, drawing on a *déjà lu*—as a painter has his *déjà vu*. If I am to cite an example, I would mention Manet's *Déjeuner sur l'herbe* in the version by Picasso. In naming Manet, however, I am doing so not just to use a model but also to refer to an archetype because, as is well-known, Manet's was in his turn a "travesty" of an etching by Marcantonio Raimondi which had been taken from

Raffaello, one that in addition had also been treated, simultaneously, by Palma il Vecchio (or, more accurately, the author of *Concerto campestre*) and was also taken up by Courbet.

It is no coincidence that modern painting was born under the sign of "travesty." And it does not suffice to say that we are dealing, in general and in particular, with a natural and traditional problem of iconography. It was "allegory" that signified a turn, brought about by an alienation effect, to use Walter Benjamin's words.

It seems to me that in *La canzone di Greta*, Luca Lombardi takes exactly that course of action. Inevitably, his Raimondi of *déjà écouté* is Schubert. But the actual encounter takes place just as in the case of Picasso and Manet, so that he profits from a veritable concatenation of allusions and alienated "travesties" that correspond completely to the intentions of the verbal material. Actually, a *Faust*, in words and in music, cannot come about other than through a metadiscourse about a myth, indeed, *the* myth of modernity par excellence. Every modern writer has dreamed of retelling his own *Faust*, if he did not already tell it again in that he positioned himself between the extremes of *Mon Faust* and *Votre Faust*. However, deep down, I would imagine that everyone dreamed of writing the last possible version of *Faust*, with a fatal lack of modesty, just as Picasso had surely hoped to have produced the last *Déjeuner*. Without that radical ambition, by the way, it would be impossible to repeat the experiment. That was probably also subconsciously my own challenge. And I think and hope that here, too, Luca Lombardi will be my accomplice, in this concert scene just as in the whole opera. And that is no excessive idea, for all myths, in order to be able to die, must somehow end in a "travesty." That is how the Odyssey ended, with Odysseus in *Ulysses*.[6]

My *Faust* opera was surely a turning point in my work as a composer, although it was, I think, a logical step in a process that had begun at the latest in the mid-1970s with my *Prima Sinfonia* (First Symphony). In that piece, I had already used some tonal material—in the shape of quotations or otherwise—in defiance of the silly, dictatorial verdict of the "Cominform of the Avant-garde" (the supranational alliance of musical conformists) regarding the use of tonality. In the opera, I applied a range of stylistic means, including tonality, in accordance with the various guises Sanguineti had recourse to in his Goethe adaptation. As a result, I have been regarded ever since as a renegade by the high priests of the pure doctrine (even more so by the not-so-high ones).

---

6   Edoardo Sanguineti, *Per Musica* (Milan: Ricordi, 1993), 232–33.

As I said, it was for me a logical consequence of my development. In a letter to Claus H. Henneberg (April 1987), I wrote:[7]

> I am Italian, brought up in German culture . . . , so that an eminently German theme like Faust, newly interpreted by an Italian poet, is one that is dear to at least two of the souls . . . that inhabit my breast. In addition, I happen to have reached a phase in my life where I am calling into question my former views. My belief is doubt. For me, it is no paralyzing force but a productive one. Namely, to go on seeking. What better companion, in this leg of the trip, than Prof. Dr. Faust? Sanguineti's text moves virtuosically on different levels of language. . . . As you know, I have taken a stand a number of times, both theoretically and in practice, for "inclusive" music that reflects the diversity of (real, philosophical, musical) viewpoints, without assuming the character of a supermarket. This music includes tonality (used not in a naive or restorative fashion), which, to quote Sanguineti, "represents today a particular form of atonality (the way a rhyme is a special case of free verse)."[8]

Some years later, in the summer of 1991—the opera had meanwhile been premiered, at the beginning of that year—I wrote:

> It has by no means turned out to be an autobiographical work (although . . . alienation and empathy morph into each other. Empathy in particular instances, alienation in the work as a whole—also the other way around). For me, Faust is also a human being, just like you or me, an intellectual, disillusioned by the theories and ideologies he had believed in. Still, he does not despair or give up but continues to try to achieve a clearer view of himself and his relationship to the world, even though now without illusions—an engaged skeptic.

In accordance with the travesty character of Sanguineti's text and my "inclusive" approach, a range of musical experiences find their way into the opera. It has serious and burlesque, sophisticated and trivial, popular and artistic features. The work's comic and tragic aspects are not in contradiction; indeed, it is difficult to ascertain whether the supposedly comic is in reality not tragic. And vice versa. I helped myself time and again to materials and stylistic moods suggested by the individual scenes, free of bias and worry. For all the diversity of its stylistic levels, the opera has a unified color, ensured also by the unity of its basic material (the Faust-, Mephistopheles-,

---

7   Claus H. Henneberg (1936–98), librettist, translator, and dramaturg.
8   L. Lombardi, "On *Faust: Un Travestimento*," in L. Lombardi, *Construction of Freedom and Other Writings*, ed. Jürgen Thym (Baden-Baden: Verlag Valentin Koerner, 2006), 501.

and Greta-chords). The schizophrenia that characterizes not just Faust but all other figures as well (not exluding the composer himself . . .) leads, on another level, to a contradictory unity. After several years of learning and wandering in the world, I have wanted to write music—as a stop on my continual travels, perhaps as a balancing act—where spontancity and calculation, complexity, and simplicity engender and define one another (just as comedy and tragedy are not in contradiction). It is perfectly clear to me that it is well-nigh presumptuous to attempt something like that today. I would not have dared to do so if the subject had been less devilish . . . The perpetually negating spirit has been of help—through negating negation, as it were—to achieve a new, hard-won immediacy of the musical gesture. I thank him [Faust] for that![9]

At the moment, I am working on my fifth opera—because of the subject I have chosen, it is alas not all beer and skittles, even though it plays in a country with plenty of beer and plenty of skittles . . . Still, I am afraid I am not interested in the easy way out but look for challenges of existential significance, something that is "true" in the sense that it has to do with real life. What is the new opera about? After paying my first ever visit to Israel in 2003 and some years later, in 2008, becoming an Israeli citizen, I began to look for a subject for an opera that would reflect this new phase of my life, also, my interest in Jewish culture and the land of the Jews. Finally, I found it in David Grossman's book *To the End of the Land*.[10]

Ofer—that is the opera's title—is the story of a great love against the background of a major tragedy. I fashioned the libretto myself, having obtained the endorsement and the help of Grossman himself, to cut the seven hundred pages down to about twenty-five. I am setting it in Hebrew, but there will be a translation into rhythmisized Italian.

The book tells the story of Ora, her love for two men and her son Ofer. Having recently been demobilized from three years of army service, Ofer volunteers to fight in the West Bank. Ora panicks, for she fears that soldiers with news of her son's death might be standing in front of her door. She seeks comfort in magical thinking: as long as she is away from home, the news cannot be delivered, Ofer cannot be dead. Her flight should protect him. She takes a youthful friend of hers, Avram, on her travels, who gradually turns out to be Ofer's biological father. Avram served in the army

---

9   Ibid., 501–2.

10   A novel (2009) by the Israeli writer, born in Jerusalem, in 1954. The literal translation of the original Hebrew title could be rendered as "A woman flees from an announcement." David Grossman, *To the End of the Land* (New York: Vintage, 2011).

during the Six-Day War and returned from his time in an Egyptian prison-er-of-war camp with deep wounds to his body and psyche.

Their travels—in a way, a magic spell of self-defense—is also one of remembrance, a conversation therapy, and the telling of a story: Ora con-jures up for herself and for Avram their son's life from the moment of his conception, in an effort to keep Ofer alive through the magical of retelling his life. The history of Ora, Ofer, and Avram as well as of other figures mir-rors that of the country. However, even though the book and the opera are linked with Israel and its neighbors, the questions they treat of are not lim-ited to that area of the globe—they are valid for other countries and other times as well—they are universal concerns of mankind.

That is what interests me not only in this new opera project but in gen-eral, in all my operas: themes that concern us because they are part of hu-man nature and history. Love and hatred, hope and despair, life and death, sin with or without atonement, power and lack of it—and, alas, again and again, war that humankind apparently cannot do without. Indeed, since the dawn of history, humankind has found itself, right up to this day, in the age of war—in a way, in prehistory. Will it ever grow out of it? At the mo-ment it does not appear so, even if Europe has lived in peace for 70 years (not counting the war in former Yugoslavia in the years 1991–95). But what are 70 years? Not much. And what are the 200,000 years of Homo sapiens in comparison with the 215 million years of tortoises or the 50 million years of bees? An extremely thin layer of time. But it helps us precious little to keep that in mind—we must attempt to come to terms with our own history and, if possible, take a step, however small, away from prehistory.

CHAPTER TWENTY-TWO

SIEGFRIED MATTHUS
(B . 1 9 3 4)

German composer

Looking at musical life in the German Democratic Republic (GDR, East Germany during its years as a communist state) from the vantage point of the Hungarian People's Republic, I gained the impression early on that its most prominent, indeed, most successful representative was Siegfried Matthus. As I write elsewhere in this book, there was of course Paul Dessau (1894–1979) with his immense authority and influence; also, Ernst Hermann Meyer (1905–88), who actually sat on the Central Committee of the communist SED (Socialist Unity Party) and was an outspoken advocate of socialist realism in music. Both of them stood out as figures of political and musical officialdom—but it was Siegfried Matthus (again, as far as I could judge from Budapest) who was actually performed with any frequency and accepted by the public, and whose jovial, easygoing manner made him a popular figure.

Unlike so many composers of the GDR who appear to have faded into oblivion since reunification, some of them during their lifetimes, Siegfried Matthus's presence has remained undiminished. One wonders what his secret might be: after all, he was permitted by the East German authorities to be elected a member of the Academy of Arts in West Berlin as early as 1976, and two years later, of the Bavarian Academy of Fine Arts in Munich. He had been elected to the East German Academy as early as 1969, at the age of thirty-five.

Matthus was showered with decorations in the GDR and, in reunited Germany, has kept up the tradition. What might be closest to his heart is the naming of a hall after him at Rheinsberg where he founded a festival of chamber operas in 1990. It is called the Siegfried-Matthus-Arena.

As for his secret—it probably lies in the fact that he writes good music.

May 22, 2015

In the late 1960s and early 1970s, I was considerably intrigued by the serial experiments of my colleagues in the West. It did not so much take courage to publicly acknowledge my interest, rather, my stance was meant as a protest against the official aesthetic dogmas in the GDR. In the mid-1970s, I noticed that this particular path had come into conflict with my desire to express myself in music. I attempted to find compositional methods of my own. That met with sharp criticism from my colleagues. They claimed I was a traitor to the cause of new music. Was I being courageous or was I merely trying to find my own way?

I want to tell you an interesting story to do with a commission. I have beeen friends with Christian Thielemann for many years. Although he was born in Berlin, he knows a great deal about East Prussia, and admires it with something of a euphoria. Whenever we meet, I want to talk to him about music but he insists on hearing about my place of birth and my dramatic flight from my native land.[1] I told him that I ought really to record those historic events but I did not think I would live to do so. Whereupon he replied: "Well then, compose them!" That is the story of *Lamento, Musical Memories for Large Orchestra and Soprano Solo*, commissioned by the Munich Philharmonic, wonderfully rehearsed and premiered by Christian Thielemann in May 2007.[2]

---

1 Siegfried Matthus was born in Mallenuppen, East Prussia. In 1944, he fled with his parents from the advancing Russian troops to the West.

2 I asked Matthus about the text sung by the soprano, and received the following reply: "One evening, as a child, I saw an angel in the window. It was my guardian angel who was to protect me in critical situations on our dramatic flight and saved me from possible death. In my composition, the soprano sings only 'ah.' The piece ends with the repetition of a single tone. Mourning? Hope?"

CHAPTER TWENTY-THREE

ROBERT MORRIS
(B . 1 9 4 3)

British-born American composer and music theorist

Robert Morris has spent most of his active life teaching composition at a number of universities in the United States, including Yale University (where he was also director of the Electronic Music Studio), University of Pittsburgh, and the University of Rochester's Eastman School of Music. He really knows what he is talking about when portraying the situation of composers in America who are anxious to make a living by joining the staff of a university music department. In recent years, he has created situations in which student composers write pieces to be played outdoors in parks and forests, the sounds of nature blending with pitches generated by the players.

As an active composer himself, over the past several decades, he has experienced the difficulties that confront creative people in their effort to negotiate the obstacles represented by the musical establishment and to get a hearing for their music. Robert Morris's survey of the music scene since the 1960s is revelatory for someone coming from Europe. But so is his detailed analysis of what he means by the notion of freedom—an analysis that was inspired by the request for him to contribute to this book.

July 27, 2015

Dear Bálint,

I have been thinking about your idea of the "tyranny of taste," and your ample illustrations of this phenomenon. I have rather complex responses to the issue, which is a reality for all creative artists (perhaps related to John Stuart Mill's "tyranny of the majority"). I have tried to condense my ideas in the short paragraphs below, but this is only the tip of the iceberg.

First, I should say that composers in music institutions in the United States have a rather different social, economic, and historical situation from composers in most of Europe, especially those in the old Soviet Bloc. The way censorship works here involves getting a job in academia and keeping it (i.e., tenure); this often forces composers to compromise. And it was true that "experimental" composers like Cage, Oliveros, Wolff, Feldman, Mumma, Lucier, and so on originally found academic employment impossible, even if they had reputations in the press and many performances. On the other hand, many "American" composers testify that these social pressures obliged them to change their styles toward serial methods in 1960s. This may be true, but I have also encountered strong reverse discrimination to serial music in the academic world in my career. Either way, there has always been pressure on young composers to adopt what is topically fashionable.

I remembered a story: A young female composer had written a piece that a senior composer had heard at a concert. He took her aside and said, "You know, you are very talented, and you could eventually win a Pulitzer Prize if you were to do one thing." The student nervously asked, "What would that be?" He said in all seriousness, "Change your style."

But this is all complicated by what is *commonly thought to be* the hallmarks of a particular style and the nature of a particular compositional method. A person (composer) may listen to a composition composed according to some method M that is usually taken (or is even intended) to yield a piece in a style S. However (since compositional methods must underdetermine the compositions that result from their application), a given piece written using M may not sound like other pieces in style S. Thus, a piece may be ignored or criticized for being written using M, and yet it doesn't "sound" like a piece in style S. Conversely, a piece that is clearly in style S may not have been written using M at all, so it may be praised or damned depending on what some person thinks of style S. For example, one might marvel, "I can't believe that wonderful piece was written using chance procedures," or "that piece may sound good, but is based on popular material so it is inherently wanting." These mistakes of identity under the operations of prejudices about M and S make the tyranny of taste a that much more vacuous and reprehensible phenomenon. Moreover, listening to music with concepts about M and S tends to make truly original pieces go unnoticed unless they are radical departures from a tradition.

Before the mid-1990s, as in Europe, an American composer's career was heavily dependent on music critics, recording companies, publishers, and performance by "major" performance organizations. One had to find a way to write music you cared about yet submit to the pressures of cash and cachet. The problem was that the distribution of one's work was dependent on these organizations and personae; you couldn't make a high-quality CD, or engrave your own music, or have direct access to performers. Computers and the Internet have changed all that, so things are easier for composers today, even if some of the software tools available are geared to popular and traditional music.

As for me, my "heroes" were composers who thought through their compositional situation carefully and with great insight. If "dynasties" arose around their ideas and music, it was because other composers were looking for some stability and identity, so they traded in their musical uniqueness for association with an "influential" composer or trend. In the 1960s many of these compositional trends were considered avant-garde, but there is a similar situation with conservative "directions" such as neominimalism, neoromanticism, "return to tonality" and various forms of "fusion." There is nothing wrong with these directions, but changing one's style to conform to them is an issue, and one that many composers eventually regret.

Then there is the problem of dualism. At one time, Stravinsky and Schoenberg were considered to be opposites, and you were either in one camp or the other. Composers such as Wuorinen and Wolpe sublated these (Hegelian) oppositions into a new "style" that had elements of both. American music and European music were considered different and opposed at various points in the twentieth century, but were eventually "combined" in later work, the same for total organization and chance music, classical and vernacular music, electronic and "acoustic," and so on.

I find my roots in the music of Milton Babbitt and John Cage—another (pseudo) opposition, and my music has elements of both (as I wrote about in my recent book, *The Whistling Blackbird*).[1] Among other composers I admire is Charles Ives, with whom I trace an intellectual tradition back to the American Transcendental philosophers and poets of the nineteenth

---

1   Robert Morris, *The Whistling Blackbird: Essays and Talks on New Music.* Eastman Studies in Music (Rochester, NY: University of Rochester Press, 2010).

century. That once—and I think still—fresh American position of individualism borrowing from European Romanticism as well as Eastern thought with an emphasis upon "nature" has been a major source of inspiration for me. It has enabled me to free myself from the tyranny of taste, and other tyrannies as well.

You also ask: "Does a creative person need courage to start writing, painting, sculpting, composing in the first place?" Well, some potential artists are literally driven to make art (they have something like "pressure of speech"); others are not. Those that are driven may find a way to power through exploiting the tyrannies of taste, and so on. Of course, a mentor or esteemed person or friend can help one develop the confidence to go forward despite (scary) obstacles. (Your other contributors have mentioned so many of these situations already.)

It would seem that a stubborn, single-minded, unbending personality would be of benefit to a creative artist, especially in times of conflict with the "establishment" or "fashion." However, I think this can result in a liability, since this type of maverick—or at least determined—personality can become insensitive to the needs of other artists, and to rule out—without much thought—other positions and trends. In this way, such a person becomes the source of the tyranny!

Clearly, the main problem is one of fear. So for me, the way of courage is not only that of combating but also eliminating fear. But there are also the problems of wanting success and fame. As I say in the last sentence of my book: "no desire, no fear, no carrot, no stick—freedom."[2]

Let me conclude with some points about the anatomy of freedom. Freedom is what is called in Zen "beginner's mind"—when you awaken to a new day; when you feel everything is auspicious; open optimism; not expecting anything particular—rather, whatever comes, it will be all right.

Freedom is space. Space has no center, or every point is the center. (No hierarchies to control you.) A free choice is made unattached to consequences. It is playing, exploring for the love of it.

To bring it down to concrete experience: Freedom yields that feeling of openness when you wake up rested and alert—without coercion and the weight of knowledge and responsibility; like when you have completed a task or escaped from danger. Freedom is not desire, but interest and curiosity; not compulsion or obsession, but connection.

Freedom comes in two flavors: "Freedom from" connotes independence, lack of restriction; "Freedom to" means one is able to live with

---

2   Ibid., 355.

contradiction and ambiguity and nonfinality. For me, "freedom to" is the more important one for manifesting creativity.

"Freedom from" means freedom without boundaries. "Freedom to" doesn't eschew boundaries. It admits them, but only if they don't block, segregate, inhibit, limit, or ignore what's on the other side. We may call them "free-boundaries." Such free-boundaries are about the permeability among things—so a thing's thing-ness doesn't inhibit its intersection with or enclosure within another thing. Anyway, thing-ness is just one way of thinking.

Free-boundaries enrich experience. They provide color and character; they encourage multiple ways of expression and connection—even to confuse and beguile the thing-ness of things. The more of these kinds of boundaries, the more interesting and useful experience becomes for many purposes and people.

But with freedom comes the responsibility to make sure the boundaries are indeed free. Choice should not inhibit another's freedom.

Krishnamurti: "All that one has to do is to understand the chaos, the disorder in which we live. In the understanding of that we have order, there comes clarity, there comes certainty. And that certainty is not the invention of thought. That certainty is intelligence."[3]

3   Jiddu Krishnamurti, "Commentaries on Living: Second Series," Fourth public talk in San Francisco, March 1973, http://www.jkrishnamurti.org/krishnamurti-teachings/print.php?tid=14&chid=761.

CHAPTER TWENTY-FOUR

OLGA NEUWIRTH
(B . 1 9 6 8)

Austrian composer

Olga Neuwirth is a courageous woman. She does not hesitate to voice her criticism of social injustice in her writings, interviews, and addresses; she also takes up the cause of minorities. Her outrage finds expression in her music as well as in her words.

Olga Neuwirth's writings reveal someone who has experienced and suffered a great deal. She is sharp-witted, tough, but also vulnerable. A fragile woman, who in our interview seemed to open up to my questions without any reservations, so that the interview made a strong emotional impact.

I hope something of that impact will emerge in the transcript.[1]

Vienna, March 14, 2016

I have read your beautiful text on Eleanor. *It is a work that particularly appeals to me—and I have the impression that it is a kind of self-portrait. Let me quote you: "For me, this composition is a tribute to all those who have dared and still dare to voice criticism despite social and political opposition."*

---

1   I wish to thank Catherine Kerkhoff-Saxon for revising my English translation.

And you go on to say: "Eleanor would . . . especially like to pay tribute to courageous women—which explains the woman's name in the title."

It also seems that "courage," "criticism," "dare" are keywords for you, as are "wound" and "fight": "The name Eleanor is a reference to Billie Holiday.[2] Beginning in childhood, her life was marked by abuse, which left deep wounds. Wounds that made it difficult to live. Her great talent, and the enormity of her soul and spirit were thus constantly fighting a sense of emptiness. Nothing was able to dull her profound nihilism."[3]

How about starting this interview with some autobiographical information? I would like to know what it was that made you the Olga Neuwirth we know. You, who—when asked if there was anything you were frightened of—said: "Of life itself."[4]

I just want to say this: I do not trust people.

Precisely. This is closely linked to the keyword "wound." You have had many disappointments. Is this what lies behind your opinion that "Man is a rat"?[5]

I must have been twenty-one when I said that. I am now nearly fifty and my opinion has not changed. On the contrary.

Why do you think you have met so much resistance? Perhaps the following quote provides an explanation: "I do not wish to take the path 'existential military service' such as many are sent off on from childhood in order to make them cheerful, happy, and beautiful. I reject all that, but it means that things assail you without there ever being a lull."[6] Those are the words of the child Olga Neuwirth, who could not and would not fulfill her parents' expectations and decided instead to do things her own way. I sense that your life has been one of rebellion, a protest against something.

No doubt it has to do, on the one hand, with the discrepancy, which began in childhood, between the exceptionally free environment that I grew up in—a society of artists and intellectuals—in a highly conservative and

---

2   The African-American jazz singer Billie Holiday (1915–59) was born Eleanora Fagan.

3   These three quotes are all from the program brochure of *Eleanor* (2014–15) for blues singer, drum-kit player, electric guitar, ensemble, and samples. World premiere. Salzburg Festival, August 7, 2015.

4   Interview with Jean-Noël von der Weid, in Olga Neuwirth, *Zwischen den Stühlen*, ed. Stefan Drees (Salzburg: Verlag Anton Pustet, 2008), 281.

5   Interview with Christian Baier (1991), in ibid., 23.

6   Ibid., 281.

xenophobic province in Austria, near the Slovenian border.[7] On the other hand, the society that my parents moved in was still very patriarchal. This was true of our own family and of their friends' families, and especially of our small town community, which was politically extremely conservative, and is still today. Yet for some reason, I was a freedom-loving, unorthodox child who did not always understand rules, nor did I always want to understand them. Rules had to make sense to me, before I would obey them. But rules, just for their own sake, forced despotically from above . . . I have always fought against that.

Isn't that a contradiction: a society of artists that lives according to rigorous patriarchal rules?

That is precisely what I mean: this odd contradiction with which I grew up. Intellectuals, artists on the one hand, who were very free in many areas of life—overly free—and, on the other hand, not free at all. As a child, I would often go over to our "normal," orderly neighbors when things got too crazy for me at home with my parents and their friends. It was all two sides of the same coin: on the one hand, very liberal, and, on the other, harsh and rough in the way they treated one another. They quarreled a lot, although they were not angry at each other the next day. For me as a child, however, who scanned her environment with great attention, it was difficult to grasp why people would behave that way—it seemed really brutal.

By "patriarchal" I mean that women had no say—whether they were "oh-so-free artists," or not. There was also a discrepancy between the artists who fascinated and inspired me as personalities, and the realization that women were ultimately supposed to keep their mouths shut and subordinate themselves to men. And so I wondered: why do these differences exist? Why couldn't we all be equal? This was why I often ran out into the fields and meadows, and created a world of my own.

Now I see why you so often speak of being "unprotected." It appears to be another one of your keywords.

Right.

Have you found some kind of protection in art—in your work?

---

7 Olga Neuwirth was born in Graz but grew up fifty-eight kilometers to the south, in Schwanberg, near the border of Slovenia.

Yes, but merely some kind of pseudo-protective place. I believe the moment I lost my instrument, the trumpet, I lost my true identity. My "first Olga." Don't forget that in the early 1980s, in the Austrian province, where nearly no women played the trumpet, not even in the local brass bands—I, rebellious as I was, decided I wanted to become a female Miles Davis. I ordered a trumpet in the United States, with a bright and clear sound, to find some release in jazz. I loved playing "Send in the Clowns" (by Stephen Sondheim from the musical *A Little Night Music*) in "my own version."

Your father is a jazz pianist.[8]

Yes, but I refused to play the piano. I was a punk in the Austrian province in the 1980s and was more attracted to the urban jungle than to mountain pastures. With the trumpet I was able to rattle these stuffy surroundings by being ironic and shrill. And then, out of the blue, there was this car crash on our way to a winter holiday. I had been adamant about not wanting to go, this was just a day after I had gotten my braces off—I had had to wear them for years. And then, after the crash, my lower jaw was gone . . .

You can no longer tell.

I used to look different, but my surgeon was fantastic. I was fifteen, in the middle of puberty, and was confined to a hospital bed for weeks. I could not go to school, couldn't talk, and had no lower jaw left—which also meant that I couldn't play my instrument any more. To be faced with all this simultaneously was a bit much. Composing became a kind of compensation. When I compose, I'm all by myself, no one determines what I may or may not do. I had the feeling at the time that in my imaginary world of sound I could at least make my own decisions, even if they were limited to a sheet of paper and my own brain. And this self-empowerment was an important place for me, a sort of refuge. Although my initial hopes of having found a secure place for myself were soon dashed: I hadn't realized that especially as a composer, you are always dependent on others who make your music heard. For composers who are not performers themselves are totally at the mercy of the goodwill of others. In other words, I found myself in a new dependency, even though that was what I had hoped to escape. Absurd.

---

8   Harry Neuwirth (b. 1939).

Writers are also dependent on publishers—if they can find one in the first place.

That is true. But once a text has been printed, it needs no interpreters.

Every reader is an interpreter.

Every reader is an interpreter, but in his or her own head. With composers, the decision lies in the hands of the musicians and the conductor (if there is one)—whether they wish to perform a piece and if so, how they are going to interpret it.

In light of this, does it take courage to continue composing?

Courage and rage. At least for me. Otherwise, I couldn't have continued. Rage has led to courage and created a need. Civilized rage sharpens awareness and often gives me the necessary energy to go on working and to escape the daily grind.

Courage is clearly something you also appreciate in others. You have, for example, detected it in Franz Schreker,[9] as you have pointed out in one of your interviews.[10] In your text on Eleanor, *for instance, you express recognition for those "who have dared and still dare to voice criticism despite social and political opposition." Once again, a kind of self-portrait.*

I have many such musically exaggerated "self-portraits." And I have always taken a special interest in particular composers because they were important for me in trying to discover who I am. Why are we interested in one person and not in another? Either because someone is wholly different from you, or because he or she feels very close. I feel very close to Schreker, Nono, Hölszky, Ligeti, Varèse. And they all, just to mention a few, had the courage to do it their own way, despite lots of resistance. They had or have an unorthodox (inner) stance that can't be pigeonholed and is dead set against the tyranny of taste—a stance that enables them to search for something for themselves and to fight for it. It is always a matter of daring. Though, as I see it, the timing also always matters: at what point do you decide to speak out or act. You don't just wait until everyone is already

---

9   Franz Schreker (1878–1934), Austrian composer, conductor, and teacher.
10 Interview with Lloyd Moore, in Neuwirth, *Zwischen den Stühlen*, 258.

shouting it from the rooftops and you can no longer be attacked. In other words, when it's "risk-free."

You mention the tyranny of taste and it reminds me of what you have said about "pseudo open-minded and liberal theater and opera house managers as well as large-scale event managers who are often unbudgeable in their opinions and believe they know exactly what is good and what is bad." The cancellation of your opera project with Elfriede Jelinek was a manifestation of this tyranny. Although it went well beyond a question of taste, of course.

Just recently I talked about that again in an interview, as I am often asked about it. In this particular case, taste was not an issue, for it never came to the point where I could start composing—because after having been invited to do so by several managing directors (administrators), I was disinvited. For a great many years I had been collaborating with Elfriede Jelinek, that fantastic, highly original writer, because I wanted to make a statement about the present. The conduct of the administrators was therefore an unmistakable indication, in my opinion, of how a standardized male system prevails in our field: after all, two women—one of them rather well-known, the other internationally famous—were summoned and told quite patronizingly: "You may now create an opera together." This was in itself rather condescending. So the writer, in her enthusiasm, writes a wonderful, poignant text, only to be told in all the complacence and arrogance of the music industry: "She is not capable of writing a text." I have this in writing. Three months later, this very same writer is awarded the Nobel Prize in literature! I wonder if we would have been treated this way if we were male? Instead, with one of my male colleagues, to make his work seem even more important, people continually stress that his male librettist is a Nobel Prize *contender*. I, on the other hand, collaborated with a real Nobel Prize laureate and we were axed. This says it all. There's no need to say more about the way women are treated in the classical music world. And this did not happen twenty-five years ago. The entire story began in 2001 and ended in 2005.

So there was much more at issue. It showed me the existing male hegemonic system in our field. *They* had approached us and knew what to expect from Elfriede Jelinek: a critical and topical exploration of an issue that had been swept under the carpet. These managing directors were, however, afraid of the subject of child molestation, especially in 2001 when we were first asked. Whether this also had to do with the fact that two women were going to work on the topic and they didn't like this? I don't know.

But you two had already collaborated on other operas.

That's right—but we were still mistrusted . . . Though, as I'm sure you know, the film *Spotlight*, which is about this very subject, won two Oscars in 2016.[11]

Fourteen years ago was just too early for a work on this topic that was so important to me: the abuse of children. Initially, we had suggested the "Children of Spiegelgrund" as the theme of our opera.[12] This was because in the late 1980s, I had taken a private guided tour that I had succeeded in arranging when I was doing some research into my family's past. In the course of the tour, I noticed some neglected-looking objects in the collection of the Museum of Natural History. It turned out I had stumbled upon the suppressed story of a collection of human remains of murdered Jewish citizens who had died as subjects of "anthropological research." I shall never forget the stench of the formaldehyde! Shocked as I was, I told Elfriede Jelinek of my discovery. She incorporated what I had told her into a chapter of one of her books, which started the ball rolling: it resulted in the first public debates on this subject, as well as restitution proceedings and the burial of the remains. But this subject was immediately rejected by the administrators . . . and we were asked to write a Don Giovanni paraphrase instead.

You are one of the few composers who do not hesitate to devote themselves to political issues. It is surely not easy to find suitable musical means that are not overly bold or blunt.

This makes me think of Luigi Nono who found a personal musical idiom for exposing sociopolitical wrongs and injustices—an idiom that is in no way overly bold or blunt. In doing so, he showed courage, for his work was, of course, not warmly received, to say the least. To my mind, an artist who lives in a particular epoch, has the duty to examine how this epoch affects people and what it makes them become. After all, we are not independent of our times and politics. It is extremely difficult and delicate to find the suitable musical means to express this. I often attempt to solve this by resorting to a kind of (ironic) refraction. In my case this approach derived

---

11 *Spotlight* (2015, directed by Tom McCarthy, screenplay by Josh Singer and Tom McCarthy), deals with the pedophilia of Roman Catholic priests in and around Boston. It won Oscars for Best Film and Best Original Screenplay.

12 "Am Spiegelgrund" is synonymous with the Nazi's child euthanasia program at Vienna's Steinhof mental institution, where sick, handicapped, and behaviorally disturbed children were maltreated, tortured, and killed by the Nazis between 1940 and 1945.

more from a literary tradition, for I was brought up with literature. At fifteen, Brecht's brand of "epic theater" had already impressed me, so I read every play of his I could lay my hands on. This is why I reject any kind of nice and soothing music that has to do with the idea of "art for art's sake."

I cannot imagine, for instance, that Nono's *Intolleranza*,[13] which premiered at the Teatro La Fenice, would be commissioned today. No opera manager would dare program this piece.

Nevertheless, I believe we are slowly getting there again—where we can discuss major social conflicts in music theater. I've been asked a number of times lately whether I would be willing to participate in symposiums on "political music, particularly in music theater." I have replied that I don't wish to participate as a speaker, for my medium is music and, anyway, all my music theater pieces have in essence treated issues of a social critical nature. Yet instead of analyzing their political content, this aspect has been played down, trivialized. I don't know why. Perhaps they were scared to confront the public with a political subject? Or because a woman is seen as unable or not supposed to think in terms of politics? It took courage, so to speak, even to suggest such subjects to opera managers. And I had to believe that with a particular kind of musical idiom I could capture audiences with such subjects. I especially also want to reach people with music theater. As I said as early as 2000 in an interview,[14] I want to understand social and interpersonal phenomena, which is why Ingmar Bergman's film *The Serpent's Egg* has accompanied me all my life. In the film, the Jewish trapeze artist foresees the "serpent" called National Socialism and says: "Anyone who makes the slightest effort can see what is waiting in the future. It's like a serpent's egg: through the thin membrane, you can clearly discern the already perfect reptile." You must want to be alert and look and listen. However, my music is largely abstract. And you cannot really say anything concrete through music without words. Music is elusive.

Though you do sometimes use the human voice—as in Eleanor, *texts by Martin Luther King and June Jordan—and therefore your message can be understood clearly.*

Now we're back at Brecht. He used a chorus to raise questions, to query the views of his characters or to make them more explicit. This is why I had fragments from Martin Luther King's speeches against suppression and

---

13 Luigi Nono, *Intolleranza: Azione scenica in due tempi* (1960), world premiere on April 13, 1961, under Bruno Maderna.

14 Interview with Stefan Drees, in Neuwirth, *Zwischen den Stühlen*, 140.

racism interrupt the musical flow of *Eleanor*. His speeches, the sound of his voice had a distinct and powerful cadence. It is almost like singing, and has its roots in the tradition of Baptist ministers.

Billie Holiday's singing is also very powerful. It exudes suffering, despair, passion—it serves as a direct means of expression. In listening to your music, it is also apparent that you use cinematic tools. No wonder—film has been one of your central fields. In your compositions, you work with cuts rather than with transitions. They happen abruptly.

This has been of interest to me since I was young and I was inspired a great deal by John Zorn.[15] From him I learned that you don't linger over a musical thought for any length of time, you don't savor it forever, but you confound the listener again and again with quick changes in the musical structure. So that they must keep up or opt out. "Musical aggressivity" has protected me from the rash attacks of others. Stroboscopic flashes of experience have shot out of my music and, even though they would often miss their goal, the structures in listeners' brains might realign themselves as a consequence. However, I work with such means less and less. All the same, abrupt "pans" into another time, another space, another state continue to play a role. Sometimes I employ brief and rather banal quotes for the same purpose. They appear like sudden memories and are gone again. Because I think that ascending into the banal and harshly descending into the profound expands musical space.

As in your orchestral piece Masaot.[16]

That's right.

Romantic as I am, I heard the beginning of Masaot *as if you were conjuring up the past with a magic wand. From the swirling and whirling of time there emerged melodies of strong associative character.* Masaot *shows a different Olga Neuwirth, as did* Sans Soleil,[17] *even though it's twenty years older. I heard* Masaot *as a piece of poetic music with short playful passages. Does it take courage for you to strike a new and different tone? One that dispenses*

---

15 John Zorn (b. 1953), American composer, arranger, saxophone player, and producer.
16 *Masaot/Clocks without Hands*, world premiere, May 6, 2015, in Cologne, Vienna Philharmonic Orchestra, under Daniel Harding.
17 *Sans Soleil: Zerrspiegel* for two Ondes Martenot, orchestra, and live electronics (1994).

with rage and is "peaceful" instead? Does it take courage to quasi betray yourself?

(*Laughs*). I've been betraying myself for ages already. That's why people often say: "With Neuwirth you never know what you're going to get." But I never wanted to be pigeonholed anyway. The music world finds this challenging because they want everything to be easily recognizable. In all my pieces, I have tried to create a paradox out of the absurd and melancholy, despair and defiance, and so evade categorization. Nevertheless, it continues to be difficult for a woman to be taken seriously.

I was a punk girl at fifteen. It was an altogether different world; I took no interest in classical music whatsoever. It was about being antiestablishment, undogmatic, singing provocative social-political songs, anarchic-ironic plays on words, and a particular kind of aggressiveness, hurling nihilism in the face of others. The rawness, the not knowing what the next moment held in store for me was important. Being undogmatic was of significance, as I have said—and you should apply this to yourself as well . . .

Trashy electronics à la Beastie Boys, a certain rawness of sound, and irony greatly appealed to me. *Sans Soleil*, composed in 1993 in Paris, takes its cue from a film by Chris Marker whom I worshipped at the time.[18] A much-traveled man, he took the title of his film *Sans Soleil* from an eponymous song cycle by Modest Mussorgsky.[19] The film is a rich mix of ideas, images, and scenes from Japan to Africa, reflecting in essay form on human existence and brutality. *Sans Soleil* is a meditation on the nature of human memory—it's why I feel so close to it. It's also why my piece has many different elements in close proximity.

In the past twelve years, I've grown milder, so to speak, and now make far fewer cuts. I give my music more time. Since 2004, the pieces have become calmer, often there are static passages. The reason could be that I felt I had said all I had to say in *The Long Rain, Lost Highway*, and . . . *ce qui arrive. . . .*[20] What I had been searching to say between the ages of twenty and, let us say, thirty-five, I had already said. After this it became

---

18 Chris Marker (1921–2012), born Christian François Bouche-Villeneuve, was a French writer, photographer, and documentary filmmaker. His best-known works are *La Jetée* 1962) and *Sans Soleil* (1983).

19 Modest Mussorgsky (1839–82), Russian composer. He wrote this cycle of six songs in 1874.

20 *The Long Rain*—a multichannel-surround video opera (1999/2000) for four soloists, four ensembles, and live electronics based on a story by Ray Bradbury. World premiere, October 19, 2000, in Graz. *Lost Highway* (2002/3), music theater to a libretto by Elfriede Jelinek, based on the eponymous film by David Lynch. World premiere, October 31, 2003, in Graz, European Capital of Culture 2003, Klangforum Wien under Johannes Kalitzke. . . . *ce qui arrive . . .* (2003/4) for voice, ensemble, interactive live video, samples, and live electronics. World premiere, October 21, 2004, in Graz, with Georgette Dee and Ensemble Modern under Franck Ollu.

difficult for me. I had to muster the courage to look for something new. It became important for me to compose music that was quieter, less restless, less forceful. This change was interpreted in a negative way. "She has exhausted herself, she's lost the ability to write, she has nothing more to say"—I heard this a lot. I really needed courage to carry on, to not become completely disillusioned. This is why it is most important for me to this day to remain undogmatic and courageous when it comes to myself and my own material; of course, I've known this for decades. For there is always the danger of getting stuck in a rut. And despite all anxieties and constraints as a freelance composer, you must not give in to the expectations of the music industry, which wants you to work faster and faster, and faster still. Yet it takes a very long time to write down what one hears in one's head— to listen to the sounds as they emerge and to render them as precisely as possible on paper. Nevertheless, you are hardly allowed to try things out, and by no means should you fail, even though it would be so important for you as a person and as an artist: you cannot develop otherwise. I attempt, at least, to continue to do things my way and to realize the visions I have in my head. But all that saps your energy.

In an interview, you said you wished to be as little integrated into society as possible.[21] Because from the outside, as you once explained, you can perceive things in a more "scalpel-like" way. Doesn't this attitude isolate you? If you consciously want to remain "outside the door?[22]

Sure. It has its consequences. The path I've chosen has many negative aspects.

It takes courage to persevere.

It does! And solitude takes courage because it leaves you unprotected.

Would you agree that you are in fact extremely strong? Strong and vulnerable?

(*Laughs*)

A last question: In the book Zwischen den Stühlen *you talk about meeting young people who listen to music differently (and to different music); short*

---

21 Neuwirth, *Zwischen den Stühlen*, 281.
22 A reference to the play by Wolfgang Borchert (1921–47), *Draußen vor der Tür* (Outside the Door), written between fall 1946 and January 1947.

numbers of two or three minutes. Young people who aren't able to concentrate on your music or relate to it. And yet you carry on . . .

I've no other choice. It was an extremely critical moment in my life. I no longer saw any sense in composing after 2004. For many years I stopped working almost entirely. In 2007, I even turned for help to the neurologist Oliver Sacks in New York, for my brain was not functioning the way it used to.[23] It was frightening: I could not compose because it was acting strange. Oliver Sacks was a great music lover and connoisseur. And this meeting was very important to me.

Such things do happen: Hans Abrahamsen also stopped composing for ten years.

I once talked to him about this at some length. About our similar experiences. It turned out that we had even read the same books about the subject. However, my problems were different. I wasn't able to hear the way I used to, and I saw, for instance, wild movements of color. It was disturbing because I used to hear my music in my head in a finished form and I "just" had to jot down the notes. This is why I thought my music also had to change. Behind me was all that I already knew, and ahead of me, perhaps around the next corner, was the unknown.

At this time I began contemplating for the first time what I would call "the notion of beauty in art." So Nono regained relevance for me, similar to when I was fifteen, but this time for different reasons. Not a kitschy beauty, but tender, fragile, with internalized rage. Music without any hollow, inflated beauty. I believe genuine beauty can anyway only be perceived by the voyeuristic, curious observer. I repeatedly tried to fathom musically what beauty was in different atmospheric shades. On top of this, it's expected that everything about a woman is pretty and proper, and that she is too. That's not for me. Nor is composing pretty and proper music. In my music, shifts and gritty passages should be perceptible! It cost me a great deal of strength to carry on at a time when I lost all footing and felt insecure.

Did Oliver Sacks help?

He helped me a great deal. But only over many many years, step by step, a new direction evolved that enabled me to compose again. But it will never be the way it once was.

---

23 Oliver Sacks (1933–2015), British neurologist and writer.

A difficult profession . . .

(*Laughs*) Yes, because everything is in your head. This is why it requires courage, at least for me, to motivate myself each time again. I sit for hours and hours just to write down precisely a few seconds of music, so that a complex web is created as I want to hear it. It is a microcosm. A microcalligraphy. Recently, in New York, I saw an exhibition on microcalligraphy, which derives from a Jewish tradition. Myriads of words make up an image. This has always fascinated me: these minute details set down with absolute precision that add up to a large, finely woven whole. Of course, it takes forever . . .

I sensed something like that when listening to Le Encantadas.[24] *A world in itself emerges, rather like in Mahler's symphonies. It is a multifarious world, in which a great deal is going on all at once. What particularly impressed me was the way you could evoke the sensation of infinity (by the way, this happens in some of your other works as well).*

That's how they differ from my earlier pieces. The infinite, the unutterable have always affected me and, interestingly, Schreker's works gave me this same feeling. Just take the title of one of his operas: *The Distant Sound*! It conjures up an intangible, distant, infinitely large, and probably unattainable sonic dreamscape.

Earlier, such a "quasi infinity" was beyond my reach because, in physical terms, I pressed everything together into solid rock. Perhaps what is happening now is the gradual disintegration of rock into another chemical state. It is also a dissolution toward an opening of space. In *Le Encantadas*, you are, so to speak, engulfed in an architecture of sound coming from all sides, live and electronically. Just as in the "organic architecture" of Gregg Lynn and the later works of Zaha Hadid.[25] This is why *Le Encantadas* is one of my major pieces after *Lost Highway*. I was finally able again to realize a sound-space vision exactly as I had conceived it, as it wasn't a commission for a specific instrumentation and duration. But this was why I had to fight for this piece for so many years as nobody wanted to believe me or had confidence in what I wanted to do—namely, that it makes sense and is possible to "capture" the acoustics of a permanently closed Venetian church

---

24 *Le Encantadas o le avventure nel mare delle meraviglie* (2015), for six ensembles distributed around the space, samples, and live electronics. World premiere, October 18, 2015. in Donaueschingen, Ensemble Intercontentemporain under Matthias Pintscher.

25 Olga Neuwirth, "Ideen für ein Raum-Musik-Projekt (London 2004)," in *Zwischen den Stühlen*, 262–63. Zaha Hadid (1950–2016), Iraq-born, British architect, professor, and designer. Greg Lynn (b. 1964), American architect, professor, philosopher, and science-fiction author.

and make the acoustics the starting point of an entire composition. I had
to persuade myself not to give up in order to convince the organizers of my
vision—for, of course, it only existed in my head. It turned into an eighty-
minute composition on sound in space. I am very self-critical, but of this
piece I am proud.

CHAPTER TWENTY-FIVE

ENNO POPPE
(B . 1 9 6 9)

German composer and conductor

Enno Poppe's lanky figure with his abundant shock of flaming red hair is a familiar figure at new music concerts and festivals in Europe, mainly in Germany and Austria but also as far afield as Russia. You see him on stage as a conductor of ensembles (mainly of the one he cofounded in Berlin, the Ensemble Mosaik [1997] but also of other formations, such as Klangforum Wien), as well as in the audience. What matters is his presence.

If you read the interview with him, you are bound to be impressed by his strong feeling of responsibility for the cause of "New Music"—so significant in the working life of this highly talented, original composer.

If you look at his concert programs, you will be intrigued by the frequent absence of his own works. He formed his ensemble not so much to promote his own compositions but, again, to serve new music. And one is impressed by his enthusiasm for his fellow composers whom he regards as comrades-in-arms—rarely does one encounter a composer who is so full of praise for his colleagues.

If you read on, you will also be struck by his immersion in the music of his forebears, such as Haydn—you may not hear it when you are actually listening to his music, but its roots do reach deep down—evidence of his searching spirit, his inquisitive mind, and, again, of his sense of responsibility toward his calling.

In thinking of Enno Poppe, I was struck by an admittedly far-fetched image—that of the Schutzmantelmadonna.[1] I have decided to mention it nevertheless for, close as I am to the past and present of contemporary music, I am reassured by the presence of the figure of someone like Enno Poppe, spreading his protective cloak over the cause to which he has devoted his life.

Vienna, April 28, 2015
Revised January 29, 2016

You must have courage—always. You must always progress a step farther, and should have the confidence to discard whatever has failed to develop its potential.

Schoenberg: he was one who was incredibly good at whatever he was doing—and whatever he was good at, ceased to interest him. He was determined to make continual progress. His orchestration was peerless, but his skill was of no concern to him. He was spurred on to set out toward new goals, in an effort to find answers to questions that had newly arisen. In my eyes, that is courage.

Or there is the composer Mathias Spahlinger, who turns his back on solutions that have proved themselves in a piece, never to make use of them again.[2] He is always seeking resistance. That is what I call courage.

What you have said about Spahlinger is just as valid for you.

It is a fundamental incentive for me never to mark time, but to pose new questions again and again.

There is an attitude typical of audiences and newspaper critics but also of some young composers: we have had that before. You often hear people say: I know that already, that is nothing new. I believe you can only say a thing like that if you have not bothered to look properly. If you listen superficially, then everything sounds alike, all string quartets are similar. Once you take a closer look at phenomena, you come upon the differences—you realize that there are white spots on the map all over the place. There is something to discover everywhere.

---

1   *Schutzmantelmadonna* is the German term for portraying the Virgin Mary in medieval iconography with her extended arms holding her mantle so as to shelter all those seeking her protection. "Schutzmantel" stands for "sheltering mantle."

2   Mathias Spahlinger (b. 1944), German composer.

There is also the attitude: you can't do a thing like that today. I must then ask: why not? Let's see if we can make something out of it after all! And in doing so, you are not looking backward but forward. Can I make use of something that might on the surface appear to be depleted—perhaps I can find something new in it? It also calls for, if you wish to use the word, courage.

It does not interest me in the least to take something old and rework it. Instead, I ask new questions, in that I explore fundamental questions and I often find such fundamental issues in older works.

Could you give me an example?

Motivic-thematic development. I was once invited by a musicologists' conference to talk about my work. The musicologists were most irritated to find that I was abusing a term that for them was closely linked to Haydn, Beethoven, and Brahms. However, there is nothing against my taking that term and examine what lies behind it, what kind of thinking it denotes, and then to transform it and make use of it differently. Just as other composers take the violin, change its technique and put the instrument to a wholly different use.

Why do you need to take over a way of thinking only to do something differently?

I do not take it over at all, I merely find points of reference for my work. I do not go back, I do not think regressively, I think progressively.

I work with the computer and have gradually realized that the use of algorithms has led me to something with an astonishing, subterranean link to Haydn without my consciously looking for it. I find that interesting because it shows how much I am bound up with tradition; it is there within me, it is my mother's milk, so to speak.

Why does one need to think progressively, what is progress in music for?

The term itself has its problems, as long as one thinks of it from a technological aspect, as in the 1970s. In other words, we need more machines, more cars . . .

. . . serial music instead of motivic-thematic development.

Progress in art does not signify for me that what came before was worse than the new. But the fact is that things are changing all the time and we move forward, we cannot stay put and pretend that the world has not changed. That is obvious.

The notion of progress is problematic as long as it is used to mean a development toward something better. I do believe we have left that behind. We cannot claim that our entire reality with all its comforts does not lead elsewhere to incredibly negative consequences and will continue to do so. Progress does not imply that everything will be better. It only means that the world changes. That is for me no question at all.

Do you select your means consciously so that they mirror those changes or do they emerge out of their own accord, so to speak?

It happens automatically, I could not suppress it at all. I will not suppress it. I do not subject reality to an analysis, and that in turn affects my music—it is not like that at all. There are artists who do that; I find that fascinating but it is not my way.

You are also different.

Yes, I also change and so does the world; we change together and I think—I am convinced—that fifty years ago I could not have written the music I am composing today.

Some composers are willing—or feel the moral obligation—to take a stand on political issues. You may remember the Requiem of Reconciliation *in honor of the fiftieth anniversary of the end of World War II, to which composers from each warring country contributed. John Adams dedicated a work to the victims of the destruction of the World Trade Center in New York City and also wrote operas about President Nixon's visit to China, the Middle East conflict, and the danger of a nuclear catastrophe. All that called for courage, as he confessed in his autobiography, especially with regard to 9/11.[3]*

A look at your oeuvre suggests that you are unlikely to accept commissions of a similar nature. Returning to our subject, is it because you do not have the necessary courage?

3　Adams, *Hallelujah Junction.*

I do not think it has all that much to do with courage. The examples you list are not really political—they are representative music, written for official occasions.

I am reminded of *Wellington's Victory*. It was one of Beethoven's most popular compositions in his lifetime, but it is not political music. Also, it is surely one of his really weak pieces, topped with an extra helping of brass, for he thought the representative event required it.

I want to make it absolutely clear that political art can be antirepresentative. There are any number of highly interesting, provocative political artists in the visual arts, in film, and the theater. There are far fewer in the field of music, for music concerns itself with intangible, non-semantic things; music per se cannot mean anything beyond itself.

Penderecki's *Threnody* is a well-known example.[4] Originally, it was called *8' 37"*, but it proved difficult to sell under that title. The publisher suggested he think of a better one and he decided to name it *Threnody for the Victims of Hiroshima*. The music means nothing, the title was devised afterward. That has nothing to do with courage, it is simply in bad taste.

Poor Shostakovich was forced to write a range of works to subjects dictated by the Communist Party, such as the oratorio Song of the Forests *or the cantata* The Sun Shines over Our Motherland.[5] *What counted was surely the text that could express what music could not. I am sure you would not consider setting texts with a "message" . . .*

No. Certainly not.

Is that because you are not a political person or because you do not think music ought to play a role like that?

Music is capable of doing that! I can only talk about myself. Others can do things I cannot do. I believe music has the power to inspire people in a way that cannot be verbalized. For instance: I have worked a great deal with non-European music, in my thinking and also in the way I write music. In my eyes, that is also a statement. I find it important that our thinking and feeling should be open beyond the European context. It is not about texts or the messages of non-European music; often I would not even understand

---

4 Krzysztof Penderecki (b. 1933), *Threnody for the Victims of Hiroshima*, composed for fifty-two string instruments (1960).
5 Dmitri Shostakovich (1906–75), *Song of the Forest*, op. 81 (1949), *The Sun Shines over Our Motherland*, op. 90 (1952).

all that. It is about the quest for that which is foreign, which cannot be grasped, with a view to questioning our own security.

The other thing: freedom. Freedom is a utopia. If art places itself in the service of a cause, if one says "I make art so that people in Palestine have a better life," art will lose its freedom. Freedom of art must be an example for the freedom of man. Art, you see, also affords a possibility for us to better understand the world. It is a wholly different kind of understanding than that offered by newspapers, television, essays, discussions, and so on.

Does courage have any role to play in your work with regard to stylistic tools? Or, let us say, ad absurdum, for you to write a waltz?

There is in my opera *Arbeit Nahrung Wohnung* a "tropical waltz," scored for four male voices and a piano duet, music to mirror Robinson Crusoe's homesickness.[6] However, he happens to picture in his mind a room in a German inn of all places, where Brahms waltzes are being played.[7] In this particular waltz there are not only no quotes, there is no triple time either.

It is very interesting that you should be asking me about waltzes right now: I am often asked why I do not return to older music, why I do not write something regressive. It is something that I refuse to consider. I find it takes courage to say: I release something into the world. There is so much music around anyway—why should we take a step farther, why write music in the first place—all that is part of it somehow.

Clearly, this is a different time from earlier when there were heated debates about stylistic issues, Schoenberg–Stravinsky or Lachenmann–Henze. Today it is no longer quite as rabid, although of course it is still there. There are composers I have absolutely no truck with, I never even meet them. That is perfectly all right. You cannot approve of everything.

Conducting has taught me, however, to expand my horizon. I think it is perfectly normal for students of composition to reject everything that differs from what they are trying to do: they must assert themselves and find their bearings. I consider it one of the most fascinating aspects of my profession as a musician to immerse myself in my colleagues' ideas and to identify with them. It is something wholly apart from my own composing: after all, I cannot write everything that interests me. I think it is great that as a musician I can have contact with so many composers.

---

6 Enno Poppe, *Arbeit Nahrung Wohnung* (Work Food Apartment), stage music for fourteen gentlemen, to a libretto by Marcel Beyer, world premiere, April 28, 2008, Staatsoper Unter den Linden.

7 Enno Poppe uses the word *Bürgerstube*.

I find it wonderful that you should never run out of ideas, that in fact you cannot keep up with the influx. It reminds me of Xenakis who was likewise never short of new ideas. What counted for him was to be able to decide which one had the potential of further development. What does it look like for you—do you need courage to settle on a particular idea?*

Of course! That is the difficult bit. When I am at work on a piece, a new idea would definitely be a gatecrasher. If one should crop up, it would unhinge the process of composition. Composing is about perseverance, following up; the abrupt popping up of a new idea is anything but helpful. I have, thank God, many openings, many commissions; the new ideas are placed in mental files. One sees how young composers pile up too many ideas—I was no different at the beginning. Selection, concentration, patience: all that is a matter of experience.

I read a lot, see films, and visit exhibitions, I take walks; that is important. Literature in particular: I have learned a great deal about form from novels. Literature is interesting because music offers a fraction of the intriguing formal possibilities that literature has at its disposal, especially as regards large form. How can you master a large form, with which you relish working for an extended time? That has always fascinated me. The same with films: they teach you a lot about dramaturgy. Surely, I perceive books and films differently from others who are interested in other things. Looking at a film as a musician means that I perceive it as a way of organizing time, rather than as a story in the first place. After all, music is time organization.

I want to say something else about courage. What really gives me courage to do what I do are the musicians. I travel all over the place, I meet fantastic musicians, with whom we progress further. They are incredibly educated and open, capable of coping with any musical problem; they want to be challenged, to learn more—and that challenges me, too, when I am composing. I have the musicians I am composing for in mind, and we progress further together, because there is all this interest.

Clearly, people like Lachenmann, Spahlinger, or my teacher Goldmann, as young composers, had disappointing experiences with musicians: they would always come up against resistance.[8] Perhaps they had more courage than we do: they stuck to their paths against all odds. At eighty, Lachenmann has now reached the stage where his pieces are played by the Berlin Philharmonic and the public is enthusiastic. That is an in-

---

8   Friedrich Goldmann (1941–2009), German composer and conductor.

credible achievement that took a great deal of courage. I cannot claim to have had the same experience because I have always had a wonderful time with musicians and it has been utterly simple. It is incredibly great: we are together, as a team; we do not work against one another. What strikes me again and again with older composers is that they grew up in a spirit of mistrust. They could not unwind with musicians, but viewed them with suspicion—it is deeply ingrained. I do not have all that in any way. Musicians encourage me to try things out that I had never even thought feasible to realize.

I think you have been talking about new music ensembles. Years ago, I heard an orchestral work of yours in Hamburg. Months later, I heard it again, with other musicians, in Vienna. The two performances could not have been more different. The second one was immeasurably better, as if I had heard a different piece. I have had similar experiences with other composers as well. Experiences like that could cause a great deal of damage for the composer, for they could make you insecure, and cause you to doubt that what you wrote can in fact be played.

That's right. Orchestras are still something of a problem. I do not really like to write for orchestras, and I keep it to a minimum. That has primarily to do with insufficient rehearsal time. I think orchestral musicians today can play anything competently, if they have enough rehearsal time. With Klangforum, we have three rehearsals of three hours or two and a half hours each for a piece of average difficulty.[9] And they are extremely well-versed in playing contemporary music. Orchestras, on the other hand, are given two rehearsals of one hour each. That cannot go well. The musicians do it unwillingly because they do not know what they are playing, they do not know the piece. That is the only reason they are not enjoying it. As for the Hamburg performance, the conductor did not know what to rehearse. He could not even make proper use of the little time at his disposal.

Thank God you conduct yourself.

I do, but I am not sure if orchestras have a future. Given the way they rehearse and work, one had better forget it.

---

9   Klangforum Wien, founded in 1985, is a new-music ensemble of twenty-four soloists.

CHAPTER TWENTY-SIX

KARL AAGE RASMUSSEN
(B . 1 9 4 7)

Danish composer

Rasmussen is a musician of many parts: in addition to his work as a composer, he has also written books on Robert Schumann, Glenn Gould, and Sviatoslav Richter. He has acted as a sort of music ambassador for Denmark, lecturing internationally on Carl Nielsen and other subjects, and has also taught composition. (I have read his Richter biography and was impressed: it is a fastidiously researched book, drawing in part on Rasmussen's interviews with people who knew the pianist, unearthing previously inaccessible material. Also, it is eminently readable.)

Rasmussen is a restless, searching spirit who has completed Schubert's unfinished opera Sakuntala *and has prepared a performing version of it; he has reconstructed what he believes to be Schubert's unfinished "Gastein" symphony as well as an orchestral version of the melodrama* Der Taucher.

His sizable oeuvre covers most genres, including arrangements ranging from Nielsen to Stravinsky and Satie.

Rasmussen's experiences as a student of composition, which he describes in his contribution to this book, gave me the idea of adding the "tyranny of taste" to the initial subject, "the courage of composers."

I.

April 2015

The concept of courage in the creation of art makes sense only in a society where certain artistic expressions may result in harm or injury, be it mental or physical, from the power apparatus. Used about the process of creating art in a modern, western society it is a category error. To claim that the elite modernist Stockhausen needed more courage to write his music than the popular Britten to write his—or the other way around—is senseless. Whereas it certainly demanded courage from Shostakovich to write his *From Jewish Folk Poetry* in the autumn of 1948, at a time when Jews were jailed and killed in Stalin's Soviet Union. The work was first performed publicly only two years after Stalin's death.

Cage claimed to have "no ear for music," he tossed coins and considered any sound to be music. It was this seemingly effortless attitude combined with his status as a world-famous celebrity that made many of his colleagues vengeful. "The whole pitch aspect of music eludes me," he told an interviewer, and whereas admitting this may have required courage, the resulting artistic activity was just an inevitable consequence, a way of turning limitations into abilities. For years he hesitated disclosing his (so-called) silent piece, *4′ 33″*, not because of artistic worries, but because of his fear that it would appear to be "a joke." His renunciation was courageous on a personal, not an artistic level.

And so, in more general terms, considering the creation of music "research" or "communication" is a personal choice, not a matter of more or less courage.

As an artist, however, you are unlikely to totally avoid a sense of pressure from whatever artistic lingua franca is surrounding you, and the fear of becoming a pariah is deeply rooted in most people. As a student of composition in the late sixties, among not particularly academic modernists, I was nonetheless acutely aware that openly admiring—just as an example—the late Strauss of the *Metamorphosen* required an assurance that I did not possess at the time. And speaking fondly of, say, Prokofiev's music was inconceivable, so you kept your fascination secret. Some of Adorno's one-liners ("you can hardly hear a note without having to hide a smile") was an ongoing slap on the wrist, creating an anxiety about always attempting "the right thing"—or nothing at all. A mind model that enveloped my every artistic viewpoint during my early years.

Altogether ignoring such ideological pressure would not have been courageous, however, it would only have led to different artistic choices. To me courage signifies the mental or moral strength to do something that involves a risk of personal danger or harm, and these are matters entirely outside the realm of art. The notion of courage in art seems to me associated with an effete attitude where the labor of art involves agony and despair to be overcome by a heroic deed. An artist will always need integrity, engagement, and ambition. But only if and when he or she represents a threat to an established power structure, is courage called for. An artist cannot be a threat to art itself.

II.

June 8, 2015

Dear Karl Aage,

Many thanks for a highly interesting comment on "courage," impressive in its depth and your marvelous command of English.

I am particularly happy with the paragraph concerning what I would call "the tyranny of taste" or "the tyranny of dogma"—it could be the subject of another book.

Courage: I wonder whether you have read John Adams's autobiography Hallelujah Junction. *It is well worth reading! There, he describes the emotional upheaval caused by a commission for him to write a work in commemoration of 9/11. There were so many arguments against facing that challenge and he needed a great deal of courage to eventually say yes. He probably also needed courage to write operas on topical political issues such as Nixon's visit to China, the assassination of a Jewish passenger on a cruise ship, or the danger of nuclear catastrophe.*

I wonder if you would be willing to consider devoting a work in whatever genre to the Muhammad caricatures in a Danish newspaper and the threats against their author—if it were to occur to anyone to commission such a piece. Does art have the responsibility to comment/take a stand on political issues? Would you need courage to quote from Strauss's Metamorphosen *in a work of yours or to arrange Schubert á la Hans Zender? Or . . . or . . .*

You may of course decide you have had your say and do not wish to devote any more time to The Courage of Composers. *I am grateful for your contribution and am very happy to have it—also, to have had contact with you thanks to this book.*

All best wishes,
Bálint

*Rasmussen was amused to hear that the paragraph on his experiences as a
student (falling afoul of prevalent tastes) had inspired me to add the subject
"the tyranny of taste" to my initial idea of devoting this book to the courage of
composers. Below are his first reaction and his answer proper.*

June 14, 2015

A.

As for "pressure from outside" it is unavoidable. Not even artists are islands
and I think we all react according to instinct and temperament. My own,
even as a youngster, was always what the English refer to as "Mary quite
Contrary," that is, doing the exact opposite of what might be expected of
you. This of course reflects just as much dependency as following the herd.

My early music is a huge patchwork of very tiny tonal idioms from all
the nooks and crannies of Western history sewn together without any pre-
existing logic—a kind of meta-tonal language; slapping Adorno (and his
"the triad is a musical lie") on the wrist, as it were.

The waltz phenomenon, in general terms, always played a strong and
permanent role in my work—for a lot of reasons, including technical ones.
My music is overwhelmingly "in three." And my admiration for people like
Kurtág (or—for a younger name: Unsuk Chin) has a lot to do with their
nonideological use of material and . . . "style." And it is hardly coincidental
that I have written books on Gould, Mahler, Cage, Gershwin, Tchaikovsky,
and Bach—and many articles on Ives.

So it is fair to say that "the tyranny of taste" has played a decisive role
in my artistic development and outlook. There is an old legend about two
diametrically opposite wolves inside any person. Which of the two do you
become?—the one you feed!

B.

Discussing the precise meaning of specific words quite often proves a dead
end. Just imagine engaging in a debate about the meaning of a word like
art.

For me "tyranny" is basically a political concept, re my views on courage as a concept, only fully meaningful when there is a risk of (physical) danger or harm. As in the case of the infamous Muhammad drawings you mentioned yourself.

My original wording was "the fear of becoming a pariah," and it referred to my situation as a student among much older colleagues. I was sixteen when I entered the conservatory, I was twenty-four when I wrote *Genklang*, finally sufficiently assured it seems to, well, to dare the risk of being excluded from whichever group.

So for me the "tyranny" was hardly anything but aesthetic group pressure, and I think gradually and instinctively resisting it during my formative years had a decisive influence on me. I was far from alone, however, I soon found kindred spirits and had open-minded teachers. And I found Charles Ives!

Addressing an audience, bigger or smaller, was never part of my reasoning, it was just a way of coming to terms with—or better, recapturing—what was my own basic impulse for creating music (sorry if this sounds more grand than intended). Something deeper than . . . taste, I think. And thus I am ending with yet another word that evades precise definition.

Comment by Allen Shawn (January 2, 2016)

As I have told you, when I was a student in the 1960s and 1970s I certainly felt the pressures that Mr. Rasmussen referred to, as he was quoted by you in your letter to me last July. At that time it seemed that a global consensus about musical language had formed, and that not to compose in a certain way meant that one was simply not living in the present. Or at least that's how we young composers thought things were. So if we were attracted to let's say Prokofiev, or to Stravinsky's *The Rake's Progress*, or to Britten or Shostakovich, we felt that something was wrong with us.

It seems to me that this issue of "courage" you raise is deeply connected to your question in *Three Questions* inspired by Lutosławski's response to hearing Cage's music. The issue here really is the "courage to be oneself" in spite of what anyone else says. No matter what pressures those of us who studied music in the 1960s and 1970s may have felt, the only thing that ever mattered about music: the integrity and meaningfulness of individual works.

Important composers such as Boulez and Stockhausen and Babbitt and Carter and the 1960s Stravinsky may have talked about compositional techniques and compositional language, and taken stands about matters of musical idiom, but in fact they were simply expressing their own natures as composers. That their natures represented their times and their historical position was inevitable, but it didn't mean that they were determining what they would say and how they would say it by first contemplating history and their place in it.

Even very strong-willed artists need permission to be themselves, and they often find that permission in other artists. Cage said as much when he referred to Rauschenberg's "white paintings" giving him the courage to present silence as music. Balanchine expressed the same thing that when he first heard Stravinsky's *Apollon Musagète* he realized that he too could leave out much that had overstuffed his ballet language ("I, too, could eliminate"). I believe that when Boulez first heard Webern he recognized himself, he heard his own voice, he identified. The music of Boulez and Berio and Babbitt and others is powerful because no one but they could have written it. They found their own voices. They were in fact writing from their hearts and passions.

Our generation had a tough time sorting out this reality because very few of our mentors reminded us of this point (certainly Boulez didn't), and innovative forms and techniques and musical vocabularies were so emphasized, and in an atmosphere of scientific aridity.

In my own case, I was thrilled by all kinds of new music, but found I couldn't compose if I censored out the influences of music I loved, including tonal music. For me music was always a dialogue with other music, and it was not a science at all, but a way of forgetting self-consciousness and thereby paradoxically discovering what I felt. In order to be "myself" I simply had to allow my unconscious free rein to percolate with memories and associations, or I would cease to compose. At the same time, I always felt that the challenging musical period through which we all passed when I was a student was essential—a purifying trial.

The idea that all of the excitingly complex and difficult music of the time (including that of Boulez) was some kind of a "mistake" offended me. I honestly felt, and still do, that music of the current time that sounds as if later twentieth-century music didn't happen is not terribly interesting. (Maybe that is my own dogma.)

We all need role models. So what gave *me* something to identify with and take courage from in the 1970s was hearing challenging works that allowed disparate influences back into the music, and seeing mentor figures associated with modern music also championing other idioms. For example with my jazz background, it was exciting to hear Rzewski's piano music, or to see Gunther Schuller conduct works of Duke Ellington. It was helpful to hear Berio's juxtaposition of Mahler with his own language; to encounter my teacher Leon Kirchner's rhapsodic and ecstatic brand of atonality. Even a chance comment from one of my other teachers, Vladimir Ussachevsky, best known for his innovative electronic works, that Britten's *Peter Grimes* was "beautifully done," opened a window onto a broader definition of musical quality than one narrowly associated with "cutting edge" innovation and historical progress. These experiences and others gave me "permission" and reminded me that the important thing was the authenticity and merit of the music itself.

CHAPTER TWENTY-SEVEN

WOLFGANG RIHM
(B . 1 9 5 2)

German composer and
professor of composition

For fifteen years, between 1992 and 2007, Wolfgang Rihm and I kept in touch on a daily basis. We spoke on the phone and sent each other faxes. (He has no computer to this day; e-mailing is out of the question.) As Universal Edition's promotion manager, I knew what he was composing, and also what he intended to write. It was a pleasurable and inspiring business relationship, which gradually turned into friendship, if of a professional kind.

My retirement at the end of 2007 put an end to our daily exchange, but it proved wholly natural for us to renew our contact when I approached him early in March 2015 to ask whether he would wish to contribute to my book. Below is our correspondence. I have included my letters because of his occasional references to some of the things I had written.

March 19, 2015

To be honest: I find there is far too much "hullabaloo" about the courage of artists. What else are they supposed to be doing other than what they are doing anyway (that is, creating)? More often than not, artistic activity is proclaimed in retrospect to have been courageous, but if you look at it closely (and if you are absolutely honest with yourself), you have to pose the question: what choice did one have?

In your letter, you recall our conversation where I mentioned the animosity with which my first compositions had been received. But I could not have written them in any other way! And—this seems to be particularly relevant to our subject—I never thought I was being "courageous." Nor did it take any courage for me to carry on.

Whatever I have been doing as a composer is rooted in my innermost obsessions, passions, desires, as well as in my very own abilities, will and also in the fact that I simply cannot do *otherwise*. There is nothing heroic or courageous about that. It is rather that one produces something within one's possibilities. Within what else? He who follows the "mainstream" has no other choice. The same applies to he who acts otherwise.

That may appear to be a fatalistic approach but in actual fact I mean something wholly realistic: that art is a human product, that there is no such thing as the "objective tendency" of the material, or a "historic necessity" that an individual can invoke for his actions. If he does so, it is nothing but hubris. For many it is unbearable to accept that *they* alone, no one but they should be responsible for their artistic effort. In the arts, we cannot delegate it to an authority outside ourselves. Naturally, the ability of an artist has objective and tangible components; as a whole, however, it is not negotiable in the sense that "it could also be otherwise." Mozart composed like Mozart, not because he might also have composed like Clementi. He had no other choice.

Well then, what is the role of courage? Surely, each one of us has to accept and endure the manner in which time treats us and our work. However, there is something comforting about that: it will all come to light! And this may be taboo but is no secret: each one of us is aware of just how much our product is really worth. In our deepest selves, there reigns merciless clarity. Again, the question has to be raised: where does courage come in?

You know, we do not mean that each one of us needs to surmount a certain degree of energy to expose ourselves again and again to the perilous test of what we are worth. But it is all relative. It melts away the moment we make artistic decisions and are keenly aware that in making our choice, we have no choice. Each one of us has arrived at that point—including those whose products are met with contempt (whether rightly or wrongly). At the moment of doing, even if our action is delegated to chance or systems or anything else, at the moment itself when a decision has been made, there is in actual fact no alternative to our decision—either to courage or the lack of it.

It is difficult to discuss these things publicly, for the public arena is dominated by a ceaseless upward or downward trend of evaluations and values. And those who speak up for *one* thing in the arts, are likely to feel the risk inherent in their taking a particular side. The same is true of rejection out of conviction. Pro and con, that is, the position takings of the day, of the market, of science, and even of (artistic) belief are of course terribly relativized through what I have been trying to demonstrate: the mercilessly individual nature, the loneliness of the process of artistic creation. Indeed, any outside interference, that is, changing evaluations, are wholly irrelevant. Nevertheless, no "divine law" comes into play, no organic gravitation, no destiny—only pure human potential that articulates itself as *none other.* Credo quia absurdum.

At the most, a courage-like behavior may be necessary to nevertheless enter a domain like that. There, games must stop. Definitively so, so that they can start again, as it were, "at the other end": as amusement. If anybody should say to you: "Oh yes, I needed so much courage to realize my artistic efforts," do not believe them!

Perhaps I need to add: all that I have put to paper here has been prompted by my intuitive perception. Naturally, all the wealth of the aesthetic-evaluative apparatus remains entirely valid. The criteria whereby works of art are viewed in evaluative comparison, perceived, valued, rejected, savored, retain their rights, above all, their right of change. But: you asked a creative person and he (that is, I) holds: "Follow your own law that you will never know. You will however grasp it in being active. Derive pleasure from it, or suffer because of it. That gives you strength."

Can you now see why I am skeptical about the icon of courage in the arts? Like a mask or a pawn? Something gestural, artificial, pose-like?

It strikes me that whenever I become part of an invigorating encounter with art (such as, visit an exhibition, hear a composition, read a book . . .), I do feel *encouraged* to continue being active in my own field. That is, to follow my own stubborn goals. Encouraged, yes. Perhaps that is why I do not need courage?

In my letter of thanks to Wolfgang Rihm, I reminded him of a different kind of courage—the one composers in the former socialist countries mustered to use advanced, "avant-garde" techniques in defiance of possible consequences to their careers. In Hungary in the 1950s, composers were required to present their new works to a commission of the Composers' Association to gain permission for public performances. György Ligeti, for instance, submitted his Six Bagatelles for Wind Quintet (1953) with too many minor seconds in

one of the movements. Predictably enough, only five pieces were allowed to be played at the world premiere.
Rihm added the following text to his initial reaction.

March 25, 2015

Dear Bálint,

Thank you for your letter. Apparently, I need to clarify. There seem to be different kinds of courage, something that I left out of account in my improvisation on this subject.

I want to make it clear that I would *never* have had courage (*this* kind of courage) to defy a dictatorship by choosing "forbidden" aesthetic means of expression, thereby jeopardizing my life and that of my family. I would be silent. Naturally, I would at the same time *try not* to have to write cantatas to words by whoever happens to be the "Führer" of the day. I did not have in mind such situations requiring courage—and one cannot but be grateful not to have been forced into one. The courage demonstrated in such situations is beyond discussion. Words fail, you bow your head in respect.

I do wish to raise the question, though: would the willing author of Führer-Cantatas have had the *artistic* chance to choose another path and write in an "advanced," "regime-critical" vein? I would say no. One simply cannot imagine that the producers of jubilant cantatas—if only they had had the courage—could have written introverted Webernesque subtleties. And Webern himself? Did his political stance not pose the danger of his moving toward Blood and Soil?[1] What would he have done? Would have . . . would have . . . Quite a conditional.

To put it briefly: I mean the frequently cited "courage" as a category of artistic excellence. And there I assert that the artist concerned has entirely obeyed his impulse, he could not do otherwise. That this frequently fails to meet with the appreciation it deserves is annoying and irksome—however, one need not fall back upon the icon "courage" to overcome any transitory sense of hurt.

When I told you how my first works had been received, no state police with guns stood at the ready in front of my house. I "merely" attempted to come to terms with lack of recognition through contact with a like-minded public and like-minded critics. That, however, never gave me the right to speak of *courage*, even though it would have made matters

---

1 Blood and Soil (*Blut und Boden*), a reference to the racist and nationalist ideology propounded by the Nazis.

simple and would—today—be instantly believed. It would be all the more embarrassing.

Vienna, June 17, 2015

Dear Wolfgang,

I am enclosing the English translation of your text, for information and correction.

Since our exchange, I have received a contribution by the Danish composer Karl Aage Rasmussen. The following paragraph might be of particular interest:

> *As an artist, however, you are unlikely to totally avoid a sense of pressure from whatever artistic lingua franca is surrounding you, and the fear of becoming a pariah is deeply rooted in most people. As a student of composition in the late sixties, among not particularly academic modernists, I was nonetheless acutely aware that openly admiring—just as an example— the late Strauss of the Metamorphosen required an assurance that I did not posses at the time. And speaking fondly of, say, Prokofiev's music was inconceivable, so you kept your fascination secret. Some of Adorno's one- liners ("you can hardly hear a note without having to hide a smile") was an ongoing slap on the wrist, creating an anxiety about always attempting "the right thing"—or nothing at all. A mind model that enveloped my every artistic viewpoint during my early years.*

I will now supplement the subject (and the title) of the book: The Courage of Composers and the Tyranny of Taste. *Actually, the complete title should read . . .* of Taste, Ideologies, Prejudices and Dogmas.

It seems to me that your whole oeuvre is proof that you do not concern yourself with all that in any way. You "may" admire Mozart, Wagner, Brahms, Mahler, Richard Strauss, and Busoni, but also Varèse and Nono. You "may" write so-called new music but also waltzes and a Music Hall Suite. *You "may" compose anything. I once remarked—and you appeared to agree—that you are a Picasso among composers today.*

I wonder if you experienced, perhaps at the very beginning of your career, the tyranny of taste? Have you acquired your freedom gradually or has it been there all along?

Perhaps you will want to add a third text to the two you have contributed so far.

With all best wishes, Bálint

Lucerne, August 17, 2015

Dear Bálint,

Thank you for your letter of June 17. I have not been able to answer earlier—Salzburg was in between, as you will have heard.[2]

So I have now pondered "taste." Your question concerns its "tyranny." If I have experienced it in any way.

It is like this: taste and "its tyranny" are always there: somebody will always have a taste, namely, his own, and wish that it were valid everywhere. That has nothing to do with "sooner or later." I perceive it every day. It is very human. And I must tell you, I can understand it very well. After all, those who create something (and I am one of them), have the natural desire that their assumptions—and that's what "taste" really is—should obtain validity beyond themselves and their domain. And those who do not produce anything, "only" perceive, will also want to be sure they are on the right track and will be glad to know their preferences are shared by other people of taste, if you like—that their inclinations are confirmed by the co-incliners, the co-inclined, those inclined in the same way.[3]

When does that turn into "tyranny"? When two forms of uncertainty take shape: the uncertainty of the creator and that of the perceiver. Through lack of certainty in their judgment of taste, the uncertain feel the desire to be reassured of the correctness of their taste. Since their desire is rooted in an uncertain position, there arises the impulse to induce certainty in the environment, not to allow any ambivalence, to prevent the emergence and the existence of possibly contrary positions. After all, these would threaten the certainty of their own aesthetic judgment. Creators react to it by ready condemnation; they banish contrary positions and excommunicate them, if not forbid them altogether, something that will be welcome by other creators, who readily join forces with the excommunicators and can in this way, at least temporarily, attract attention that otherwise, on the basis of their own work, they would never get. Those on the receiving end react in a similar way, with some delay.

The problem appears to consist primarily in the fact that uncertain people possess an influence in the domain of the arts that they exercise in

---

2 The Salzburg Festival programmed a highly successful new production of the opera *The Conquest of Mexico*. (The premiere of the new production by Peter Konwitschny took place on July 26, 2016. The conductor was Ingo Metzmacher.)

3 This is my rather feeble attempt at rendering Rihm's witty way of putting it: "das er in seinen Neigungen bestätigt wird durch Mit-Neiger, Mit-Neigende, Mit-Geneigte."

order to confirm their ability to pass judgments of taste even though they are aware that they are not really in a position to do so.

It is therefore extremely important that no uncertain people should have the power to make decisions as members of juries, editorial boards of newspapers, cultural managers, directors of institutions. However, who on earth should decide *that*? It is all so hopeless. For the bosses, the democratically elected decision makers/determiners are, as a rule, even more uncertain. And is uncertainty basically evil? I do not think so.

After all, uncertainty is one of the important (the *most* important!) prerequisites of the production of art. It is the insecure and uncertain tread that creates the really productive path. The "confident stride" makes at the most a deeper-trodden track. What would artists be without their genuine uncertainty? Genuine? Yes, because there is also such a thing as acquired uncertainty through prejudice and arduously gained ignorance. In contrast, the uncertainty of artists, of art is rooted in the uncertain-making movements of the material itself, something wholly outside the range of confident perceivers or of extremely confident judges of art.

Media figures confident of their judgment—like Reich-Ranicki some years ago—were interesting precisely because they did not have the faintest idea of the creative process; in their inviolate virginity they only came "in touch" with used-up energies, from which they deduced their canonical judgments and, in their apparently unchallenged certainty, projected them into the future.[4]

But let us stay with music. The composer, productively uncertain, but certain of his powers, creates works that will be released into everyday reality with its continual struggle for "the right thing." If the public today looks down superciliously on the public of whatever past age when composers adulated today as gods (Mozart, say, and the rest of them) were not accorded due respect and esteem, then they forget that each past was once a present. And whatever is created in each present cannot yet be recognized for what it will come to mean—valid, perhaps canonical, expressions of art—when the future in its turn will begin to turn into past.

What do I mean to say, Bálint? Yes, there is always a dominating taste, it changes and becomes tyrannical when those who [would dearly love to] determine it (critics and perceivers) exert pressure out of uncertainty and

---

4   Marcel Reich-Ranicki (1920–2013), Polish-born, German literary critic. He survived the Warsaw Ghetto and moved to Germany to work for the *Frankfurter Allgemeine Zeitung* and *Die Zeit*. Reich-Ranicki is regarded as the most influential critic of his time.

the creators let themselves be tyrannized out of (other kinds of?) uncertainty. Tomorrow, another taste will reign supreme and if, all of a sudden, my work should match it, it is neither here nor there, because the day after another taste takes over, and then another . . . In other words, it never becomes *really* valid. It reigns, perhaps, for a time. Rather like carnival kings who will be killed after the feast. We should not delude ourselves. I believe I have written you about this: taste is by no means a kind of conservative mask. The taste masquerade of progressive positions is just as silly—the nearly identical forms of terror in both hemispheres. The only possibility is to do your thing and keep an eye on what is going on around you: attentively and not without interest, that is, in a friendly way.

And as for "may": in art, no one may do anything, unless they are doing it.[5] Doing, acting, are beyond most people anyway. I would much rather opt for "taste" as a liberating form of inactivity. Don't you agree?

And another thing: poor Adorno will always be cited when it comes to prohibitions and permissions. He wrote some of the best books on artistic creativity. You have to acquire the art of reading them so that you relax your standing at attention and realize that their autocratic character can manifest itself in regarding as absolutes the highly opinionated views of an enthusiastic individual—Adorno. As if the initiates would never stop uttering, "Aye aye, Captain Adorno!" The reading of Adorno can be extremely encouraging: to adopt creative obstinacy.

That should do.

I hope I did not inundate you with too much redundancy. I wish you a pleasant time for the rest of the summer.

Yours Wolfgang

Vienna, September 13, 2015

Dear Wolfgang,

I have just returned from several months away from home, to find your letter in my mail. Thank you for a wonderful text! I must reply straight away.

You remind me of our various conversations over the years—for instance, about Max Beckmann. You think highly of his art and have since devoted a composition to him. I still cannot quite fathom why you respect him so deeply; his colors, his motifs are wholly alien to my innermost self. I believe we have

---

5   "May" is a reference to my letter.

to do here with a difference of taste in its purest form. This is no question of certainty or uncertainty—it is simply like that.

Another time we talked of Gruppen—*a seminal composition of postwar music. All the composers I know hold it in awe. Once again, I am at a loss to really comprehend the reasons for it, but I think this is not a question of taste but perhaps of musical intelligence. I simply cannot hear what I ought to be hearing, perhaps because I am not a composer myself; I have not analyzed the score (nor am I capable of doing so).*

I was sitting with Heike Hoffmann in the Berlin Konzerthaus, listening to Lachenmann's piano concerto. She said the music gave her sensuous pleasure and I felt so frustrated, indeed, downright angry with myself—why was the music beyond me? Was it a question of taste? Or of musical intelligence? I simply do not know.

I believe you can afford to be uncertain in your private capacity. It is of no importance whatsoever. As soon as you are in a position, however, where your taste manifests itself as judgment, with far-reaching consequences for creators, you ought at least to be able to buttress up your judgment—whether you turn your thumb upward or downward—through unassailable knowledge. You write about this yourself.

In the book, I have also posed the question to music critics: after all, they exert an influence on the taste, the judgment of the public. How far does their own taste have a bearing on their judgment of, say, a new composition?

I hope to see you in Donaueschingen, so that I can thank you in person.

Yours Bálint

September 24, 2015

Dear Bálint,

In your letter of September 13, you cite three experiences of your own. I find them highly characteristic and important if one is to comprehend what "taste" is. You name Beckmann, Lachenmann, and Stockhausen. Their art represents, to put it simply, a very German type of artistic expression.

If we replace Beckmann with Matisse, Stockhausen with Boulez, and Lachenmann (to simplify it even more drastically) with Sciarrino—all of them representatives of the Romance sphere of art—the picture will be altogether different. In its manifestations, the figurative and the ornamental assume a more decisive significance. Its forms of articulation are no less radical but possess a larger inherent energy of communication. This art carries in its very appearance the core of its communication, the transitions are less "abrupt," the idiom is altogether more unified; to simplify: more balanced, more "moderate."

In this case, taste would mean a sensorium for the forces of balance, rather than for building up contrasts. Taste would therefore signify the working of a will of moderation. Everything that is sharp, with hard edges, abrupt contrasts, dialectical tension, and the like, would make for a problematic perception of the artifact with its apparent fading out of the energies of balance, all of them negative features from the point of view of taste perception. (As I pointed out: on the basis of perspective simplification—in this case, by me.) The perception of Mahler by Debussy, Dukas, and others surely rested on similar contaminations.

And now back to work. Perhaps a last thing: for some time now, I can experience how pieces that I wrote some forty years ago—at the time regarded as aesthetically highly problematic if not "tasteless"—are played and perceived today by interpreters and the public as classically balanced texts. Most recently, the *Music for Three Strings* at the Musikfest Berlin last week.

See you soon! Yours Wolfgang

CHAPTER TWENTY-EIGHT

REBECCA SAUNDERS
(B . 1 9 6 7)

British composer

The moment that has stuck with particular vividness in my mind during our conversation in Rebecca Saunders's rather Spartan studio in a no less austere block of flats in Berlin where she lives with her family was, when in her emotionally charged way, she suddenly pointed at three short sketches in the manuscript spread out on her desk. Faster than I could really follow, she indicated in quick succession the sketches and said: "I could pick this one or this one or that one." The choice was hers and at that moment, the loneliness of the long-distance (i.e., professional) composer was brought home to me with tremendous force, as never before. Loneliness coupled with barely suppressed excitement. I felt I was eye- and earwitness of a creative moment in Rebecca Saunders's life.

Yes, the choice was entirely hers and it was really up to her judgment, her talent, her musicality, to make a final and definitive decision. Did courage play any role there?

Of course, the story of revised versions is as endless as that of world premieres; making a decision does not mean that you hew a piece out of a block of marble and are left with an unchangeable result. I remember the world premiere of Berio's Alternatim *for clarinet, viola and orchestra in Paris in 1997. It left Berio rather morose and soon enough he added a beautiful highly expressive solo for the viola to redress the balance between the two instruments: the clarinet had proved too prominent. He had made a decision in his study at Radicondoli and, when faced with the sounding result, he realized he had miscalculated.*

In his essay "The Anxiety of Art," Morton Feldman admits that artists have many anxieties, "trying to make something, trying to find safeguards against failure." There is even, he says, an "anxiety of Art."[1]

No wonder, then, that sitting at her desk with her manuscript spread out before her, Rebecca Saunders was torn between choosing a way to go forward in her work, fully aware of her responsibility toward her art. She was probably unaware right at that moment that she might make changes afterward. You cannot live in a permanent anxiety of art. You must have the courage to overcome it and live with the result.

Berlin, April 22, 2015
Revised October/November 2015

In your reply to my first question—whether the encounter with a work of art has evoked a radical change in your musical thinking—you actually used the word courage *twice.[2] You described the impact Galina Ustvolskaya's compositions, the Duet for violin and piano in particular, had made on you, her "frightening courage" to write music reduced to the "absolute essence." You added that Ustvolskaya had reinforced your convictions and given you courage to sketch out the outlines of your future path as a composer.*

I wonder if you have ever consciously considered "courage" as part of the creative process or whether the word came to you intuitively in that particular context.

I cannot remember the exact wording of my reply, but if you ask about courage, the music of Ustvolskaya does certainly come to mind.

There are many different ways in which composers can forge their own way forward and develop a personal voice. For me personally, Galina Ustvolskaya's ability to reduce her musical form of expression to such a skeletal-like structure; the essence, the purity, the absolute directness of her art, that is incredibly courageous. Nothing is superfluous, nothing trying to charm or please—just exactly said. Or not said. Because I don't think she is saying anything. Exact and without compromise, she goes *beyond*

1   Morton Feldman, *Give My Regards to Eighth Street: Collected Writings of Morton Feldman*, ed. B. H. Friedman (Cambridge: Exact Change, 2000), 32.
2   Varga, *Drei Fragen an 73 Komponisten*, 298.

the superfluous, beyond language. Perhaps this is the said "courage," to approach the essence, to face herself.

Composers must have courage to launch themselves into the unknown. Face the emptiness, trace the edge of the "abyss." Wolfgang Rihm didn´t teach me technique, no compositional tools in that respect, but he showed, implied, and suggested, that one ask questions, seek answers, and these you can only know yourself, and that if you fail, if you fall, if you succumb, then try again. And again. Learn to stand alone, and go on. And on, as Beckett says.

Composing traces a process of thinking, a deeply explorative means of creating new virtual spaces, acoustic structures, and models, but it's also a process of asking questions and seeking answers, and it is definitely about creating these acutely necessary moments of "in-between," suspended outside of the normally experienced flow of everyday life, it's about creating environments where an otherness is given space to breathe and to unfold, to explode, and to mutate.

One needs courage perhaps to be directly and truthfully critical toward oneself and one´s work. One must stay humble and fresh, as if for the very first time, to decide absolutely what is necessary and what is superfluous. And the courage is, really, to risk, and inevitably to fail. With every piece you confront the unknown, create and enter an as yet unknown virtual world, and, quite banal, create something out of nothing. Without the risk of failure little of value comes about, I think.

It is necessary to filter and to be careful to follow your own voice. Pursue and define your own language, approach your obsession. This may take many years. To come to this point, you have to know yourself, which requires strict honesty and much discipline. And that, as we all know, is hard.

One needs courage not only to discern beauty in the ugly but also to incorporate in one´s work that which is unbearable—ever-present but unacknowledged: fear, hate, jealousy, sorrow. That which each of us carries within. That's human. That´s mortal. Perhaps one role of an artist is to give this a voice. It´s about creating those *places-in-between*—revealing or forcing open new ways of experiencing, listening, thinking, feeling. Virtual spaces.

Does composing help you to write all those negative emotions out of your system?

God no. I hope I didn't imply that—it is expressly not a therapeutic thing, quite the opposite: it is a celebration of something very human. It isn't about getting rid of something, curing something: it is the articulation of that which is there.

I am Anglo-Saxon, Protestant, even if not christened, English. Born into a society that aspires above all to at least *seem* to be nice, and good. A good girl, you know.

Jane Austen . . .

Yes. The English Protestant soul has many similarities to the Protestant German one, but the English can be frighteningly politically correct and can be desperate to at least seem to be good. It's terrifying. But this ideal has of course nothing to do with reality. There is above all no place for contradiction. No dialectic. It's not about expressing certain emotions, but, rather, acknowledging the inherently unresolvable. We need to give voice to everything beyond the norm, which surrounds the human condition, which is fragile, which is fallible, which is deeply human—create a space to breathe and expand this world. It is not about me, not about needing to put some aggression or sadness into my work. It is merely a possible function of art, and is perhaps a necessity for a society that functions, albeit only relatively.

You are part of a community of composers. In writing music, you must be aware that it will be commented on, judged by your colleagues, and that it creates a context in which your work will thrive—or not. Does that influence you at all?

No, not at all. It may be a question of generations. At least I hope so, for it would be very disturbing were we all loaded with such expectations. Perhaps I am sufficiently autistic and manage to ignore this. Of course there are certain pressures to avoid certain means of expression. But basically we are all so different, the spectrum of music is enormous. And that is a wonderful thing. One does not care what kind of music it is but it has to have that quality, a certain element, an essence that makes people believe in it and want to hear it, that reveals other possibilities, that leaves something precious behind. It does something, changes something, reveals.

But yes, returning to the act of courage . . . Hopefully every piece is an act of courage—or it should be. If it isn't, it will probably not turn out so well. To force oneself into the unknown is always an act of courage. It is always difficult and I hope it will always remain difficult. It does not get any easier, and it is good so, I think. And if it does get easy, I must take a step back and ask myself: am I complacent? Am I arrogant? Why am I doing this then? Not that it is a kind of masochism. It is because the process is so complex.

Returning to colleagues . . . I respect my colleague Enno Poppe very much. He said very clearly once in an interview about composers of our generation, "We are not in competition with each other. It does not exist anymore. It is not about one being better and the other being more extreme than the other." Something like that. There is no jealousy—or if it is there I ignore it. I look away. In fact I think there is an extraordinary curiosity among colleagues regarding what the other is doing, and how different and how fascinating that can be.

On the other hand, I don't belong to a group or clique, am not part of a music institution in Berlin, not a member of an ensemble, I don't work in an improvising community, I don´t conduct. I lead a very restrained, reclusive life. I live with my family and with music.

Is it a conscious decision?

It is probably half and half. I write my music, but I also have a family. Having children means I inevitably engage in society in a very different way from my childless colleagues, obviously.

Xenakis told me that getting new ideas was no problem for him, he could think of any number; it was far more difficult for him to discern the one with potentialities for a new composition. Does this ring a bell for you? And does it take courage for you to single out one idea and start working on it?

Absolutely! These are my sketches—this is (*we were sitting at Rebecca Saunders's desk in her Berlin studio and she showed me an A3-page of graph paper*) a wonderful sound fragment for the bass flute for Helen Bledsoe. Finally—I have *finally* found that sound! And I have found the notation and the way in which I can work with it. I can begin to feel the way in which I can explore the potential of that sound. (*She points to a system in the sketch*) Here I have a series of dyads—they are normally terribly quiet, gentle, fragile, unstable bi-tones and I have created a way in which they can be overblown according to a graphic distribution, changing the dynamics, changing the accents and the consonants, exploring the different facets of this one single sound. And I am beginning to see the way in which it will be revealed in the score. It is a long process. To have the courage to take just that one sound, discard all others, and put it in a completely new context—that's the composing, that's the work. On the other hand, here I have five different sounds, all of which are stunning timbral fragments—but to actually make that decision, what do I discard? Do I want this one, or this one or this one? I could say, I'll have a little bit of this, a little bit of that, (a), (b), (c), (d), (e), (f), finish, end of piece. That's too easy. Look, you see? I can make a little melody out of this, I can do some rhythm out of this, I can do these "waa waa waa" long sounds here, and then I can end with my dyads at the end. Yes, it may sound cynical, but what do I get from that? Nothing. It remains on the surface, is complacent, obvious, it does not open up a new space, there is no startling interstice, nothing unexpected, neither surprise nor risk.

The exciting, courageous thing is also the whole reason for doing it. Perhaps that is the point. I see a whole world opening up in front of me—a world in which new possibilities become visible, audible. So I am expanding, exploring a space that was never there before, I go into that space, I enter that space, and I begin. That's what composing is about.

Do the fine arts have any relevance for you as a composer? Has any work of art given you an impetus, given you courage the way Birtwistle has been encouraged by Picasso's reworking of Velazquez's Las Meninas *to arrange Machaut, Bach, and other of his predecessors?*

There are moments when I discover something in a medium other than music, and it gives me the distance and the clarity to approach something when I compose, that for me perhaps was previously unclear, was blurred, unfocused. A simple example: When I was in New York in 1995, I went to different museums to look at Rothko pictures, I observed how the rectangles of different colors or shades of the same color are placed on top of each other as if they are floating; the depth and the vertical tension created through these quite simple forms; how they create a perfect unity—how the tensions pull toward and away from each other. The juxtaposition of three tableaux is completely classical, a triptych, and the luminosity of color and of form of this abstraction is a most simple juxtaposition. But the tensions and the depth he created enabled me to reconsider my approach to form. Later I wrote a series of pieces that didn't simply have movements one, two, and three, but were juxtapositions of three entirely different timbral palettes worked out to their absolute limit, but nevertheless conceived so as to coinhabit the same shared acoustic space. For example, in the piano solo *crimson* from 2005, although there may be a few fleeting moments of cross-references in the whole piece, or rather points of reference, the three parts have little to do with each other. What they do share though, is the way in which resonances, echoes, layers of pulsating silence, pauses, are treated. One becomes very aware of these moments-in-between, of resonating pauses and fermatas—the waiting. These movements are the three rectangles, suspended in a shared acoustic space and they pull—and push—toward and against each other. My response to Rothko´s late abstract paintings in *crimson* was entirely intuitive. His seemingly simple formal approach to juxtapose different weights—that spoke to me very strongly.

Also the late short prose works of Samuel Beckett have had a very strong impact on me. Beckett weighs each and every word and its shadow, its echo. His writing has an intense lyricism, and his profoundly reduced, almost skeletal prose, is both mercilessly direct and yet exquisitely fragile. This aspect of his writing I found mesmerizing. I began at first unconsciously, to collect fragments of sound that had the potential to be fragile, elusive, and incredibly quiet, and, although still very unstable, these sounds can also become brutal and direct. Discovering traces of sound with this dialectic built into them fascinates me particularly at present.

An "act of courage" for me was writing my first melody, *blaauw*, a trumpet solo for Marco Blaauw (2004).[3] Years earlier when I left Scotland and began to study in Karlsruhe, I had decided that melodies are just not on, you just don't write melodies. In fact, I only wanted to write one tone, to go inside that single tone and explore its timbral potential. I was obsessed by it. It was very exciting to hear and explore music from a radically different perspective. So I wrote one tone for a very long time, many years really—often juxtaposed single tones—but one tone; central tones—moving away from any idea of vertical harmony and certainly no melody. And then at some point I had the courage to return and to write a melody. I think it had something to do with the natural lyricism of the trumpet. When Marco plays, I close my eyes and I hear a voice, not an instrument. As if he is singing. A strange one, but still a voice. The melody in *blaauw* is maybe twelve notes long or so, and it is elongated over ten minutes and then also timbrally differentiated to the point that timbre is the decisive parameter, but nevertheless it is a simple lyrical line and it is clearly visible. And it really took an enormous amount of courage to take that step.

It was liberating.

It was liberating, but once I started writing it was so easy, because I had been waiting to do this for fifteen years. So that was fun.

---

3   Marco Blaauw (b. 1965), Dutch trumpeter.

CHAPTER TWENTY-NINE

ALLEN SHAWN
(B . 1 9 4 8)

American composer, pianist,
teacher, and author

In his very first sentence, Allen Shawn confesses to suffering from phobias. In the next one, he mentions he has written some books. Those who wish to have an idea of the ordeals of someone whose life has been an uphill struggle to achieve a semblance of normality in his day-to-day existence, should read Shawn's achingly beautiful, disarmingly honest and upsetting memoir, Wish I Could Be There *(London: Penguin Books, 2007). His music, as far as I know it, bears no trace of any lack of balance. It can be full of joie de vivre; the presence of jazz in a range of compositions lends them an unmistakable American flavor, but his lyrical slow movements refuse to be pigeonholed: they are universal in their humanity.*

July 29, 2015

As someone who lacks physical courage, and who has anxieties about many ordinary situations (I suffer from phobias), I know that I often have to summon "courage" just to follow through with the most mundane tasks. At the same time, I have devoted my life to composing music, an activity that is not highly rewarded in our society, which I have supported by teaching, playing the piano, and writing a few books. You might say it takes courage to pursue an activity that is poorly rewarded, is not part of the cultural mainstream, and is utterly intangible. But I wouldn't say that. I make music not because I am courageous, but because doing it is what comes most naturally to me, makes me feel most alive, and helps me make sense of being alive. When I compose a decent piece, or even a decent phrase, I feel that I have justified being on this earth. It is my way of celebrating being alive, and also of participating in the huge world of music. Although the composing itself is solitary, being a part of the world of music and participating as a composer, performer, and teacher is a connection on the deepest level to the world and to other people, past and present. I am therefore very lucky that somehow I have managed to keep composing, and that the urge to do so was not thwarted by circumstance or by my feelings of discouragement and inadequacy.

We all must summon courage to face life and whatever befalls us. It is not only composers who must sooner or later come to terms with their mortality and their insignificance in the universe. But when I think of what many people have gone through and are going through in their lives, I don't think that those of us who have had relatively fortunate lives, like myself, have much right to speak about courage.

I want to express a few more thoughts, if I may. I think that precisely because we so-called serious composers do something that is marginalized in today's world, we are often a bit self-conscious when we talk about composing, and sometimes, without meaning to, speak of it defensively, as primarily a science. This holds true in the public realm, but also in the teaching realm, where this kind of deracinated approach runs the risk of cutting students off from the very love of music that put them in the classroom to begin with. I myself suffered from this kind of teaching as a music student in the 1960s and early 1970s.

There is no question that to compose music is a huge intellectual endeavor. But when we dig in our heels and act as if our enterprise is somehow disconnected from the music making that is a huge part of almost everyone's life, this attitude of disconnection represents a danger: the risk that we deny our own simple humanity, our intuition, our sense of pleasure, and the truth that, for us, this so-called serious music is also simply music, like any other music; that it is our natural mode of expression, our release, our refreshment, and that just like any music, it starts with what we *like*, and with the same impulse to sing and dance that all music everywhere has at its origin.

How can we speak honestly, and also unsentimentally, about the desire we have to mold sounds, the love of working with sounds?

As absurd as it is to read writings about music from the Romantic era, which equate music with bubbling brooks and twittering birds, there is also a danger in thinking of music and describing it as something completely isolated and pure, as a "composition," which is either "interesting" or "not interesting." The danger is that we lose our connection to the mysterious essence of music itself that can make the succession of only a few tones in the voice of a mother singing a lullaby penetrate to the core of one's being. If we composers need courage, perhaps it is the courage to remain innocent and natural, and to remain open to being touched by any and all music.

As soon as one tries to verbalize what it is to compose or play or to listen to music, one risks being dishonest about it. Do we even know what music is? It seems to me that music is a power that expresses itself in an astonishing variety of ways, unpredictably, and a term that can't be easily defined. Focusing on this or that definable component of musical vocabulary is to neglect the total experience.

Two nights ago I heard a concert in which the "Holidays" Symphony of Ives was performed. In the middle of "Decoration Day," the intoning of "Taps" on the distant muted trumpet was extraordinarily moving. "Taps" could be described as "nothing" but a "simple" major triad. But here, in this context—and I write this as a deeply unmilitaristic person—its effect was overpowering.

It is of course is deeply depressing to read long discussions of music that never even refer to music itself, let alone its intellectual side. Sometimes in discussions of rock music, for example, complex and artful songs are described exclusively in terms of their lyrics. The opposite tendency emerged during the 1950s, 1960s, and 1970s, during which some composers wrote about their music purely in terms of numbers and rarefied compositional techniques. Although some of these techniques derived from Schoenberg, his own writings are utterly holistic, natural, and full of humanity, and even irrationality. Even today, many composers write about what "concerned them" when they were composing. They write about their compositions from a vantage point of what they *intended* to do, what they *knew*. I think this is terribly misleading. What about what they *didn't* know or intend? What about all those aspects of self that are revealed in their music—as in a high resolution photograph—about which they had no conscious knowledge? The pace at which they walk; their state of tension and relaxation; the music they first loved as a child; the music that has actually stuck with them; what they most deeply relish; what they most deeply need; how they hold a lover's hand, or make love?

Whatever its manner and sound world, music is a physical act as much as a conscious intellectual one, and it is inseparable from our needs as human beings. As a student I learned from watching the full physical, spiritual, mental, and human involvement Nadia Boulanger and Leon Kirchner brought to their piano playing as much as I learned from anything they said in their classes. I learned from watching Stravinsky's face, arms, and hands as he conducted the final movement if his *Symphony of Psalms* in Lincoln Center in 1966. The physical effect of his inexorably slow tempo in the final pages has stayed with me to this day.

How refreshing it is that we don't have program notes from Bach, Beethoven, Haydn, and Mozart. How refreshing it is to find a letter of Mozart in which he writes about the Minuet of a fellow composer simply that it was "charming." Perhaps particularly when facing neglect or a feeling of being marginalized, it takes a kind of courage for the so-called learned composer to be that simple and straightforward.

Can we write honestly about the fact that we need many kinds of music in our lives, and different music at different times and for different reasons? Joyous music in which to cut loose; music in which to reflect; music of mourning; wild and sensuous music; music of primitive coarseness; of lofty purity; music of quietly hermetic intricacy? It is remarkable how even within the work of a single composer the force that is music expresses itself in a variety of ways, yet always—in the great composers, anyway—somehow carrying the composer's full life force with it. To take an obvious example, how can one write honestly and unsentimentally about what lies behind such diverse pieces as *The Art of The Fugue*, the D-minor solo Violin Partita, and the *Brandenburg Concertos*—namely, not only the unparalleled musical intellect of J. S. Bach, but also his *life* as he was living it?

I was lucky to experience many different kinds of music firsthand very early. When I was a child my parents took me to hear Thelonious Monk, Duke Ellington, and Charlie Mingus, as well as the Budapest String Quartet, the New York Philharmonic, and countless concerts of all kinds, and also to the New York City Ballet. Those early experiences had their intellectual side. But they were also rituals. They were human and social encounters. They were experiences of the physics of sound in spaces of different sizes and contours, and as harnessed by different musical instruments. They were ways of experiencing the strangeness and amazement of being a transient human creature. If it weren't for the often jovial, lighthearted, humorous, and sometimes anarchic moments they contained, one could say that they were akin to religious ceremonies. Music passing through space, heard in a community, provided a unique way of experiencing being alive.

CHAPTER THIRTY

JOHANNES MARIA STAUD (B. 1974)

Austrian composer

The closer you grow to someone, the harder it is to portray them. It takes a conscious effort for me to try to write this introduction to my conversation with Johannes Maria Staud because I am clearly biased in his favor: since my retirement from Universal Edition (UE), our relationship has become a friendship.

I met Johannes when he was twenty-five. I (together with Otto Tomek) was instrumental in his being invited to join UE's roster of composers and did my very best to launch his career. He is now forty-two, has achieved international recognition, and I am watching his progress from the sidelines, so to speak.

In addition to his music, I have admired Johannes's wide range of interests, which have fed his creative thinking. He is passionate about the arts from Leonardo da Vinci to Bruce Nauman, about literature from Dante to Bruno Schulz, and about political issues. His orchestral work . . . gleichsam als ob . . . was actually written as a protest against the participation of the extreme right-wing populist Freedom Party of Austria (FPÖ) in the Austrian federal government in 2000.

Johannes is passionate about many other aspects of life as well, including natural beauty, whether of the Austrian Alps or the Sea of Sardinia, and, indeed, about music. I have never known him when he was not engrossed in the intricacies of a particular compositional problem. He is not only

passionate—he can be choleric (a word of his choice), and a simple conver-
sation can morph into a heated debate in uncompromising defense of his
convictions.

I am not really a suitable partner for such discussions—in private life,
and not just as an interviewer, I am a good listener rather than a talker—but
Johannes can get carried away under the influence of his own arguments, and
my presence is more or less reduced to a hand holding a microphone.

Vienna, April 19, 2016
Revised May 6, 2016

Is courage of any relevance for your work as a composer?

I do have reservations about it in this context—I find it too grand, somehow.
As I see it, courage applies to people who stand by their ideals under the most
adverse political and social circumstances, those who resist, who rebel, and
are incorruptible in their dedication to humanity, to helping the needy.

Composing itself is not really courageous. It is at best honest—radically so. Above all, it must have no truck with the current taste—if there
is such a thing—or with any trend. It must solely follow one's own imagination, the pleasure one derives from reveling in one's play instinct and
obeying one's striving for perfection, in other words: observing one's compositional ethics.

There is of course such a thing as "cowardly, conformist composition"
(and here I am being inconsistent). I mean an attitude of wishing to please
the public at any cost. An attitude like that underestimates the public, that
mysterious, hybrid entity made up of so many individuals, tastes, and prejudices, and, on the other hand, it abuses it for one's own dishonest goals.

When I was a student, new music had not fully established itself in
Vienna. You came across composers all over the place who would be com-
plaining about a supposed dictate from Darmstadt in the 1950s and 1960s.
They never tired of citing their struggle for a return to tonal music, music
"for the public." I could not fathom those people. They abused the notion
of "courage" in writing banal, uninspired, and anachronistic music devoid
of any creative passion.

Years ago when the FPÖ formed a coalition with the Austrian People's Party
(ÖVP), you wrote an orchestral work titled . . . gleichsam als ob *. . . It was*

openly directed against the participation of that extreme right-wing, populist party in the government.[1] *Were you aware of any courage in taking a stance against it?*

A political stance was spelled out in my program notes as well as in an interview I gave at the time. . . . *gleichsam als ob* . . . turned out to be an aggressive piece. It was an attempt to channel, to transform into music my rage over this revisionist, anti-Semitic, xenophobic party entering the government. Of course, I abstracted it and created an autonomous model—that is what composing is about.

It was surely nothing courageous: after all, the overwhelming majority of the population was against the new coalition. Today I am no longer so sure. A staunchly right-wing, German national candidate of the FPÖ won 50 percent of the votes in the runoff of the presidential elections.[2] It is a devastating reminder that extreme right positions have once again arrived in the middle of society—it saddens and enrages me at the same time. An artist can articulate himself with texts—interviews, articles, and other statements. The same is open to others in public life.

With the increasing influence of right-wing populist and radical forces all over Europe, I think it quite feasible in the near future for contemporary art—and New Music—to be once again branded as degenerate, decadent, in violation of "healthy popular sentiment."[3] Let us hope that this will never

---

1   The Freiheitliche Partei Österreichs (FPÖ), under its then leader Jörg Haider (1950–2008), won 26.9 percent of the votes at the parliamentary elections of 1999. Having emerged as the second strongest party in Austria, it joined the government under Chancellor Wolfgang Schüssel (ÖVP—Österreichische Volkspartei, a moderately conservative party in Austria that represents the middle class, as well as farmers, and is marked by its proximity to the Catholic Church), with Susanne Riess-Passer (FPÖ) as vice chancellor. Composed in 1999–2000, . . . *gleichsam als ob* . . . was premiered on September 20, 2000, at Schwaz, Tyrol, with Dennis Russell Davies conducting the RSO Wien (Vienna Radio Symphony Orchestra).

2   With the mandate of the Austrian president Heinz Fischer running out in July 2016, elections took place on April 24. They ended with the devastating defeat of the coalition parties (leading to Chancellor Werner Faymann's resignation on May 9 and Christian Kern's taking over the helm, also of the Social Democratic Party), and the emergence of the extreme right-wing FPÖ's candidate, Norbert Hofer, as victor. In the runoff on May 22, he competed with Alexander van der Bellen, a former leader of the Green Party. Van der Bellen won the election with a narrow majority of the votes and succeeded Heinz Fischer as Austria's next president—that is, until the election was contested by the FPÖ on formal grounds and the Constitutional Court upheld their appeal. New elections were held on December 4, 2016, and to the relief of Austrian and international public opinion, Alexander van der Bellen once again secured victory. Populism could after all be contained.

3   Staud refers here to a notion in currency at the time of National Socialism: "gesundes Volksempfinden" ("healthy popular sentiment" is my attempt to render it in English) would be attributed to "the people" in whose name the fascist authorities purported to be acting, such as branding modern art as "degenerate."

happen—but if by any chance it should, only then will it be possible to assess whether an artist has courage or otherwise. Seventy years ago, Richard Strauss was certainly not one of them.

Did it occur to you that your critical stance might diminish your chances of enhancing your career—that commissions might not come your way?

That did happen earlier on. Some years ago, I wrote a "Letter to Tyrol" for publication in the *Tiroler Tageszeitung*, in which I sharply attacked the then minister of the interior, Günther Platter, for his base and vicious policy against asylum seekers.[4] As a result of political intervention, my letter was removed from the paper's website on the very day of its appearance. In addition, the projected coproduction of my opera *Die Antilope* with the Tiroler Landestheater was canceled overnight. The administrator, Johannes Reitmeier, who until then had been well-disposed toward me, was all of a sudden unavailable. It does not take much imagination to figure out what had gone on behind the scenes.

In hindsight one might perhaps claim that it was courageous of you to leave the possibility of ostracism out of account.

I received a great deal of positive feedback on my letter, from worried and critical citizens of civil society—but also from Tyrolean composers and artists who, unlike me, had no international career and were as a result dependent on state support. They had no choice but to refrain from making political statements critical of the government. It appears as though we were not living in a democracy after all—very sad indeed.

In my own experience, music can indeed play an important political role. My brother, who defected in 1956, still has the songs he learned in the pioneer movement in the early 1950s vividly in his memory and can sing them at the drop of a hat. The same is true of me, of course. They had a political message in accordance with the goals of the ruling communist party. But the music was appealing, written by some of the best Hungarian composers, and eminently suitable for motivating people (not just the young generation). In France, the "Marseillaise" has become a national symbol, perhaps on a par with the tricolor. I still have goose bumps when I think of the way it was sung by masses of people as a sign of their determination not to be intimidated

---

4   Günther Platter (1954) was federal minister of the interior as well as minister of defense, before being elected governor (Landeshauptmann) of Tyrol in 2008.

by terrorist attacks in Paris. It was uplifting: music has a unifying power; it is perhaps best suited to creating a communal feeling, a feeling of shared identity.

I do not believe that music by itself is suited to playing a political role. It does of course have a revolutionary potential due to the text that has been set, which creates the feeling of "us against the others." I do admire, incidentally, the choral pieces written by Hanns Eisler shortly before Hitler's coming to power. That music has retained to this day its ability to get under your skin. To have written such music with those texts—that was truly courageous.

Political music as such does not really work, even with Nono, because politics happens on different level from music—from art. Music is far more complex, far more multifarious. To be able to compose music, you need calm. You cannot be worked up all the time. It was painful for me to realize that. What music *can* do is to set a poetic and complex, multifaceted and human alternative against a prosaic and threatening reality.

Does it require courage for you to face—and overcome—a horror vacui *at the start of composing a new work?*

No. Composing is a compulsion neurosis, a beautiful compulsion neurosis. It does not take courage to get going: I have no other choice. There are of course pieces that prove a hard nut to crack, but on the whole, the difficulties you have to surmount are part of it all; in fact, they are rewarding. I was once considering taking a year off, just to absorb culture, to read, and so on . . . Sounds fine but actually, I abhor the very idea. It is simply unthinkable not to compose for a whole year.

Now let us consider a sociological aspect of being a composer. You earn your living by writing music, provided you have no other sources of income. Can you afford to say no to a commission? Are you afraid to turn down an offer, in case no others come your way?

Black Moon was premiered in 1998.[5] I was still a student at the time and I remember talking after the concert to a well-known composer (I prefer not to name him). He gave me the advice, "If ever you were to turn down a commission, you would be out of the running straight away." I was

---

5   *Black Moon* (1998) for bass clarinet, commissioned by Tyrol Province for the festival Klangspuren. World premiere, September 18, 1998, Ernesto Molinari, clarinet.

thinking at the time, why should I be "out of the running?" The older I get, the more clearly I see that his advice was wholly misguided.

I admit I have not always managed to say no; there were times when I took on too much. But then what can you do if, for instance, you are asked to write an orchestral work for Pierre Boulez? You cannot possibly turn it down. One falls back on energies one may not actually have. That is how *Contrebande* came into being.[6] He was a composer whom I have respected ever since my student years—it was an offer that made me leave everything else aside. I have also noticed, incidentally, that interesting pieces do not necessarily require all the time in the world, with you chiseling at it at leisure. Often, they arise under tremendous pressure, so that it is a question of "sink or swim." Of course, it is flattering to be asked—I do not mind admitting that.

"Admitting" reminds me: you have in the past admitted on two occasions to have needed courage in composing particular sections of your operas Berenice *and* Die Antilope: *they have the character of light music.*[7]

Let me go back to the time when I was in my teens—between fourteen and eighteen. I was every inch a rock musician, playing in bands and writing one song after another. I do not think many classical composers have had a similar experience. Rebellion, resistance, being loud, wearing shoulder-length hair—all that was extremely important for me as a young man in a provincial, Catholic Tyrol ruled by the ÖVP, and marked by beer-induced stupor at student clubs. I remember I learned a lot at the time about the nature of sound—I profit from it right up to this day. Of course, I have not become a full-time rock musician, it would have been too dull, and I quickly found my way to serious music—that is where I am at home.

Later on, I lived for just under four years in London and took an interest in the rock music scene.[8] I was well up on young alternative bands. They exerted a certain influence on me, even though I continue to have a problem with crossover and quotes from pop music. I do not like that. However, I do appreciate the authentic; I am all for authentic rock music.

---

6   *Contrebande (On Comparative Meteorology II)* (2010), for orchestra. The premiere was conducted by Péter Eötvös in Paris, with the Ensemble Modern Orchestra, November 6, 2010.

7   *Berenice* (2003–4/2006), opera based on a story by Edgar Allan Poe, with a libretto by Durs Grünbein. World premiere, May 12, 2004, Munich Biennale. *Die Antilope* (2013–14), opera, with a libretto by Durs Grünbein, conducted by Howard Arman, Direction Dominique Mentha, world premiere, September 3, 2014, Lucerne Festival.

8   Between May 2004 and January 2008.

With regard to using songs in both of my operas, I have followed an altogether different concept. I am not out to integrate heterogeneous material in a polystylistic whole, but rather to include a few small stylistic islands into an otherwise stringent overall concept, in the interest of the dramatic idea, the stage. It is something I have mulled over a great deal. I have certainly drawn lessons from films—Fellini, Billy Wilder, David Lynch, and Spike Jonze, to name a few.

Berenice has a show element to it: Egaeus, the protagonist, who maintains an incestuous relationship with his cousin Berenice, enters the stage, grabs the microphone and sings—a simple, easy-to-grasp, melodic and groovy song, but in no way a mixture of light and serious music. It is over in no time and the opera takes up its course once again.

As a young man, I already realized that I had a talent for writing pithy melodies. I suppress it in 95 percent of my pieces. In operas, however, it may very well emerge onto the surface without any inhibition. It is of course not pop music—it is far too complex for that, in its modulation and instrumentation. But it is all invented by me; there are no quotes—I am against them on principle. I dislike quotes used by other composers as well, with the exception of Bernd Alois Zimmermann: he may do anything.

You have yet to explain why you needed courage to compose those inserts.

Perhaps I wanted to provoke to a certain extent. Some people at the world premiere cut me afterward. There were concert organizers there who had shown an interest in my music before and dropped me after the premiere—some of them came back later on. So it was not too bad after all. I think I have fought for and eventually achieved a freedom that is very dear to me. Actually, concert managers ought not to be sure what they are going to get from me. After *Berenice*, I composed *Apeiron, Towards a Brighter Hue*, and *Violent Incidents (Hommage à Bruce Nauman)*—wholly different kinds of music marked by a harsh, wild sound world.[9] Ten years later, when *Die Antilope* was premiered, those stylistic islands went down without a hitch. Times change.

---

9   *Apeiron* (2004–5), music for large orchestra. World premiere, June 15, 2005, Berlin Philharmonic conducted by Sir Simon Rattle. *Towards a Brighter Hue* (2004) for violin solo. World premiere, September 9, 2005, Munich (participants of an international competition). *Violent Incidents* (2005–6) for saxophone solo, wind ensemble, and percussion. World premiere, September 9, 2005, Schwaz, with Marcus Weiss, saxophone, Windkraft Tirol, conducted by Kasper de Roo.

There we come to taste, ideology, prejudice . . . They are still there to a certain extent and cause quite some harm.

Bálint, I have them too. I also have prejudices. I have an enormous prejudice against minimalist music, against new simplicity, the neo-neoclassicism of postmodern music. I sometimes try to consciously listen to music I dislike but that nevertheless has quality and a personality of its own. I let myself be provoked and then do something fundamentally different.

Clearly, everyone has prejudices. What I find problematic is for decision makers to use their prejudices as a yardstick.

I cannot see any problem here, for there are many decision makers, many different points of view, many festivals and concert series. And times have changed since the 1950s and 1960s. It is no longer just the avant-garde and reaction, but there are many other kinds of music in between, a kaleidoscope of nuances. A discussion of the kind that took place between Hans Werner Henze and Helmut Lachenmann would be unthinkable today, because the times have changed. At that time, of course, it was enormously important.

There are many decision makers—you were not really hurt by the reaction of those present at the premiere of Berenice, *I presume.*

Of course I was hurt. Bad reviews also hurt me but with the passage of time I do not take all that very seriously anymore. Also, as a composer, one thinks in the long term. Concert managers come and go, some switch to a different field of activity altogether. There are also some who continue to devise programs on an extremely high level—such as Harry Vogt.[10] He is open in his thinking and makes wonderful programs.

I must say I admire composers who avail themselves of a suitable opportunity and come out with a piece of a consciously provocative character, like Harrison Birtwistle did with his *Panic.*[11] I find it absolutely great. He knew precisely what he was doing. To have written a piece like that for the Last Night of the Proms—that was quite something. Since I lived in

---

10 Harry Vogt (b. 1956), German radio producer. He has been new music producer at WDR Cologne since 1985. He took over the artistic directorship of the Witten Festival of New Chamber Music in 1990; in 1998, also that of the concert series Musik der Zeit in Cologne.

11 Harrison Birtwistle, *Panic* (1995), a dithyramb for alto saxophone, jazz drummer, wind, brass, and percussion. World premiere, September 16, 1995, Last Night of the Proms, with John Harle, saxophone, Paul Clarvis, drum kit, and the BBC Symphony Orchestra under Andrew Davis.

England for a time and am familiar with the preference of the public for the pastoral tradition, I find it very amusing indeed. It must have been a slap in the face. It was in any case a scandal. Courage is one thing, but the will to provoke and "épater le bourgeois" is something quite different. Of course, it is nothing new for artists and is always beneficial, refreshing.

I am reminded of Marcel Duchamp's Fountain, *a commercially available urinal.*

I am not talking of music in connection with politics, the powers that be, or society, but of music that provokes in its own domain of concert organizers, interpreters, and the public—the concert situation as such. And there are pieces that simply *must* provoke the public with their intransigence—pieces that cannot but polarize. It is also important for the development of music.

Now on to a different subject. You have written a piece for members of the Berlin Philharmonic, with the strings having to play percussion instruments with their feet.[12] Interestingly enough, it proved quite a challenge for them. In any case, does it take courage to confront musicians with unusual tasks? After all, a poor performance could harm the music.

It probably required no courage, also because no work is written just for the first performance. The Scharoun Ensemble did eventually do justice to the piece, admirably so. No, courage played no role. My bias toward the combination of "high-tech" and "low-tech" occurs every now and again in my compositions, such as in *Esquisse retouchée (Incipit II)* for trombone solo, where the soloist has to play a bass drum with his foot.[13] It has to do with my enthusiasm for combining a highly sophisticated sound world with a rather brutal, not so sophisticated, archaic one. It is like combining a smart jacket with a pair of jogging pants.

---

12 *Configurations/Reflet* (2002) for eight players. World premiere, October 22, 2002, Berlin, Scharoun Ensemble, conducted by Henrik Schaefer.
13 *Esquisse retouchée (Incipit II)* (2001–2), for trombone with bass drum. World premiere, September 15, 2002, Innsbruck, Uwe Dierksen.

CHAPTER THIRTY-ONE

MANFRED TROJAHN
(B . 1 9 4 9)

German composer

Here is one composer who does not speak in terms of courage but rather stay-
ing power, not about tyranny of taste but about chicanery. Manfred Trojahn
would thus seem to have been unaffected by what other composers with
weaker nerves might have experienced as atrocities; indeed, he appears to
question the raison d'être of this book.

Looking objectively at the examples he cites from his life, though, I do
believe that those subjects have nevertheless had their relevance for Trojahn.
He may have developed a protective shield with the help of his irony and ar-
rogance, but it is hard to believe that the incidents he recalls have not left a
trace. He certainly remembers them vividly.

I think those incidents must be of interest for students of recent music
history: how young composers could be hounded by apostles of so-called
New Music, how those composers might have been made hopelessly insecure
through diametrically opposed expectations by critics, were it not for their in-
ner certainty—and how that inner certainty can nevertheless yield to nagging
question marks that can produce a blockage in their minds. Even Manfred
Trojahn admits that he stopped composing for a year, he was so unsure of
himself.

If you look at his worklist, you cannot but be impressed by its dimensions
and diversity. He is one of the most successful opera composers in Germany
and has made his way in other genres as well, in a niche of musical life that

exists side by side with and wholly independent of the avant-garde scene. Trojahn has also had a fair share of official recognition in the way of awards and positions: he was president of the German Composers' Association for several years and was also deputy director of the Composers' Section of the Academy of Arts.

March 2, 2016

On consideration, I have come to the realization that courage is probably not the best word to describe what an artist needs to do the right thing. I have never had to live under conditions where my activities would have created life- or even existence-threatening situations. Such conditions would have required courage for me to stay upright and I do not wish to know if I would have been able to muster it. In the security of our lives, it is all too easy to castigate the weakness of those who adapted themselves and to demand an apology in that unbearable fashion that you encounter nowadays on all sides. Excuses change nothing. Few of us were born to be martyrs, but most of us are good at raising our forefingers to admonish others.

I am not in a position, then, to describe that sort of courage.

It was not courage, rather inner a necessity, to turn down participation in a discussion following the world premiere of my Second Symphony in Donaueschingen in 1978. The clamor of fifty know-it-alls whom I deprived of the chance to composer-bash with their arguments at the ready did not really interest me. It was more awkward when, after a performance in Metz, a critic actually detected neo-Nazi tendencies in the symphony—when in fact it engages with that all-out Nazi Gustav Mahler . . . Ever since, in France where I lived at the time (and where I still have an apartment), I have been considered a neo-Romantic composer. That was easier to live with.

The composition had an aftermath in Germany as well where I became a longtime lodger in a pigeonhole with the inscription "Neo!" I conducted it some thirty years later in Hamburg, with Mozart and Ravel also on the program of the Philharmonic Orchestra. A critic opined that one ought not to be regaled with such avant-garde stuff; one should rather listen to beautiful music by Mahler . . . Such coincidences give one food for thought but they certainly do not provoke anxiety against which one would need courage.

I believe an artist requires a great deal of time to observe how his inner needs are changing. One can measure those changes by the way one's attitudes to other arts are transformed. Those one may have rejected in the past can all of a sudden assume importance and become indispensable. No one should tell me it is all a matter of rationality—in any case, I have not been able to find out what is actually happening there but I do know that a range of highly complex and interconnected factors are at work.

One's own writing changes, but that is not rooted in courage; it simply happens and there is nothing you can do about it.

A friend of my son's, a severely handicapped spastic whom we have known since he was seven or eight years old and sang in the children's choir, set his mind on becoming an actor. In the tortoise-like slow tempo that marks his life, he has reached his goal. That is courage. One has to bow one's head before his courage to face life.

The likes of us, however, in reasonably good health, adequately talented and long enough at it, do not need much to invest, certainly nothing that could be called courage. I do not mean to say that anything has fallen in my lap. This profession makes for high blood pressure: it comes from permanent stress at one's desk and in post-processing. But those who will have none of it: keep that in mind when picking your career!

Manfred Trojahn's text provoked three e-mails from me in quick succession. He in turn sent a detailed reply that to my mind has added another facet to the book.

March 2, 2016

E-mail 1

In composing your Second Symphony, were you aware that your musical idiom would meet with indignation and rejection from some listeners? If you were, didn't you need courage to carry on nevertheless?

Do you need courage to get started on a new work? Courage to write an opera or a string quartet, in view of the tradition of those genres that you are about to add to? Write a work that is to be different or similar—in what way different, in what way similar?

I have found that there is such a thing as courage toward oneself. When Kurtág said, some thirty-five years ago, that his goal was to dare to compose with yet fewer notes, he was thinking of no one else but himself.

Hans Abrahamsen said something similar: as a young man, he did not have the courage to write the simple music he actually had in mind.

You will remember that the book should be called The Courage of Composers and the Tyranny of Taste. *The examples you cite indicate, I think, that you have never let yourself be tyrannized. That also presupposes courage, an inner certainty that you are doing the right thing. To be sure, you have had sufficient positive feedback (also from your publisher) to confirm the goal you have set yourself.*

E-mail 2

You write it was not a matter of courage for you to have rejected participation in a discussion following the world premiere of your Second Symphony. Could it have been cowardice?

E-mail 3

Martyrdom . . . I feel very strongly about this subject. After all, it was through sheer luck that my family survived World War II; many relatives were deported and murdered in Auschwitz. They were martyred as were all those composers who left their lives in concentration camps. None of them wanted to end like that. And I must think of all the artists who might have opted for silence but instead adapted themselves to the dictatorships they lived under, and produced works that were bound to be short-lived (compositions, plays, novels, and so on). Architecture is somewhat different in that many buildings survive—Moscow's Lomonosov University or its counterpart in Warsaw come to mind. They are by no means short-lived, unless they have been demolished since.

Several of the composers who have contributed to this book cite the example of Shostakovich and his Stalin Cantatas. But he also composed "courageous" pieces.

I must also think of composers who went on producing for the drawer (Braunfels, Kaminski) and of painters with their "unpainted pictures" (Nolde felt close to the Nazis but they did not want him; Gurlitt also curried favor with them, with no success, and eventually settled in Japan).

A difficult subject.

March 2, 2016

Dear Mr. Varga,

I do not think I was anxious to avoid anything at the time. Much rather, I wanted to make it clear that calls to justify myself did not impress me—such demands were no less vociferous in the so-called socialist countries at the time, especially among the left wing. Of course, our own leftists did not have the same possibilities as those in the East and as a result, my refusal in Donaueschingen provoked a broadcast by a bearded left-wing journalist with the head of Karl Marx in which he attacked me as "that would-be composer Manfred Trojahn." Coping with that was not a matter of courage but of staying power. If you read my book, you will come upon many passages of justification.[1] When the texts were published in the book, years after the actual events, the journalists whose attacks had motivated those justifications posed the question: why does he keep on justifying himself? . . . c'est la vie. It takes no courage to come to terms with that, but humor and irony. I possess both, I think, in abundance. Self-irony as well.

If at the age of fifty-five Kurtág still needed a bit of daring to do what he was convinced of and you describe it as courage toward himself, then you are extending the notion a bit too broadly and equating such slightly vain narcissism with genuine problems that composers in dictatorships with their tyrannical policy were experiencing at close hand. Kurtág was one of them, wasn't he? Perhaps it was more of a political than an artistic problem.[2]

Decades ago, when Killmayer suggested that I compose a Lied with the piano part reduced to a single tone, I followed suit.[3] I needed no courage to do that, just imagination. Actually, I carried it off a few years ago in the *Schlegel-Lieder* (2012); all other attempts landed in the wastepaper basket.

I never needed courage to compose a symphony or a string quartet or even an opera; the relevant compositions of music literature did not weigh on me in any way—on the contrary, they have helped me.

I have never asked myself whether I should produce or avoid similarities; if they emerged, they were obviously necessary at that point.

I have always felt sorry for colleagues who suffer under the burden of tradition. Rihm's laconic reply: "Awareness of the past is only cumbersome

---

1 Manfred Trojahn, *Schriften zur Musik*, ed. Hans Joachim Wagner (Frankfurt: Stroemfeld Verlag, 2006).
2 I decided not to start a discussion with Manfred Trojahn about Kurtág. In the 1970s, writing with fewer notes had no political relevance anymore; it was purely a psychological issue and you need to know Kurtág closely to understand its implications.
3 Wilhelm Killmayer (b. 1927), German composer.

for those who lack imagination." I have had my own, highly personal tradition (incidentally, the only one any of us can have) and it has given me
wings rather than scared me.

You should know that I heard *Don Giovanni* at ten and decided to become a composer. I never doubted for a moment that this was precisely
the right thing for me to do and I rigorously worked toward it, until I published my first pieces at twenty. It has remained that way since. It could
have been naiveté but I think not inflated self-confidence, for I do have
self-doubt once in a while, which can lead to ceasing to write for a whole
year because I am so unsure of myself.

It was clear to me that my musical idiom would come up against resistance on the part of some listeners. Should that have upset me? I knew all
along that everything I was going to do would find friend and foe. Should
I bury my head under the blanket because of that catastrophic experience?

I think the story of the Second Symphony in France and the fact that
until about four years ago I was not performed in that country (I am now
played there with increasing frequency) shows that of course I was tyrannized; I would actually prefer to call it chicanery. This is just aesthetic
ostracism that I need to sit out, evanescent fashions—you do not need any
courage for that.

However, I had no other choice but to bow to what you call "tyranny,"
and what I prefer to call chicanery. I continue to be persona non grata at a
number of radio stations, but am I really to fear someone who has made it
as a radio producer? I am far too arrogant for that.

When Abrahamsen says he did not have the courage to compose simple music it only shows that he was insecure. It required no courage: one
was not imprisoned for something like that, at least not in the West. If one
is so much afraid of arguments that one does things one would rather not
do, that is deplorable and perhaps it does take courage to overcome one's
anxiety. That is, however, a private psychological phenomenon, I would not
want to mix it up with the notion of objective courage.

There has never been a tyranny of taste. There has been a wide range
of different concentrations of taste. After I had ceased to have anything
to say in the field of avant-garde music, my works would be played by
larger and smaller orchestras and chamber music groups. They never programmed the kind of music that was performed at avant-garde festivals. In
other words, there were diverse aesthetic fields that never overlapped. To
begin with, composers of new music displayed a dismissive attitude toward
opera; Boulez's misinterpreted sentence plugged up many people's brains.
Later the first wave of chamber operas emerged, and then, when I was also

confident enough to embark on my first opera, that is, when I had at long last found a subject, having perused world literature beforehand, the large theaters were suddenly prepared to offer considerable fees for new operas. As a result, everyone seems to think they are opera composers really. To my mind, there is far too much courage there and far too meager métier. Métier can to a large degree replace courage.

To conclude: God has been kind enough to implant the subtle trait in me not to believe that I have been chosen to do the only right thing. Otherwise I would probably have decided to go into politics. I do what I like to do and I do not ask myself if it is the right thing as long as it fulfills me.

I have always found somebody to take an interest in what I do and to produce it. If it is going well, the publisher is also happy—it is, however, particularly happy with each opera whose costs it does not have to advance, that is, those that will not be composed.

Best wishes,
MT

CHAPTER THIRTY-TWO

JÖRG WIDMANN
(B . 1 9 7 3)

German composer and clarinetist

The interview took place in the lobby of Jörg Widmann's hotel in Donaueschingen, on the eve of the premiere of Mark Andre's clarinet concerto über—*a piece that Widmann had initiated. He was also responsible for its considerable technical difficulties: he had shown Andre many of the feats the clarinet was capable of.*

Our conversation was inserted with some difficulty into his schedule as he was desperately trying to complete his work on a viola concerto: the deadline was the very next day. I was grateful that he should have squeezed in the time for it and I had concomitant pangs of remorse. It was a relief to hear a few days afterward that he had brought it off: the viola concerto was ready on time.

I have known Jörg Widmann for many years without our ever having conducted a proper conversation. There had been friendly greetings at Donaueschingen, Salzburg, and Vienna, but it was all too fleeting for me to form any reliable picture of his personality. The forty-five minutes we now spent together gave me some idea of the phenomenon Jörg Widmann.

This interview ought really to be heard and seen rather than read. The aural and visual aspects are very much part of it: the many nuances and registers of his voice, his innocent purity, his willingness to open up without any reservation, the musicality that imbues every word—all that captivated me. I sensed his vulnerability, a kind of defenselessness that deeply moved me; the interview itself proved ideal for the purposes of this book.

The next day I was impressed by Widmann's interpretation of Mark Andre's clarinet concerto. I was once again struck by his total identification with the music that also manifested itself in his body language. Respect for the music, humbleness, concentration—inspiring for the listener, to try to likewise identify with the work.

In recent years, I have encountered an encouraging phenomenon among younger composers, of whom Widmann is one, together with Enno Poppe, Rebecca Saunders, Mark Andre, and others: their mutual support and appreciation for one another's work, an attitude that was more or less absent in my initial years at Editio Musica Budapest in the early 1970s. Widmann's interpretation of Andre's music was an act of friendship for a colleague and also a service to the cause of New Music.

Donaueschingen, October 17, 2015
Revised Budapest, January 2016

I hit upon the word courage *just once in your conversations with Markus Fein.[1] In connection with* Lichtstudie, *you say:[2] "At the end, after just under an hour, the Icarus metaphor is conjured up again: the piece is irradiated by light. A dazzling, bright light, in a broadly arching culmination. I had never had the courage to write an ending like that."*

Why courage?

I can understand both extremes in the many examples you list. To begin with, however, I would tend to agree with Lachenmann, Rihm, and Cerha. I am a Schoenbergian through and through: art comes from compulsion. I have no other choice but to follow the inner voice. That is the crucial point.

When I was listening to my first interview, I remember how my own voice struck me as foreign. When, as a fledgling composer, I first heard a piece of mine, I was puzzled rather than elated. Also as a clarinetist—musicians have radar ears, extremely focused—sometimes, when I listen to a recording, I am disappointed, for I thought I had played a good concert

---

1   Markus Fein, *Im Sog der Klänge: Gespräche mit dem Komponisten Jörg Widmann* (Mainz am Rhein: Schott, 2005), 54.

2   *Lichtstudie I* (2001) for orchestra. Widmann followed it up with five more compositions, which make up the cycle *Lichtstudie I–VI* for five soloists (violin, viola, accordion, clarinet, and piano) and orchestra.

and find myself confronted with mannerisms that I had assumed I had long gotten rid of.

In the beginning, you have courage. Although children are sometimes afraid of going into the water: fear of entering a place is a well-known phenomenon. It is also a question of upbringing. Children are warned not to touch a hot oven, they do so nevertheless. Once one has burned oneself, one might be cautious next time. (I am trying to approach the subject from different angles.) And I can also remember that as a teacher, just as much as a student, it is one of the most difficult things of all to find one's own voice. That does have something to do with courage, also with one's encounters on one's path to music.

I was lucky enough to make the acquaintance of Günter Bialas in Munich.[3] He was a great composer, who, alas, is hardly ever played nowadays. His late work especially is fantastic music. For us young composers, he was one who was always there. He attended all our performances. My colleagues will also confirm this: he would always be present, would come backstage and make a comment. He would always say: "Good job." He gave us courage. And, before leaving, he would add: "Take a look at that passage with the woodwinds, you might . . . it is not heard well enough." Or something to that effect. He said things like that to the others as well.

Was he always right?

Always. That is what hit us so hard (*laughs*). But what mattered was that he gave us courage. I think one does need people who encourage one on one's path, for the path is indeed thorny.

Perhaps, as a very young composer, one can fearlessly put something on paper. The daring of youth, maybe. One may put something down without thinking about it, without pondering it and it will still exude the charm of youth. There will, however, come a time when that will no longer do. That is when reflection and doubt set in. For my composing, my thinking, doubt plays an absolutely central role.

Have you experienced doubt as conducive to your work?

Not always. On the whole yes, but it does frequently turn against me and paralyzes me. Strictly speaking, it recurs each time I start a new piece. I call it incubation time.

---

3   Günter Bialas (1907–95), German composer and professor.

I think it can be explained in the following manner: the original idea is innocent. It is just there, to begin with. But what comes next? Then come all the counter-ideas, not just one. And until one actually gets going—honestly, I do not have a clue whether it has anything to do with courage. To play a bit with the word: sometimes one needs the courage of despair. In my case, it is like this: at one point the magnetism radiating from my desk grows to unbearable proportions and turns against me. It will reach a stage of the "point of no return" where the magnetic vectors change direction and I simply must go to my desk. And from then on I stay put.

Frankly, once I am there, I no longer need any courage. But at the start of a piece: already the second note is wrong! I do wish I could simply get going. That is something I have not managed to do right up to this day, including the Viola Concerto. Apparently, I have no problem getting an idea to start with. But then—the fear of my own courage . . .

And, you know, while we are talking about courage, Furtwängler comes to my mind. There are innumerable stories about him. He is said to have hesitated before giving the upbeat. The story goes that members of the Berlin Philharmonic were asked how on earth they knew when to begin playing. They answered: When the baton reaches the third buttonhole. Once they were touring Italy. Furtwängler came onstage and was marking time. Someone from the audience called out to him: "Coraggio, Maestro!" I find that wonderful! If only I had someone who would once in a while shout—without Maestro—"coraggio" to me . . .

Just at the start. After that I am fearless. Aesthetically speaking, I am fearless at the weirdest places, where I am most likely to be particularly sharply criticized. See my Babylon opera, for example.[4] The music got a terrible panning in the press—I think also *because* the public loved it so much. It has tonality, it has singing, it has pathos, it has irony, it is an overwhelmingly colorful piece. It ends with a tonal chorus—I am totally fearless about something like that. I just do it. I must live with it—can in fact live with it—if it is badly criticized, for I know precisely what I am doing—and, perhaps, also because it is forbidden. Some people go out of their way to draw a line that is not to be transgressed. That kind of thinking is far too narrow for me, it is too limiting. Those supposedly forbidden zones—what you may not do, what you ought not to do—have always intrigued me. There I am too much of a child.

---

4 Commissioned by the Bavarian State Opera House, *Babylon*'s world premiere took place in 2012 in Munich. The librettist was Peter Sloterdijk.

That is where the subjects of the book: courage and ideology, courage and prejudice, meet.

If you look at publications about me, this seems to be a recurring subject. It is something I do not consciously provoke only to take pleasure in the reaction.

I am familiar with both worlds, the criticism voiced on both sides. Sometimes people ask me: "Listen, you play the clarinet so marvelously, why do you write this ugly music?" And sometimes I would hear people say: "Is that really modern music? It is heard by so many people, it is so popular." Well yes, because the music is performed by large orchestras, and . . .

. . . is it really suspect because it gets many performances?

I think for some people it is. Clearly, the old prejudice is still in place: when people are enthusiastic, the music must be bad. When ten performances are sold out and the audiences love it . . .

Peter Sloterdijk and I have apparently broken taboos with this opera. It appears that a code of conduct continues to hold sway within modern music theater: it determines what it should be like, what it may do. It is bound up with the subject matter of *Babylon*: we decided well in advance that we would not exclude anything. I did not say from the outset: that is taboo, that sphere must not be allowed in.

To my mind, the character of Inanna, the Babylonian goddess of love, lends itself to demonstrating what I mean. She comes very close to a trivial sphere. You can of course say you abhor that sphere and with it Inanna's figure: she is very Babylonian in her love life, you would not want to identify with her morals. As a music dramatist, as a composer, however, I have availed myself of the possibility of taking that sphere very seriously.

We were lynched for those very passages on which I had flogged myself to death, and had worked for days, weeks, and months on the instrumentation. For of course everything is clearly audible in those tonal areas. You always hear everything anyway, but you have to be particularly careful with those passages. I composed them with the greatest precision and love, I cannot put it any other way. That is why I find it too narrow and small-minded to say: "You cannot do that!" You can criticize anything; I am all for discussion, I love controversial exchanges, anything else bores me, but I think it is intellectually wanting to say, well, that goes too far, that is beyond the pale. That appears to have happened with the opera.

Why do I say this? Because that particular section took me no courage to compose whatsoever. I did not say to myself: Oh God! Let us forget about it! I was fully conscious of what I was doing, but I was wholly fearless. I must take any negative reaction in my stride.

A chorus at the end starts with a quote from the Book of Ruth: "Where you go, there I will also go." Very simple, very plain. There I can't (*he mimicks "modern" music, with wide interval leaps and a raw voice*). I have put love music in there. At the conclusion of the opera, it was very important for us to make at least a possible reconciliation between the Jewish and the Babylonian peoples happen, a possible utopia of a peaceful coexistence. That has of course nothing to do with historical truth.

And then we added something that is absent from the Book of Ruth: "Where you go, there we shall also go." And all of a sudden, the Jewish chorus returns to the stage and they sing together. Now that I am telling you this, I have goose bumps. That is the spot that was particularly criticized. But why does it need to be so beautiful? Because a minute later, the Tower of Babel collapses. If I had written dissonant music before that happens, nobody would have noticed. In our opera, the Tower of Babel does not collapse as punishment by an Old Testament God whose wrath has been provoked by all the sins of the hedonistic people of Babylon; in our piece it collapses out of sheer happiness. Sheer happiness! And that is the kind of music I attempted to write for a hundred-strong chorus, soloists, and a huge orchestra.

We are talking here at Donaueschingen; I would be nowhere but for the festival. The world premiere of *Implosion* in 2001 was a pivotal experience for me, also because it afforded a chance to become acquainted with this orchestra.[5] My *Second Labyrinth for Orchestral Groups* also received a fantastic premiere here in 2006.[6] In other words, I am part of this world, but I am also aware that many of the people here would reject those sections of the opera without a moment's hesitation, for they probably think: that won't do, that cannot be. But, as I have said, I worked on those very passages without any fear.

So you won't allow yourself to be tyrannized by tastes, by prejudices.

No! That would be surrendering. Also in the contrary sense, I must add. When in 2004 I was composer-in-residence in Salzburg, together with

---

5 *Implosion's* first performance was on October 21, 2001, with Sylvain Cambreling conducting the SWR Symphony Orchestra Baden-Baden and Freiburg.

6 *Second Labyrinth for Orchestral Groups*, world premiere, October 2006, SWR Symphony Orchestra Baden-Baden and Freiburg, conducted by Hans Zender.

Kurtág, the Young Friends of the Festival—that is, students who accompanied me—posed the question: "Do you think you might one day write normal music?" (*laughs*). Whereupon I asked them: "What is normal music? Perhaps I find your music not normal!" (*mimics the monotonous rhythms of Muzak*). I would be selling my soul if I would only compose music to appeal to the masses . . . I have pieces that only three people will listen to, I must write them all the same. I have played numerous premieres of new music, so I am really familiar with that situation. But, of course, I am just as familiar with giant sold-out halls. It is not for me to carry out public opinion polls—I can only write music I have faith in.

I conducted the very first interview for this book with John Adams. He related how he had hesitated to accept a commission to write a work in memory of the destruction of the World Trade Center. He had to muster his courage to eventually say yes, similarly to his other compositions that concern topical political subjects. How about you? Would it take courage for you to write a piece, say, about the unification of Germany? Or any other similar subject— music to be programmed on national holidays.

The first thing that comes to my mind is that I have in fact performed Wolfgang Rihm's Clarinet Quintet in the building of the Reichstag (today's Bundestag) to mark the Day of German Unity. The acoustics were poor but, of course, it was a great event.

On another occasion, I composed a piece that I knew would be played on a Day of German Unity—an extreme, unwieldy composition not easy on the ear—*Chor* for orchestra, premiered by Kent Nagano and the Deutsches Symphonie-Orchester at the Berlin Philharmonie, on October 3, 2004. The occasion has since slipped my mind, your question now brings it back. My cycle *Lied, Chor, Messe* has a logic of its own; it is a comment on the fundamental European idea of "Brotherhood unites all men." It is a comment infused with doubt but it leads to a desperate, affirmative culmination.

But what is *Chor*? Is it a synonym for people or society? It could also be a cacophonous chorus, a dissonant chorus of pain, a chorus of accusation, a *turba* chorus like Bach's.

Of course, that is no answer. To tell you the truth, I have never thought about writing something representative. Sometimes it is implicit: I am going to compose a piece for Kent Nagano, for the opening week of the Elbphilharmonie concert hall in Hamburg. It will be the only work on the program. He might easily have picked Beethoven's Ninth or Mahler's Second. Instead, he opted for a large-scale contemporary composition for soprano, baritone, chorus, and orchestra. It is quite a challenge and I am beset by a great deal of doubt. It would be out of place today, I think, to produce something in the vein of Beethoven's *Consecration of the House*.[7]

The problem of the refugees that we are currently experiencing is cutting me terribly to the quick. In every sense. From a human point of view especially: this misery that cries out to heaven! But I also understand those who have anxiety. I can certainly not understand the politicians who have caused it all: we supported the US air strikes in both Gulf Wars. Thank God, we at least stayed away from bombing Libya. It is all man-made and we are seeing what it has all led to: a frightening, misguided policy.

Sometimes I wonder if I should perhaps make a music theater piece based on all that. After all, I have devoted my earlier works for the music theater to similar subjects. My first opera, *Das Gesicht im Spiegel*, concerns cloning—that we can now reproduce ourselves.[8] It is an expression of criticism, if you like, but I do find that mere criticism by itself is not sufficient, a stage poetry should be pitted against it. Criticism alone does not do; criticism is always cheap. If I cannot create an alternative realm in my art, I have no raison d'être as an artist. I should at least work toward that goal. Magic!

In other words, I would not reject composing music of political relevance out of hand, because I am intrigued by going out on a limb. That was how I grew up, especially as a composer: I was always thrown into cold water und never had a chance to wonder whether I could swim in the first place.

I wrote my very first piece to receive a public performance for a chamber ensemble of the Munich Philharmonic, Variations on Mozart's *A Girl or a Little Wife*. It was played on a tour of Japan and in Europe, as part of an all-Mozart program. The musicians then turned to me:

"You are a composer! Why don't you write a closing piece for all the young soloists of the evening?" They were exquisite instrumentalists made up of first-chair players of the Munich Philharmonic. That was the first time I had the chance—and the assignment—to write for the horn. I thought to myself: "An F-horn—you will have to transpose!" I was devastated. No courage left at all. That happens early on, once one senses one's own limitations. Then I do worry sometimes. It is something very intimate, if you

---

7   Beethoven composed the overture *Consecration of the House*, op. 124, for the reopening of the Josefstädter Theater in Vienna, first performed on October 3, 1822. The premiere was led by Beethoven himself, seated at the piano.

8   *Gesicht im Spiegel* (Face in the Mirror), composed in 2003 to a libretto by Roland Schimmelpfennig. The revised version premiered on April 17, 2010, at the Deutsche Oper am Rhein in Düsseldorf.

like, but it happens to every artist. Artists know what they can do, also what they can do especially well, but they are also aware of their shortcomings.

I know from your conversation with Markus Fein that you actually welcome the chance to expose yourself to extreme challenges, that you consciously attempt to measure up to tasks that are wholly new for you.

That is true. If I had set my sights on a comfortable life as an artist, I would not be doing it. At the beginning of our conversation, I told you of the extreme situation I am facing currently and you noted it was nothing new for me. It was rather brusque—but you hit the nail on the head! (*laughs*).

You cannot do otherwise, can you?

I rather suspect it is up to 90 percent true.

You are out to prove to yourself that you are up to it.

Well . . . there is a grain of truth in that. But I swear to you, I often fear I am not quite up to it. At least at the start of a piece, I think I won't manage. I may have just finished a work for the Berlin Philharmonic two weeks before and am about to get started on a new piece. It is really no false modesty but once again I have the feeling I am beginning from scratch. Nil! It is because I attempt in each new work to create a new cosmos. That is bound to produce a feeling of exposure, in a desert or a storm. It might appear trite but I am very familiar with the situation where, at the start of a new piece, one feels the mountain facing one is too high. I can only rid myself of that anxiety and lack of courage by taking the plunge. This process of getting started is sometimes as painful as it is to ceaselessly pack my suitcase and acclimatize myself to new places and people in my day-to-day existence. My life looks like this: I set off from somewhere, travel home, stay there two days and am off again. Hardly arrived and leaving again: it is my own choice and still it is a difficult thing. But as soon as I am seated in a train, I realize that that is precisely what I need. Changing places. I know that feeling extremely well and need it as much as I need air to breathe.

CHAPTER THIRTY-THREE

CHRISTIAN WOLFF
(B . 1 9 3 4)

American composer

Audiatur et altera pars *has been a principle that has guided my activities as an interviewer. It was tremendously thrilling for me to confront John Cage with Morton Feldman's remarks about him, or to check with Witold Lutosławski the veracity of Earle Brown's claim that the Polish composer had been influenced by Brown's notation.*[1]

Similarly, I was fascinated by Karl Aage Rasmussen's report on his experiences as a composition student in Denmark—how he was frowned upon for expressing what at the time were considered unorthodox tastes. I sent the relevant paragraph to all the composers who had contributed to the book so far and thus inspired/prompted them to express their own views.

The interview I did with John Adams for this book led me to forward the text to Christian Wolff who had answered my three questions in a highly interesting and thought-provoking manner back in 1984. Little did I know that Adams had been Wolff's pupil of beginning Greek at Harvard University. Later on, John Adams was to organize a performance of Wolff's Burdocks in San Francisco, at the Music Conservatory where he led the contemporary music ensemble. As the older composer remarked: "How differently our musical lives have gone!"

---

1 Varga, *Three Questions for Sixty-Five Composers.*

I sent the Adams interview to Christian Wolff, especially because I was anxious to have his views on Charles Ives, a pioneer whom Adams sees in a more critical light than one would expect. That was indeed the first subject Wolff commented on, before getting down to "the courage of composers."

April 21, 2015

Two responses to J.A.

1. The criticism of Ives I think is a serious misunderstanding (it's not new: Elliott Carter—who learned a lot about rhythmic procedures from Ives and knew him personally—also asserted that Ives's composition techniques were inadequate, too crude). Ives, though his work can, I think, sometimes be uneven, is still a great composer. And the "murky," "overloaded" patches were surely that way because that is how Ives intended them, and/or he was deliberately trying something new. He speaks of "mud" as sometimes a desirable quality in music (and refers to Brahms!). (People used to complain similarly about Schumann's orchestration, also Mussorgsky's.) There's grit in the music and it's what makes it really good. Or, to put it another way, Ives had courage.

2. I do agree that courage may be a kind of persistence, never giving up on one's work, regardless of external circumstances. And I like the remark about a composer always hoping that the next piece may be the best one. That feeling is a basic part of what keeps me working.

I am probably one of the few people who has addressed questions to Christian Wolff without asking him to comment on his relationship with John Cage and the other composers who have come to be known as the New York Group. Still, courage and taste are apparently subjects that are bound to involve a reference to at least Cage, and I am glad Christian Wolff brought him up of his own accord.

I remember talking to Georges Auric in Budapest several decades ago, and the patience with which he explained, clearly for the umpteenth time, that his music and that of his friends (Poulenc, Milhaud, Durey, Tailleferre, and Honegger) had very little to do with one another; it had merely been the idea of the critic Henri Collet to refer to them as a group and call them Les Six.

I believe Cage, Feldman, Brown, and Wolff likewise created independent musical worlds for themselves and did not necessarily expect to be regarded as a group. However, there was probably more to it than with Les Six, for—as Christian Wolff explained in an interview—they were so different from the rest of the musical world in the United States, it was comforting to be able to rely on one another for support. In fact, they would often write their pieces for one another. He also referred to his collaboration with the choreographer Merce Cunningham as "encouraging and supportive" in that their ideas about structure were related—and I detect the word "courage" in "encouraging" . . .

Another feature they might have had in common was the need to start with a clean slate, a departure that was probably more radical than that of their European contemporaries. When I did an interview with Boulez about the New York Group shortly before his death (in the end, he decided against allowing it to be published), he found the "métier" missing in their work, and remarked that probably Earle Brown alone possessed it to some extent.

That is indeed what differentiates the music of these American composers from that of their European counterparts. Here is a quote from Christian Wolff:

> *One day I said to myself that it would be better to get rid of all that—melody, rhythm, harmony, etc. This was not a negative thought and did not mean that it was necessary to avoid them, but rather that, while doing something else, they would appear spontaneously. We had to liberate ourselves from the direct and peremptory consequence of intention and effect, because the intention would always be our own and would be circumscribed, when so many other forces are evidently in action in the final effect.[2]*

Innumerable other ideas could be quoted to demonstrate the originality of Christian Wolff's thinking. I just want to single out his commitment to political ideals, which has led to politically motivated pieces of music. He became involved early on in the civil rights and antiwar movements and this led logically to writing relevant music. He used texts to begin with but relinquished words at a later stage, for he was not interested in writing vocal music. He is in fact one of the few composers contributing to this book with an avowed political concern.

I am happy to have been able to persuade Christian Wolff to participate in this project: it lends the book a historical perspective and represents a unique approach to what composing music is about.

I.

Now as for "courage" in one's musical life: basically, I think it's a willingness to take chances and to risk failure. It can apply to (1) aesthetics and

---

2   Christian Wolff, *Occasional Pieces* (New York: Oxford University Press, 2017), 46.

(2) social and economic conditions. John Cage used to speak disparaging-ly of composers who primarily made a living by means other than music. So, for instance, Ives was making a lot of money working in the insurance business. And he could have included me (but he never did), taking up full-time teaching, at first of literature, not music. Cage himself showed extraordinary courage in making the music he did before he finally (at well over forty) started to be successful. When I met him (he was thirty-eight), his economic situation was very bad and yet it was just then that he stopped writing in what was really his most accessible way (e.g., the prepared piano music, the first string quartet) and went to the chance operations and the really difficult (from every point of view) pieces that followed. I think of that as his truly heroic period. Courage in both the aesthetic and social/economic sense.

That's all I can think of to say about the subject at the moment. It is not so easy to talk about. Courage is a virtue, and so it's difficult to talk about in relation to oneself. I would connect courage with experimental music (and I should say that I regard all really good, authentic music, of whatever time, as experimental), that is, a music that tries to be free of pressures from established aesthetic and social conditions, that is, takes risks and attempts new things.

Addressing certain political issues in one's music may also take cour-age, though that would depend mostly on larger historical contexts. Shostakovich sometimes clearly showed courage and risked his life as a composer under Stalin. I think, for example, of his using elements of Jewish music in one of the piano trios at a time when official anti-Semitism was the rule. I also think of Cornelius Cardew who risked his reputation and living as an avant-garde composer when he turned to political activ-ity and a music to support it, a music that was thought old-fashioned and regressive by many of his former musical associates.

II.

A.

I think the question of "tyranny of taste" is rather a side issue to the ques-tion of courage. I have trouble responding because I've never been much bothered by anxieties over what I should admit to liking or not, and most of my musical friends have not either.

The question of "taste" could be interesting, especially as it is some-thing that is impossible to discuss or really explain. Why do I decide that something I have composed is good or not (and it's not uncommon for me to find something not good or not good enough, and so I discard it)? Apart from obvious factors like careless or not concentrated writing (usually because one is too tired to work properly), I just don't know. And with taste, one changes one's mind, and often doesn't agree with others. As I say, I don't see where courage comes in. What might come in is capacity for judgment and the use of intelligence.

June 30, 2015

B.

You've moved a ways from the notion of courage. I guess what's left is the courage to stand by/act on one's "taste," that is, one's own sense, very hard to describe and perhaps to account for, of what's "good." That is, apart from simple matters like technical competence or obviously unworkable ideas, poor judgment.

As for accepting and appreciating "music that is wholly foreign to [my] taste": well, I think that if one is devoted to and works with music, one should have as extensive a knowledge of music, of all kinds, as possible. Accepting and appreciating is not the point. Rather it's about being informed and knowledgeable. I can listen to music that I find second-rate or just not to my taste and still learn something from it (say, the use of an instrument, or, negatively, what not to do with a series of loud chords for a climax).

By the way, you mention Barber's *Adagio* and Shostakovich and Britten. The *Adagio* is fine, though it's been shamelessly exploited, used, and played much too much. Shostakovich I mostly like and admire, especially his ability to do much with apparently simple means. Britten I find less engaging, though he writes very well.

As far as adverse effect of prejudiced opinion (I assume you mean others' prejudiced opinion): of course my "career" has been affected. For instance, my association with John Cage was enough for many musicians simply to write me off. Though later, when Cage was appreciated more widely, the reverse was the case. Or the music I've made with explicit political material has surely been rejected by some who don't share the politics (and conversely, some who shared the politics found themselves appreciating the music).

PART TWO

CRITICS

When I think of critics, the name of Aladár Tóth (1898–1968) is the first one to come to my mind. In my youth in Budapest, he was regarded as *the* Hungarian music critic, even though he had stopped writing reviews in 1939: Tóth was married to the Jewish pianist Annie Fischer, and the couple had to flee to Sweden before the outbreak of World War II.

In the nearly two decades between the two world wars (1920–39), however, Aladár Tóth's reviews proved highly influential in securing recognition for the music of Béla Bartók and Zoltán Kodály. In fact, Tóth was the first to realize the significance of those composers, and in his articles he created a climate conducive to their creative work.

In other words, Aladár Tóth was far more than a music critic in the accepted sense of the word. He had a mission that went beyond registering his impressions of the concerts and opera productions he attended. He was a fighter for the cause of new Hungarian music.

Tóth and Annie Fischer returned to Budapest in 1946, and in 1947, he was appointed director of the Budapest State Opera House. One of his first acts was to invite Otto Klemperer to be the theater's music director (1947–50), initiating a high point in its history, only comparable to the directorship of Gustav Mahler (1888–91). In his new position, Aladár Tóth continued his fight for Béla Bartók's stage works, then under a cloud with the communist authorities because of their supposedly "formalist" features.

Paul Bekker (1882–1937) played a similar role in Germany, first as a music critic (1906–22), later as administrator of the opera houses in Kassel and Wiesbaden. In both capacities, he was a vocal advocate of the music of Gustav Mahler, Franz Schreker, Arnold Schoenberg, and Ernst Krenek. He published a book on Mahler's symphonies ten years after the composer's death as well as a study of Schreker's music theater as early as 1919. During his time in Kassel, Bekker premiered the twenty-six-year-old Ernst Krenek's opera *Orpheus und Eurydike* (1926) and programmed Schreker's *Die Gezeichneten* in 1927. In Wiesbaden, too, he was faithful to Schreker, with seven performances of *Der singende Teufel* in 1929. No doubt about it: Paul Bekker was more than a music critic: he was a potent patron as well.

In the United States, Paul Rosenfeld (1890–1946) championed the cause of modern American music, but was uncompromising in his criticism of Arnold Schoenberg's dodecaphonic work. Elliott Carter cites

Rosenfeld's view that Schoenberg's compositions "baffle with their apparently willful ugliness and bewilder with their geometric cruelty and coldness."[3] Carter notes: "This attitude persisted to the very end of Schoenberg's life in this country and succeeded in restricting his influence to a much smaller circle than he deserved and kept most of the composers discussed from coming to grips with his music."[4] Amazing, really, is the extent to which the judgment (taste? prejudice?) of a single music critic can harm the career, the standing of an artist on a national scale, in a country as vast as the United States.

In my years with Universal Edition, Vienna (1992–2007), I soon learned to respect the reviews of Gerhard R. Koch in the *Frankfurter Allgemeine Zeitung*. I sensed a purpose in them that went beyond the concert he was discussing, as if he were out to teach, to educate his readers. That is why I have asked him to define his credo: "As a critic, my goal is to ensure that readers, having perused my reviews, have become better listeners, better thinkers and, above all, rid of their prejudices. That is: doubters, questioners, less certain of themselves. In short: more open to discourse."[5] I invited some critics to reply to the question of whether they are aware of the subjectivity of their judgments, and if so, whether they strive for objectivity, consciously trying to leave their personal tastes aside.

---

3   Elliott Carter, *The Writings of Elliott Carter*, ed. Else Stone and Kurt Stone (Bloomington: Indiana University Press, 1977), 233.
4   Ibid.
5   E-mail to the author, March 31, 2016.

CHAPTER THIRTY-FOUR

PAUL GRIFFITHS
(B . 1 9 4 7)

British music critic, author of
music books and fiction, librettist

Paul Griffiths has been a friend for over three decades. He was chief music critic of the Times *of London when we first met; subsequently, he was on the staff of the* New York Times *and the* New Yorker, *before becoming freelance.*

The first of the above two sentences is a private statement of fact. The second could be taken from an official curriculum vitae. This headnote is bound to be in turn subjective and objective; a mixture of the two is probably not possible (can one be subjectively objective?)

I admire Paul's supreme mastery of the English language. His letters to me, especially since his move to Manorbier in Wales, where he begins his days with an early morning walk along the coast in the company of his dogs, are veritable gems in that they describe nature as he observes its colors, shapes, and sounds.

An impression of his poetry can be gained from the poem printed in the interview with Hans Abrahamsen: drawn from Griffiths's unique Ophelia *novel, let me tell you, it inspired the Danish composer to create a song cycle for soprano and orchestra, which won the Grawemeyer Award in 2016.*

Paul's critical writing is represented by a quote from the third edition of his Modern Music and After, *chosen to underpin what I have to say about*

George Crumb.⁶ That is of course just the tip of the tip of the tip of the iceberg. Paul's oeuvre is huge; a fraction of his output fills a shelf in my library. He has written on a wide range of subjects, perhaps most notably contemporary music. In any case, he is probably the only writer on music to have been honored with the rank of OBE (Officer of the Most Excellent Order of the British Empire): this occurred in the Queen's New Year's Honours in 2014, for his services to contemporary composition (as well as to literature).

Literature: yes, Paul Griffiths has written a range of novels. The first one, Myself and Marco Polo *(1989), inspired Tan Dun to compose an opera. The libretto, fashioned from the novel by Paul himself, was followed by further essays in that genre, the most prestigious being* What Next? *written for Elliott Carter (1997–98). Paul Griffiths has secured his place in music history.*

What follows is Paul's response to my request for a comment on the job of a music critic. He wrote it on a train journey across England and Wales, with the sun shining on the computer screen and blinding his eyes. I think it is an instance of Paul letting his thoughts wander freely, improvising on the subject in a capricious and witty manner, and arriving at some fascinating insights. Perhaps I am being subjectively objective here.

on taste—for B.A.V.

STATEMENT

I liked it.

COMMENTARY ONE, ON "I"

We have had at least two centuries to get used to doubting how single is the first person singular. Schumann, in his critical writings as much as in his music, invited Florestan, Eusebius, and other characters to debate issues of taste, judgment, and response, all from within the many intercommunicating chambers of his own mentality. The views of these figures could never be unanimous; rarely, even, could their voices harmonize. Though we may lack Schumann's virtuosity as a polyphonist in prose, still we may

---

6   In 1981, Paul Griffiths published *Modern Music: The Avant-Garde since 1945* (New York: George Braziller). In 1995, he updated it in *Modern Music and After: Directions since 1945* (Oxford: Oxford University Press). Fifteen years later, the updated third edition was published (from which I have quoted), *Modern Music and After* (Oxford: Oxford University Press, 2010).

recognize how our simple affirmations come, at best, out of silenced con-flicts, in which "I like it" spars with "I do not like it," or "I so much want to like it," or "I am not sure I like it," or "I am not sure I dare say I like it," and so on.

ANECDOTE ONE: The critic, typically rushing to leave the concert hall as soon as the final applause has started, is stopped briefly by an acquaintance with a question: "Did you like it?" "I don't know," comes the reply, "I haven't written my review yet."

COMMENTARY ONE POINT ONE, ON ANECDOTE ONE: Much more probably the question would have been voiced as: "*How* did you like it?' which asks not just for a yes/no answer but for some touch of a more detailed and supported evalua-tion: "I thought the slow movement wasn't slow enough," or "Well, she was expressively way over-the-top, wasn't she?' or "He just doesn't have the voice for Manrico," or, just possibly, "Oh, she's always terrific."

COMMENTARY ONE POINT ONE POINT ONE, ON COMMENTARY ONE POINT ONE, ON ANECDOTE ONE: Note that in these examples, invented at random and not with the intention of allowing this observation, the negative remark always says more than the positive. The critic, or the armchair opinionator, feels the need to justify a negative reaction, whereas a positive one can be simply stated. This has implications for the usefulness of criticism from the past.

COMMENTARY ONE POINT ONE POINT ONE POINT ONE, ON COMMENTARY ONE POINT ONE POINT ONE, ON COMMENTARY ONE POINT ONE, ON COMMENTARY ONE, ON ANECDOTE ONE: Star ratings, of course, are senseless.

But it is more complicated yet, because—and maybe this matter needs to be raised as COMMENTARY ONE POINT TWO, ON ANECDOTE ONE—the critic's "I" is a more complex figment than usual, one in which the individual is modulated, probably self-modulated, by the forum within which that individual is required to communicate. A popular newspaper, a "quality" newspaper, a specialist magazine, and a learned journal imply dif-ferent readerships, readerships that, having different levels of involvement with the topic at issue, require different voices from the critic. A paper or, more likely, a magazine may also have a personality, which its contributors will knowingly or unknowingly want to substantiate or challenge. ("This doesn't read like a *New Yorker* piece.")

OK, let this be COMMENTARY ONE POINT TWO POINT ONE, ON COMMENTARY ONE POINT TWO, ON ANECDOTE ONE, with reference also to COMMENTARY ONE POINT ONE POINT ONE, ON COMMENTARY ONE POINT ONE, ON COMMENTARY ONE, ON ANECDOTE ONE, only please don't ignore it for that reason, because it's important: Professional criticism is different from armchair opining precisely in the measure to which it is communicated in public. To the reader, taste is of much less concern than judgment, which of course will be colored by taste but also educated by knowledge and experience, besides being enlivened, one may hope, by writerly skills and flair as well as conditioned by the forum and by the public nature of that forum. Professional criticism is not just one person's opinion; it is a very particular person's opinion, an informed opinion, delivered under circumstances demanding control and expertise.

> COMMENTARY ONE POINT TWO POINT ONE POINT ONE, ON COMMENTARY ONE POINT TWO POINT ONE, ON COMMENTARY ONE POINT TWO, ON ANECDOTE ONE: Taste is immediate, like pain. Judgment has to be arrived at. This will partly explain the rushing critic's inability to answer a question that is at once too simple and too complicated. Unwilling to pronounce a view in the time frame of taste (to pronounce it, and thereby to run the risk of henceforth feeling committed to it, or having it usurp all authority), that rushing critic has not had time yet to form a judgment.

>> COMMENTARY ONE POINT TWO POINT ONE POINT ONE POINT ONE, ON COMMENTARY ONE POINT TWO POINT ONE, ON COMMENTARY ONE POINT TWO, ON ANECDOTE ONE: Or, one might better say, for a judgment to form of itself, because there is another essential difference between criticism and armchair opinion, which is that the former is, in general, written. (Even a radio review is likely to be, if not fully scripted, prepared in advance, some phrases readied for use.) Writing has its own ways of doing things: rules and conventions, of course, but also a kind of fluency that may seem at times independent of the writer. When we speak, we feel the words to be immediate to us (though, of course, we may be deluded in

this); when we write, there is a separation. We have surely all had the experience of the writing taking over. (It is doing so now, to some extent.) And perhaps it is impossible to write without the writing taking over (yes, to some extent, let it just be to some extent).

Other considerations, too, may impinge. To give one example, we will want to give the benefit of the doubt to the newcomer: the singer straight out of the conservatory, the composer having a first professional performance. On such occasions we may want to dunk the hot response of taste in the pool not only of reflection but of hope.

COMMENTARY TWO, ON "LIKED"

Is it just the existence of this word that allows anglophones to be so miserly in their enthusiasms? But what verb, then, does taste want to wield? The more potent "love" has an edge of condescension, which will suit some potential love objects better than others. "I love Satie." Fine. "I love the St. Matthew Passion." Not so sure.

In its favor, "love" has the immediacy of taste, the unconsideredness, the eluding of any barriers of thought. But it has, also, the urge to possess. You can possess Satie all you want. He will not object. He may even enjoy the experience. Who knows? But the St. Matthew Passion . . . ?

Turned into the past tense, of course, the verb's sense changes. "I loved her Mozart sonata" no longer strives to possess, for the experience and the reaction to it are both wholly in the past. However, the immediacy of taste is still implied, for it would be possible to say, for instance: "I loved her Mozart sonata, but when I thought about it, I wasn't so sure." Again, taste responds all at once; judgment takes its time and its thought.

Yet, once more, some things are too big ever to have loved. An account of a Mozart sonata will probably have accepted the embrace, and gladly, but you cannot get your arms around any performance of *Don Giovanni*.

What about "admire," then? Or perhaps not. It presupposes the workings of judgment, and does not work at all for taste. You can admire something you do not like—a dual response that once more neatly encapsulates the difference between taste and judgment, which difference is even virtually implicit in the use of "admire" without qualification. (Example: I greatly admire the playing of Teodoro Anzellotti, to which it is hardly necessary to add: "but I don't like the sound of a solo accordion.")

But "admire" is also too cool. What then? "Enjoy"? It has become as vacant as a wide-eyed open mouth: "Enjoy!"

We can shift the burden to an adjective or adjectival form, but does this help? "I find/found it interesting." As Helmut Lachenmann has laconically remarked, "interesting" in this context means "boring." An "interesting" piece of music is probably one that, eliciting very little response, leaves the listener outside observing, being interested, being bored. A composition or performance that catches the interest pulls you in, and is no longer interesting. Taste, of course, is not interested in being interested, is too quick to be interested. Judgment sagely ignores such a level of engagement.

So what else can we find music? Let's stick with the positives: moving, bewildering, spellbinding, elegant, powerful, disturbing, logical (or illogical, which can equally be a plus), fascinating, deep, playful, reminiscent, unexpected, sensuous, economical, thoughtful and thought-filled, colorful, atmospheric—to mention only terms aiming to define more a response to music than the music itself, though of course the border here is fuzzy.

Of course, too, any real music is likely to evoke all these responses at once, or severally—and more besides, for to the list we should add "open-ended." To listen to music is to be in the presence of a multidimensional maze, in which there are holes where we are not yet listening fully or thoroughly, holes where next time we may find more of the maze, and more holes.

COMMENTARY THREE, ON "IT"

It, then, is inexhaustible.

Taste strains to go there again, to have the same experience, which will be more of the same, as taste steadies and develops into judgment. Taste leaps at the first encounter. Taste is love at first sight (hearing). Taste is promiscuous.

Judgment also looks forward, more patiently, to the next reacquaintance. Judgment may be suspicious of the first encounter and prefer the second, the third, the twentieth. Judgment knows it will not tire. But judgment, too, of course, is promiscuous. For yes, judgment may accept both Satie and the St. Matthew Passion, only, to be sure, knowing there is a difference.

It remains. Generally speaking, it remains. There is, to be sure, music that taste and judgment, expressed widely enough, can bring back into circulation or take out. Most of what we know as "classical" music, though, is immune to swerves in popularity. We are free to exercise on it our tastes and our judgments—or, rather, to have it exercise our tastes and our judgments for us—but it will go on. That, after all, is the definition of a classic. Exercising our tastes and our judgments will be important to us, for music is partly a mirror, telling us who and what we are. But the mirror does not remember what was reflected in it. Only we do that.

CHAPTER THIRTY-FIVE

WOLFGANG
SCHREIBER
(B . 1 9 3 9)

German music critic

Wolfgang Schreiber and I used to meet at important new music events from the early 1970s onward. He was writing reviews for newspapers and magazines in Vienna, where he spent the first seven years of his working life. In 1978, he joined the staff of the Süddeutsche Zeitung (SZ), *a major German daily published in Munich, and that is where he spent the next twenty-four years. His articles have earned him prominence in German musical life and they carry weight up to this day. I have profited from his prestige: the sales of a book of mine rose after he praised it in the SZ.*

It was therefore logical for me to approach Wolfgang Schreiber for a contribution to this book. He had intended to expand on his short text but never found the time to do so. No wonder: he writes and edits books, the most successful of which is titled Great Conductors.[1]

May 29, 2015

To my mind, the phenomenon "taste" as prejudice or judgment has to do with philosophy, language, and the environment in which we live. One

---

1   Wolfgang Schreiber, *Große Dirigenten* (Munich: Piper Verlag, 2006).

could engage in enjoyable and endless discussion about it all, for it is entirely rooted in the subjective.

I think the notion is difficult to grasp in an objective fashion, for its basis and premise are bound up with one's taste and individual background, and the structure of one's consciousness and ingrained reactions. Personal "taste" always plays a role in forming a judgment as a tacit or overt judgment-in-gestation, in most cases hidden or subcutaneous.[2] Criticism, too, as any professional and institutionalized judgment, is very possibly always linked to a category like taste, but also with the capacity to think and to speak, as well as with knowledge, experience, intelligence, and so on.

I wonder if I have been able to help you . . .

---

2 "Prejudice" in German is *Vorurteil*, made up of the words *Vor* (pre) and *Urteil* (judgment). Wolfgang Schreiber had this etymology in mind when he spelled the word "Vor-Urteil." You cannot play with it in the same way in English: "pre" does correspond to "vor," but there is no such thing as "judice." I might perhaps have opted for "prejudgment" but it is just as unconvincing as the solution I settled on: "judgment-in-gestation."

CHAPTER THIRTY-SIX

ARNOLD WHITTALL
(B . 1 9 3 5)

British music critic
and music theorist

It is curiously schizophrenic to be writing about a critic who has published critiques of my own books in the past. I do not mind admitting that I was rather overwhelmed by his detailed scholarly dissection of my Conversations with Xenakis *(published by Faber and Faber in 1996). It was obvious that my way of interviewing was found wanting. Another book of mine,* Three Questions for Sixty-Five Composers *(University of Rochester Press, 2011), fared rather better.*

In fact, the publisher noted with palpable relief that this time Arnold Whittall was more positive in his judgment than he was known to be.

And now here I am, writing what must needs be a sketchy portrait of the man. But the Arnold Whittall I have gotten to know through our correspondence over the past years is rather different from the severe critic one encounters in his writings. He may set extremely high standards in his own works (he has published a number of books), his reviews, and his teaching (he is professor emeritus of King's College, London, having previously lectured at Cambridge, Nottingham, and Cardiff), but he is also generous and warmhearted. I have the impression that as a true teacher, he follows the careers of his former students with eager interest, taking pride in their successes. He is also a keen observer of the contemporary music scene in Britain and derives personal pleasure from coming upon promising new composers and compositions. I imagine he is a kind of father figure to many of those active in British music today.

Arnold's generosity was apparent the very first time I approached him. In preparing my book of interviews and a memoir, From Boulanger to Stockhausen *(University of Rochester Press, 2013), I asked him if he would be willing to write the preface. Much to my delight, he replied by return post in the affirmative, signing his letter with his first name. This informality is of course nothing unusual in the English-speaking world, but it is something that I, coming from Central Europe, still find to be an honor and an unusual sign of goodwill. Even more important, in agreeing to cooperate, Arnold gave up many hours of his time to read the book and then to actually formulate an introduction to it, with no expectation of financial gain.*

Arnold Whittall's generosity has extended to contributing the essay below. I have reason to be grateful.

July 24, 2015

Taste and Judgment

As far as I'm aware, the development of civilized legal systems has depended on the belief that the judgment of those empowered to pronounce on guilt or innocence is as objective as possible, seeking to counter any tendency to prejudice by laying down principles and procedures for the evaluation of evidence. Even here, "judgment" might not be entirely free of bias, emotion, lack of balance. But, to the extent that judgment seeks to minimize the involvement of instinctive reactions, to counter the inherently irrational with the systematically rational, it might be thought to resist what in the aesthetic sphere we tend to describe as "taste." Judging a work of art is less a matter of coolly working through a sequence of logical steps to form an opinion by weighing up pros and cons: taste is something irresistible, immediate, and all the more decisive for not being reached only at the end of some kind of intellectually plausible evaluative process.

There is certainly a sense in which musical "taste" cannot be explained—just as the physical sense cannot be easily described when we refer to the taste of an onion or of a strawberry: we "know" what the taste is, and any further analysis is as impossible (save in the narrowest scientific terms) as it is pointless. To propose that this is the case is to argue that any kind of aesthetic preference is inbred, instinctive, involuntary: and even if it is claimed that tastes can be acquired (that is, emerge), or change, the argument from genetic predisposition is not thereby invalidated. After all, there may be reasons for resisting the lure of an already-felt enthusiasm—learning that Wagner was anti-Semitic, for example. But the basic ability to love or loathe, or to be indifferent, to Wagner or any other composer is—the argument goes—somehow built-in to the individual's psychology and personality.

To define taste as essentially involuntary suggests that it involves the kind of preference that still distinguishes it from addiction—a need for something that is hard if not impossible to resist. But it would be unwise to assume that taste as instinctive preference cannot change, if circumstantial conditioning makes that possible. In my own case I would say that my doubts about the more mechanistic aspects of later baroque music—Bach and Handel, for example—intensified after I got to know the much earlier baroque style of Monteverdi. It would nevertheless be difficult to say that a taste for Bach turned into positive distaste for Bach. Absolute distinctions between loving and loathing might be quite common where musical taste is concerned, but there are also shades of taste and distaste: for example, mild enthusiasm for Holst, mild dislike of Delius, both of which I would find difficult to explain on technical grounds alone.

As someone closely involved in contemporary music I'm often asked about my musical preferences, and after a performance of a challenging or complex work that has puzzled or irritated the person asking me the simple question "did you like that?" or "do you admire that composer?" I often reply (on occasions when I wasn't bored or otherwise convinced that the music was not to my taste) that I certainly respect and appreciate what the composer in question appears to be doing. This leads to skepticism about the (for some people) unusually wide range of my musical interests: and I've come to wonder whether the fact that I admire and enjoy works as close in time and as different in manner as Strauss's *Metamorphosen* and Schoenberg's String Trio (along with Britten's *Peter Grimes* and Vaughan Williams's Symphony No. 6) helps to explain my lack of success as a composer. Does this mean that successful composers are inherently narrow-minded, and more prone to bias in their instinctive musical preferences than critics or musicologists? I suspect that it might!

FESTIVAL DIRECTORS

CHAPTER THIRTY-SEVEN

HEIKE HOFFMANN
(B . 1 9 5 8)

German scholar of
culture and theater

Heike Hoffmann is artistic director of the Schwetzingen Festival. In past decades, she was active in a similar position with the Musik-Biennale in Berlin, the Berlin Konzerthaus, and the Salzburg Biennale.

I first met Heike Hoffmann in Berlin, probably at the beginning of 1991. I had taken up my job as deputy director of the Hungarian Cultural Institute in January that year, shortly after the fall of the Berlin Wall. Haus Ungarn, as it was then called, found itself in a vacuum, its once faithful visitors having decided to take advantage of their newly won freedom and revel in the rich cultural life offered in the western half of the city, from which they had so long been cut off.

Hoffmann was an "Ossi," as former citizens of the German Democratic Republic were referred to and, in a way, so was I, coming as I did from what had been the People's Republic of Hungary. She and I shared a similar background and an effort to establish ourselves in the new order of things.

She succeeded to a remarkable degree: born in northern Germany, she started life as an assistant in a private music shop and worked her way up to become a leading light of German musical life.

Hoffmann visited me in the spring of 1991 as representative of the Berlin Biennale, looking for a Hungarian composer from whom the festival could commission a new work. I was in my element: after all, I had been responsible for the promotion of contemporary Hungarian music until a few months before. Our contact produced Elegy *for wind quintet and string quintet by András Szőllősy (1921–2007), a piece of enduring appeal, for it continues to be played at regular intervals in Hungary.*

I am not sure whether our professional association in the succeeding sixteen years or so was similarly successful from my point of view. In any case, I visited Hoffmann each time I was in Berlin as promotion manager of Universal Edition, Vienna, and informed her about the activities of the publisher's composers. She was friendly, apparently interested—and adamantly impervious to suggestions. She knew exactly what she wanted (and still knows)—a self-assured woman who reminds me slightly of another self-confident lady of iron will, who grew up, like Heike Hoffmann, in the German Democratic Republic and has for several years now been guiding the destiny of the German Federal Republic and, to a certain degree, of the European Union—of course, I mean the chancellor. Angela Merkel.

February 2016

Does programming festivals require courage to the extent that you commission controversial or wholly unknown composers, that you select works that are expensive to produce and unlikely to be successful? Or to implement ideas that you are not entirely convinced of but could theoretically be of interest? Ideas rejected by people whose opinions you value?

For me, it was not so much a question of personal courage; I was simply convinced that I was doing the right thing. In most cases I was proven right, in others I was not. Interestingly enough, flops mostly arose where I had let myself be persuaded. But this is not really unequivocal: artistic success or lack of it cannot necessarily be measured by the immediate response of the public or by ticket sales. Sometimes the public is happy but the concert organizer is not. Or the other way around. Not to speak of the press: reviews can be wholly controversial. Of course, there were ideas that turned out during the course of their realization to be not feasible. It is part of the job, flops should be acceptable, provided one has done one's work in a dedicated and painstaking manner, creating the best possible conditions for the creative work of the composer. It should be remembered, however, that at the end of the day, it is the creative person who is responsible for the work's quality, not the facilitator or mediator—for that is how I see my role.

Still, I believe that over the years I have developed a flair for recognizing quality and originality, and for deciding whether a project is worth risking. As a result, I allow myself to be influenced less and less. Also, I no longer justify why I do *not* underwrite a project. I only explain why I dedicate myself *to* an artistic idea, or a composer. There are of course many people whose judgment I trust and whose advice I seek. Their opinions do have a part in the decision-making process. It does not mean that I always act upon them; critical opinions may serve to confirm my own convictions.

Has it ever occurred for you to be perplexed by the overall success of a composer or a particular work you could not appreciate? Would you eventually ignore your instincts—your taste? Is it at all possible to form an objective judgment, regardless of one's personal taste?

Yes, it has happened once in a while, but accumulating experience has strengthened my courage to defend myself against outside influence and to make decisions based purely on my personal conviction—or taste, if you like. It is in my view not at all possible to disregard one's personal taste, one's personal preferences and to form objective judgments. What criteria should one apply?

I find any form of objectification in art wrong. How often have judgments been formed on the basis of apparently valid criteria, which later turned out to have been mistaken? Music history is full of them. Artists are often ahead of their time and it is our duty to engage with their new works, for the assessment of which there exist no criteria as yet. It involves a profoundly subjective process. This is one reason that one cannot expect a curator to be objective.

Is it admissible for a festival director to say: I stick to my judgment; after all, there are any number of festivals where composers may place their works. You said recently: "Twenty-five years of Armin Köhler meant that particular composers were supported over a long span of time; some unknown ones were also given a chance, others however had to accept that they would not get a performance in Donaueschingen half their active lives."[1]

It is not only admissible—it is a must! It is a subjective selection that lends a festival a profile and gives its program a specific direction. I am against committees, regardless of their makeup, deciding on programs, because if

---

1 Armin Köhler (1952–2014) was artistic director of the Donaueschingen Festival between 1992 and 2014.

one agrees on the smallest common denominator, one will steer clear of risks and never come up with programs beyond the mainstream. A curator or artistic director must have complete freedom of decision. It takes a certain time for their individual style to become apparent. In that respect, personal continuity and secure planning are highly valuable. After a number of years, however, each of us will show signs of exhaustion. Ten years, I should say, is a reasonable span in which one can develop a profile and put it to the test. After that, one should really look for new challenges.

CHAPTER THIRTY-EIGHT

SIR NICHOLAS KENYON
(B . 1 9 5 1)

British music administrator,
editor, and writer on music

It is, I believe, part of the British education system—and, indeed, of British thinking—that you study one thing and end up doing something wholly different. Education is supposed to teach you to think, it hones your brain; having a specialist knowledge of any one field is less important. Paul Griffiths, for instance, has a degree in biochemistry from Lincoln College, Oxford, which has not prevented him from devoting his life to music. Nick Kenyon majored in history (less far removed from his eventual career) at Balliol College and on graduation joined the English Bach Festival. He was subsequently active as a music critic—for the New Yorker, *the* Times *(of London), and the* Observer—*before finding employment with the BBC.*

That is where I first met him. As representative of the Austrian music publisher Universal Edition (UE), the "Controller, BBC Radio 3," was an essential contact for promoting the catalog—with, for, or against. Nick became an absolute must when, in addition, he assumed responsibility for the Proms, the most substantial and high-profile music festival in Great Britain. He filled that position for most of my time with UE, 1996–2007.

I cannot say I achieved much for our composers: Nick was impeccably polite and frustratingly noncommittal. I suppose we both played the roles allotted to us by life the best we could.

He has very impressive credentials to prove he has played his role with
singular success: to begin with, he was entitled to put three letters after his
name, CBE, standing for Commander of the Most Excellent Order of the
British Empire (New Years Honours 2001), and three other letters were ap-
pended before it when he was knighted in 2008. On leaving the BBC in 2007,
he was appointed managing director of the Barbican, a prestigious music cen-
ter in the City of London. I am happy that he has agreed to sum up his views
regarding his profession in the following essay.

London, November 22, 2015

Taste is not a tyranny. Taste is a measure of our changing sensibility. As T. S.
Eliot so memorably put it, "sensibility changes from generation to generation, but expression is changed only by a man of genius."[1] The question
for a promoter of concerts, or a programmer for the radio, or a publisher
bringing new music to the public, is: What music being written now best
captures the expression that will resonate with the audience? It will challenge an audience, it may even baffle an audience, but at some level it will
make a connection that impels further exploration.

There are many different audiences with many different tastes. But
somehow, we observe that collective taste changes and this collective taste
shifts inexorably. Think of the way that Mahler, once regarded as eccentric
and overblown, has now entered the center of taste among concertgoers.
Similarly with Shostakovich, whose music now speaks to audiences; his music fills halls in the way that Tchaikovsky used to do. Think too of the way that
performance style shifts with the public: at one point the reference point for
Mozart may be Karl Böhm and the Vienna Philharmonic, for the next generation it is Christopher Hogwood and the Academy of Ancient Music. Why
does this happen? (It cannot be, as sometimes argued, because audiences
are fully aware of the historical arguments around period performance: we
simply like the noise it makes.) The influences on this ever-changing taste are
many and varied, and deserve to be explored in greater depth.

Composers write what they must write, with personal conviction. I
would not say for a moment that a composer must first write to please.
The composer who writes only to please will end up with the lowest common denominator of taste, and that is bad for everyone. A composer must
have fierce integrity and clear vision, and must take his or her chances on
whether that is recognized by the listening public. They can write for the

---

1   T. S. Eliot, "Poetry in the Eighteenth Century," in *Pelican History of English Literature*, vol. 4, ed. B.
    Ford (London: Pelican Books, 1957), 271.

future, or they can believe as Edgard Varèse did that they write for the present while it is the audience that is fifty years behind.

The responsibility of the concert promoter here is to be discriminating, to make judgments, to foster talent, but always to look wider than their own personal taste (however that has been formed) would suggest, always (as that great impresario William Glock put it) pushing their boat further out to sea than they might be comfortable with.

There is an extremely complex and subtle combination of influences that determines what a promoter offers the audience. It is not just one person's taste, but neither is it a random choice of allocating valuable resources and scarce performance time to anyone. For example: what do performers want to perform and conductors want to conduct? One has experienced unwilling musicians forced to play things for which they have no sympathy and understanding, and it is not a pretty sight. On the other hand, when a totally committed performer gives a powerful insightful performance of music with which the audience is totally unfamiliar, this can be a thrilling act of communal exploration. It is always important, for example, to ensure that a conductor is in sympathy with the aspirations of a composer—otherwise he will give a performance that is merely mechanistic, and (as observed backstage after one premiere) throw the score to the floor with the wish never to see it again.

Yes, there is subjectivity at work here. But there is no such thing as objectivity in matters of artistic judgment. What one hopes is that by balancing different views, different opinions, being alert to what composers are writing and what they could write, and the reaction of audiences when their music is performed, there can be a result that makes a difference. Sometimes you get it right, and sometimes you get it wrong. Sometimes it works, and an audience is held, concentrated and alert, by a new experience. Sometimes it just doesn't, and is forgotten by the second half of the concert.

So it is the function of an impresario to push on public taste with conviction. But you do that in collaboration with performers, publishers, festival directors, and the composers themselves who have a vision of where that taste should lead. Here is an idea that could work; here is one that just feels out of tune with the temper of the times. Here is a composer who with support could create something unique; here is one who with the best will in the world is not pushing the art form forward. Decide which is which, and take the risk: that's your job.

When running the BBC Proms in a very particular era of taste (1996–2007), I felt it vital to reflect the widest possible spread of good music—the repertory was expanding hugely in all directions, away from the core classical Western canon, back to explore early music, sideways to explore non-Western music. In that context new music was a vital part of the mix. But it was a different mission from, for example, the Proms of William Glock's time in the 1960s, where there was a single line of musical adventure he wanted to bring to audiences. I did not work alone: each year we would discuss with artistic administrators, conductors and other commissioners, with those who edited new music on Radio 3, with those who ran the BBC's orchestras, where the most exciting possibilities lay.

Increasingly, in order to ensure that major international figures were represented, we would co-commission works. Elliott Carter, Harrison Birtwistle, Luciano Berio, and later Magnus Lindberg, Esa-Pekka Salonen, and others—that was the best way to ensure their presence. For British composers there were particular ones who had relationships with the different BBC orchestras, from Jonathan Harvey and Judith Weir to Peter Maxwell Davies and Oliver Knussen. There were others whose music one spotted in other performances and simply asked them to write: Joseph Phibbs for the last night of the Proms, Julian Anderson, whose outstanding work sprang from a close relationship of support with the BBC. The range of new music that we commissioned, or in other cases of which we gave the first UK performances, is something of which we were all pretty proud (all recorded on the BBC Proms website at www.bbc.co.uk/proms/archive).

But inevitably there were many choices, both in terms of composers and repertory, with which others disagreed. There is a long history of controversy particularly around something so visible, and so central to British musical life, as the Proms. Glock often had to defend the absence of, say, Delius from his programs; I had a noted lack of sympathy for certain corners of the more conservative English repertory, which would provoke regular moans of discontent. Fortunately, my successor at the Proms, Roger Wright, did not feel the same way and was able to redress the balance. Certain composers I just strongly felt, on the basis of works I and others had heard, weren't very good, and we didn't commission them, causing complaints from them and their supporters. Maybe the future will prove us wrong, but I don't think that because of that we should be prevented from exercising our taste. Taste must be exercised with responsibility and judgment, and must reflect a genuine relationship with the listening public. Then the judgment will be that of posterity; but it will not be a fixed judgment, as music shifts in and out of fashion, influenced by great performances, recordings, and the development of technology. The rest, as they say, is history.

E P I L O G U E

Rainer Nonnenmann (b. 1968) and Bálint András Varga (b. 1941)

I do not hesitate to contact critics who have commented on my books in one way or another. Those who praised them, receive a short letter of thanks from me; those who took issue with some of their aspects, will receive a note in which I attempt to explain why I did what I did.

Rainer Nonnenmann was not all that happy with my book Three Questions for Sixty-Five Composers, *and true to form, I contacted him. Later, when the idea for the present book struck me, I wrote and asked him what he thought of it.*

He had many reservations, as you will see in his essay. I went on with the project nevertheless and am now rather curious to see what he will have to say about it.

In any case, having gotten this far in the book, you will learn from Nonnenmann, why it was not a good idea to do it in the first place.

Rainer Nonnenmann: The Anxiety of Composers and the Plurality of Tastes

Born in Ludwigsburg, Rainer Nonnenmann is a German musicologist, music journalist, and university professor. He is editor of the journal *MusikTexte* and author of a number of books on the music and aesthetic of the nineteenth, twentieth, and twenty-first centuries.

Cologne, August 2015

Dear Mr. Varga,

We have exchanged some e-mails about your latest book, *Drei Fragen an 73 Komponisten* (Regensburg, 2014) as well as your current project, with which I wish you every success. You have now invited me to contribute a text and asked me expressly to formulate my critical remarks and doubts. I have followed suit. My reservations will probably be invalidated by the views of some of the composers—I certainly hope so! For I have taken your wording "the courage of composers" seriously and have only considered composers in general, mentioning certain artists as an exception. Without meaning to, I may well have lumped them all together, even though a thorough look at each case by itself might have brought to light individual differences.

The fact of the matter is that I regard my brief not so much as to talk about one or another composer in a detailed manner; I am a musicologist and music journalist who has been closely observing the music of the twentieth and twenty-first centuries, and as such, I wish to point up structures and mechanisms that have worked on a more general level—those that in my view constitute the Achilles heel of the subject "the courage of composers" beneath its heroic surface.

The thematic impulse is bound to provoke comments that will approach the subject from a wide range of aspects and shed light on the thinking of composers in and about music. However, it differs from the questions you raised in your previous books, in that this time, you have not posed any question at all. Instead, you have put forward a moot idea and a number of reactions to it that set out to prove that artists, in particular circumstances of their lives and work, need courage to overcome the dominating opinions and styles of the time. Most composers should be able to relate experiences to do with the current institutional conditions of the production, distribution, and reception of music, that is, with the mechanisms of judging, assessing, selecting, or indeed turning down and rejecting music. I doubt, however, that your choice of subject for the book, *The Courage of Composers and the Tyranny of Taste* is suitable to address the core issue of artistic creativity. In my view, you see, the categories of "courage" and "taste," and especially talking of a "tyranny of taste" fail to touch upon the aesthetic, technique, intention, content, and impact of music. Much rather, they concern the psychological traits and mindset of composers and their individual manner of coming to terms with their environment. In addition, confronting the "courage of composers" with "the tyranny of taste" does not work, for one thing because composers are not courageous—if at all, they are driven by anxiety—and, for another, because the days when one taste dominated over all others have ended.

György Ligeti is right (in the statement you have quoted) that a composer needs no courage, he needs merely to write what he thinks and hears, ignoring any reaction his work may provoke. Arnold Schoenberg's laconic reply also comes to mind, to the question of whether he happened to be "that much-debated composer" who had done away with tonality. He said, "One had to be it, nobody wanted to be, so I volunteered."[1] Schoenberg's pointedly unheroic reply does not stem from courage, but simply from his realization of the necessity to take the step toward atonality. Whether or not he was right, he was led by insight and self-knowledge, in other words, the analysis of his own work against the background of the situation music history found itself in at the time, bound up with a clear vision of a new music of a fundamentally different kind. Schoenberg's epochal decision is representative of all basic changes within an individual oeuvre and in music history as a whole—changes that disrupt canonized forms, techniques, sonorities, and playing techniques, leave well-trodden paths behind, and cross hitherto accepted boundaries. In all that, courage appears to be of secondary importance as far as artists are concerned. For if they resolve to leave their own doubts and scruples out of account, they do not act in a courageous but in a negligent fashion, spurred by immature ideas. If they had considered them properly, they would have every trust in the rightness of their revolutionary undertaking. If, on the other hand, they take a drastic step despite their own fears and against their better judgment, they do so out of insecurity and indecision, or indeed, to consciously provoke their environment by breaking with ideas they still adhere to—something that makes for the inconsistency of their position and deprives it of credibility.

The Anxiety of Composers

As a general rule: he who has anxiety needs courage. The fearless are not courageous but are possibly unaware of the lurking dangers. Courageous is one who defies the uncertainties and risks inherent in a situation. Part of it is the self-assertion of the individual against a majority and their overt

---

1   The English translation is from Joseph Auner, *Schoenberg Reader: Documents of a Life* (New Haven, CT: Yale University Press, 2003). Kindly provided by Therese Muxeneder of the Arnold Schoenberg Center, Vienna.

or covert group pressure. However, all this does not render courage an aesthetic category. For those who make a public statement as artists, politicians, scientists, journalists, or in their private capacity, independently from the occasion and in whatever function, must face possible rejection and critical reaction. In pluralist societies, no product that reaches the public sphere is guaranteed an all-around positive response. That is why it is questionable whether there is such a thing as "the courage of composers" in relation to genuine musical activity and communication. Presumably, one demonstrates courage not as a composer but simply as a person with individual temperament, character, and stamina. Courage is not the breaking of taboos or rules out of historic insight, aesthetic logic, or inner conviction, merely the way the artist comes to terms with the likely or concrete reactions.

Conversely, it is also true that one who shows courage, in actual fact has anxiety. Behind the subject "the courage of composers" lies the complex one of "the anxiety of composers." Confessing to justified, real, diffuse, or imagined anxiety does take courage, for it touches on an area of artistic creativity and musical life that is usually treated as taboo. If in reality we are talking of anxiety rather than courage, we should be asking: which composer has anxiety of what? Does this anxiety stem from objectifiable facts? Or does it derive from the individual psychological disposition of a particular composer?

In general terms, it is safe to say that each composer has his individual character and behaves accordingly in situations that make for anxiety and require courage—anxiously or courageously. Like any human being, composers, too, will be able to relate such experiences. But beyond chance personal traits, many composers possibly share similar anxiety about failure, rejection, indifference of the public, the media, or concert organizers as well as about concomitant objective and personal conflicts. Needless to say, such anxieties occur in other professions as well: interpreters, managers, editors, publishers, teachers, musicologists, music journalists, cultural politicians, financiers. Even those with safe jobs are familiar with anxiety about personal weakness, incompetence, loss of motivation, lack of new ideas or orientation, ignorance, misguided decisions or, having made a decision, being left alone, exposed to the wrath of others.

It is wrong, however, to regard courage as the answer to such anxieties (covered up by some through a pretense of adamant conviction about a step they have taken or through apodiptic statements). After all, composers are not more courageous than other people, rather the opposite: they do not make life-and-death decisions, in contrast to the daily routines of physicians, paramedics, firefighters, police officers, extreme athletes, or workers operating dangerous machines under perilous conditions.

There remains the anxiety of composers in the face of the "tyranny of taste," and the courage they need to defy it. Apart from differing individual tastes, taste is a historically, socially, and culturally determined system of intersubjective categories, norms, and criteria that have found overall acceptance—ones that might harden into a veritable "tyranny of taste" given its increasing rigidity and narrowness. There is no question, then, of absolutist monarchs, totalitarian rulers, extraordinarily influential artists, domineering "judges of art," whose dictates allow only a limited range of artistic endeavor, but of the majority of the members of a particular scene, society, nation, or an entire cultural environment that share a complex of traditions, experience, ideas, preferences, and aversions. Their validity transcends individuals, is binding internally and confining externally, so that any deviation can be punished, if it comes to the worst, by exclusion. Artists need only to have anxiety about dictates of taste if they themselves are not free from the demands such dictates imply, either because they have no faith in their own actions or because they expose themselves to very real dangers in totalitarian regimes.

The Freedom of Pluralism

Taste is rarely displayed consciously and offensively; it works in a subliminal manner and remains unfounded, which is why it often tends to produce prejudices and ideologies that may lead, just as intangibly yet perceptibly, to blind support or animosity. Still, it would be wrong to infer from that the emergence of a tyranny of taste because today there is simply no taste that dominates over any other. Since postmodernism in the 1970s, the composition of music has been characterized by an attitude of "anything goes," from pluralism and internationalism, and an increasingly global breakdown into innumerable trends, subtrends, and stylistics right up to the private aesthetic worlds of individual composers, interpreters, ensembles, festivals, and concert organizers. Over the past fifty years, the composing, improvising, installing, conceptualizing, and performing of music in a great many directions have branched off into an immeasurably rich "multiversum." Ever since, it has been part of the very nature of new music that its constituent features could just as well be wholly different. Instead of a "tyranny of taste" there reigns total freedom that in turn results in entirely different problems, such as total arbitrariness: anything is possible, but nothing is really necessary. Total freedom does not mean that any material or forum is accessible to any composer. However, in view of the thousands of ensembles, festivals, concert series, and Internet portals the world over, everyone ought to find their form of expression and means of presentation.

In the past, a generally binding taste was defined either by a consensus, specific to a particular epoch, of central aesthetic aspects—such as in the Renaissance, the Baroque, in Classicism, and Romanticism—or it was determined through the philosophy of history. The last effort in that direction was undertaken by Theodor W. Adorno in his *Philosophy of New Music* (1948) with his theorem of a historically objective necessary tendency of the musical material. In the early 1950s, Pierre Boulez deduced from that his claim for the serial approach to be the sole representative of the dodecaphony of the Viennese School, one that he regarded as the most advanced method of organizing the musical material. In his essay "Schoenberg Is Dead" (1952), Boulez decreed with a generous helping of music-historical self-confidence and sense of mission: "No hilarious demonism but rather the most ordinary common sense leads me to declare that since the Viennese discovery, every composer outside the serial experiments is *useless*."[2] Boulez measured the "usefulness" of composers according to the extent to which their work could be put into the service of serialism in its integral incorporation of ever more parameters of music—a process that put the system at the spearhead of music's progress. His statement is one of the few surviving quotes by a serialist composer that goes so far as to exclude and disparage all those who did not subscribe to the "serialist efforts." But did that establish a dictatorship of taste?

It was not Boulez's intolerance as expressed by his historicoteleologically motivated absolutist claim that was decisive but his conviction, formulated in the first-person plural so that it appeared to represent an entire school, that was meant to further the development toward the total organization of material that he regarded as historically and objectively necessary. That did not mean, however, that other composers were forced to follow that dictum or to feel tyrannized by it. After all, they had every right to offensively represent whatever they regarded as valid and necessary; others were similarly free to decide that their colleagues' arguments were not cogent and reject them as fallacies. However, instead of relativizing serial techniques as the private affair of a small group that tended to act in an arrogant manner, their doctrine was perceived by many as undue interference and—because

2   English translation taken from, Pierre Boulez, *Notes of an Apprenticeship*, trans. Herbert Weinstock (New York: Knopf, 1968), 274.

they could not find the arguments to refute it—basically accepted it. Also, it should be remembered that Boulez, Nono, Maderna, Pousseur, Stockhausen, and others were at the time—for all the powerful support they received from the Darmstadt Summer Courses, radios, certain concert series, festivals, journals, and publishers—exposed to massive hostility from the press, the public, and other composers. The serialists had to defend themselves against accusations of being the extremists and sinners of new music. That they in turn attacked their attackers was a legitimate way of defending themselves and as a defense mechanism transparent enough.

Meanwhile, composers born in the 1940s and 1950s could be the last generation to assert themselves against the serial avant-garde's claim of exclusive validity—an avant-garde that had quickly established itself in concert life and music academies. However, those today who think they have to protect themselves against the intellectually underpinned progress of the material and deterministic control mania—and this is not infrequently the case—mount a sham fight against an opponent that has long since ceased to be one. For the serialists soon enough recognized the narrowness of their integral constructivism and their purist ideals and, as early as the 1950s and especially in the 1960s, developed techniques that integrated more open and differentiated materials. Today, the brave fight against the serial tyrant is mere shadowboxing with a pale ghost. That touches on the delicate issue of myth creation and self-stylization.

Fictions and Self-(De)constructions

Instead of concentrating on one's own work and trusting one's own experiences, thoughts, instincts, intentions, and ideas, some composers attempt to define their position through distancing themselves from supposed dictates of taste, which, in spite of the de facto dominating pluralism, apparently continue to wreak havoc. However, artists who look too much to the left and right to see what others are doing, are likely to end up trying to pilfer recipes for success, looking for recognition, immortality but also for obstacles, opponents, and scapegoats that can be blamed for their own failure. Pitching "the courage of composers" against the "tyranny of taste" is bound to encourage leanings toward egocentricity, vanity, and self-stylization, which in turn easily give rise to untruths as a means of self-protection. Those who (from their own viewpoint with justification) feel deprived of the recognition that is their due can quickly develop theories of conspiracy. After all, each composer fights a courageous battle—let us remember Richard Strauss's *Ein Heldenleben*—for his own work against a horde of ignorant opponents. And in doing so, some strike melodramatic, others more subtle, poses as great solitary figures, outsiders, underdogs, outlaws, unrecognized geniuses—lamenting the tyranny of whatever taste is symptomatic of composers who feel they have not made it and endeavor to blame others for their failed careers. This lament is also possibly a sign of lack of independence and freedom from one's own inner constraints mistaken for outer opposition.

Nonetheless, a fictitious dictate of taste can become effective and anxiety can determine the creative work of a composer: mostly it is the fear of being submerged by the masses of composing contemporaries, outdone or ending up as epigones of successful styles and ideas, that is, obeying the tyrant of taste; or having established oneself against the masses, that is, defied the dictates of taste, the anxiety to be nevertheless alone, with no interpreters, supporters, fans, and pupils. For a composer has a chance to become a celebrated avant-gardist only if he has followers in his quest. If, however, an artist remains without successors, his work will not be regarded as a step onto uncharted territory, merely a mistaken move onto an uninhabited desert where the supposed avant-gardist will die of hunger as a lonely prophet. The road toward a revolutionary future will turn out to have been an impasse, off the beaten track, marginal, spurious, soon blown over by the sand and wind of history.

Popular mass cultures are possibly more in ascendance today than they were in the past, with far more presence in the media and commercially far more successful than art music. They affect the long-term choice, perception, and appreciation of music by broad masses of people. This, however, has no bearing on the composition of new music because few composers—except the younger generation—respond to pop music or react to it in their creative work. On the other hand, new music also knows phenomena such as fan following, trends, hype, and fashions. They arise in part from the tendency for major innovations to attract groups of adherents: the innovations can only find acceptance through communities, or when outstanding artistic personalities often further the emergence of veritable schools. In recent music history, that mechanism was at work in the case of Serialism, Spectralism, New Simplicity, Postmodernism, Minimalism, Concretism, Complexism, and most recently, New Conceptualism. They have been motivated in part by the increasing pressure to achieve success, and the decreasing willingness to take risks in the face of a growing lack of money and waning public interest as well as vanishing political support. Instead of sacrificing themselves as solitary fighters, composers, primarily of the younger generation, are acting in networks of communication with a view to better realizing the identical or at least similar artistic goals of their groups. It is doubtless possible for a particular taste to achieve predominance within a certain trend. It does not mean, however, that any one composer is forced to jump on the bandwagon: a composer can assert independence from the community anytime.

Today it is valid more than ever before: the tyranny of one taste overthrows that of another.

Vienna, September 2015

Dear Mr. Nonnenmann,

Let me comment on some of the points you make.

It does not necessarily take a question mark to imply a question. I can simply say "we are having nice weather today" and if the addressee feels impelled to respond, he or she will do so. In submitting to composers a series of examples demonstrating that some of their colleagues, in particular situations, have needed courage to (re)act, I implicitly posed a question. Clearly, in my accompanying correspondence I did ask them to comment. The quote from Karl Aage Rasmussen was added later—another question without a question mark. I might have called the book Two Questions for . . . Composers, but I find the one I have settled on more informative.

The examples I have selected have little to do with courage in the face of dominant opinions and styles, as you assume. For Birtwistle, it simply meant: if Picasso could get away with it (that is, offering a novel interpretation of a masterpiece by a painter of the past), so could he. Petrassi, too, was encouraged by an artist (Alberto Burri) as well as by a fellow composer (Bruno Maderna) to expand the confines of his world. Those are highly private decisions. I picture creative artists in their studies or ateliers, alone with their work in gestation—insecure, hesitating, seeking enCOURAGE-ment. The example of a colleague, whether a contemporary or one of the past, could serve as badly needed help. The same could well be true of writers of fiction, or indeed, of any creative artist.

To my mind, deciding for or against a sonority, for or against a single tone, are matters of life and death for an artist at a particular juncture. A novel harmony could open up vistas for future work—or indeed, if it fails to produce the expected result, it could spell the death of an idea, all hopes for future exploitation dashed.

A young Austrian conductor told me how he had decided to program a work by Béla Bartók at a concert with a Viennese orchestra. The board would have none of it: they had played a work by Bartók the previous season, that should do for a time. Bartók did not sell tickets. The conductor was required to do a symphony by Prokofiev instead, even though it did not appeal to him. A clear case of the tyranny of taste, in the first years of the twenty-first century.

The director of a German festival of new music confessed to me after the premiere of an orchestral composition that he liked it very much indeed, even though music of that particular cast was not supposed to appeal to him. Another instance of the tyranny of the so-called ruling taste.

In my own work as promotion manager first in Budapest, and later in Vienna, it took a conscious effort for me to ensure that my taste did not interfere with my work on behalf of the composers in the catalog. Every now and again, works that did not appeal to me met with general acceptance, even considerable success. If I had acted otherwise, I would have been guilty of letting the "tyranny" of my own taste get the better of me.

During the decades of my promotional activity, I would come up against the personal tastes of people in leading positions. "I like it"—thumbs up—could signal the beginning of a promising career. "I don't like it"—thumbs down—could mean the end of an international career before it even started. I am exaggerating a bit, of course, but it is a fact that during the Cold War years, Editio Musica Budapest was the only music publisher in Hungary and I was responsible for single-handedly carrying the torch in the shape of scores and recordings to the far side of the Iron Curtain. My promotional tours produced performances and commissions for some, and nil for others. An absurd situation, really, that was bound to disappoint and antagonize some composers.

Working on this book, it has struck me that ideologies in totalitarian systems could be regarded as the outcome of institutionalized taste. I believe that the bulk of Bartók's oeuvre, for one, that went beyond folk music arrangements, was as alien to communist party officials as it was to the public at large. They fabricated an ideology out of it, stating that Bartók's abstract works, just as those of Schoenberg, Webern, and others, were "formalist" and not to be programmed in Hungary in the 1950s. Ideology morphed into censorship with fatal consequences—see the history of Hungarian composer János Viski as related by Péter Eötvös (in "Prompts"). Clearly, Zhdanov's doctrine of antiformalism played a role in all that: it was enforced in Hungary as in all other socialist countries.

I think that should do. I am pleased to have conducted this "debate" with you and thank you for taking time to formulate your reservations in detail about the subjects of my book.

With best wishes,

Bálint András Varga

INDEX

Eastman Studies in Music

Ralph P. Locke, Senior Editor
Eastman School of Music

Additional Titles of Interest

Claude Vivier: A Composer's Life
Bob Gilmore

A Dance of Polar Opposites:
The Continuing Transformation of Our Musical Language
George Rochberg
Edited by Jeremy Gill

Intimate Voices: The Twentieth-Century String Quartet
Volume 1: Debussy to Villa-Lobos
Edited by Evan Jones

Intimate Voices: The Twentieth-Century String Quartet
Volume 2: Shostakovich to the Avant-Garde
Edited by Evan Jones

Leon Kirchner: Composer, Performer, and Teacher
Robert Riggs

The Music of Luigi Dallapiccola
Raymond Fearn

The Pleasure of Modernist Music: Listening, Meaning, Intention, Ideology
Edited by Arved Ashby

The Sea on Fire: Jean Barraqué
Paul Griffiths

The Substance of Things Heard: Writings about Music
Paul Griffiths

The Twelve-Tone Music of Luigi Dallapiccola
Brian Alegant

A complete list of titles in the Eastman Studies in Music series
may be found on our website, www.urpress.com.

Bálint András Varga is perhaps the world's most respected interviewer of living composers. For *The Courage of Composers and the Tyranny of Taste: Reflections on New Music*, Varga has confronted thirty-three composers with quotations carefully chosen to elicit their thoughts about an issue that is crucial for any serious creative artist: How can one find *courage* to deal with the sometimes tyrannical expectations of the outside world?

The result is an imaginary roundtable at which we encounter fresh, revealing, previously unpublished statements from such world-renowned composers as John Adams, Friedrich Cerha, George Crumb, Sofia Gubaidulina, Georg Friedrich Haas, Giya Kancheli, György Kurtág, Helmut Lachenmann, Libby Larsen, Robert Morris, and Wolfgang Rihm. Also represented are composers who are becoming more prominent with the passing years—for example, Chaya Czernowin, Pascal Dusapin, and Rebecca Saunders—as well as conductor-composer Michael Gielen, festival director Sir Nicholas Kenyon, and music critics Paul Griffiths and Arnold Whittall. In *The Courage of Composers and the Tyranny of Taste*, composers and other insightful individuals comment on choices made, traps avoided, unforeseen consequences, proud accomplishments, occasional regrets: the whole range of experiences central to artistic creativity.

"This book is a must for all who care for the future of classical music."
—Iván Fischer, music director, Budapest Festival Orchestra and Konzerthausorchester Berlin

"Despite what they may or may not wish to admit in public, all genuine artists know that the responsibility of their gift is an arduous burden, the shouldering of which constantly forces them to tread the lonely path. Bálint András Varga's intriguing book, enabled by his unique experiences at the heart of contemporary music creation over many decades, offers us a rare opportunity to experience firsthand the soul-searching that society—or is it God, or the Universal Chi?—requires of the Artist."
—Jonathan Nott, music and artistic director, Orchestre de la Suisse Romande, and music director, Tokyo Symphony Orchestra

"I enjoyed this book enormously. The diverse landscape of musical composition comes into crystal focus through the inquiring lens of Mr. Varga's questions. This is an essential work to understand how composers think."
—David Robertson, chief conductor, Sydney Symphony Orchestra, and music director, St. Louis Symphony

Bálint András Varga is the acclaimed author of *György Kurtág: Three Interviews and Ligeti Homages*; *Three Questions for Sixty-Five Composers*; and *From Boulanger to Stockhausen: Interviews and a Memoir* (all available from the University of Rochester Press).